'Cookery School

°Cookery School

from channel 4

with recipes by richard corrigan

photography by mark read
and tricia de courcy ling

MICHAEL JOSEPH
an imprint of
Penguin Books

MICHAEL JOSEPH

Published by the Penguin Group

Penguin Books Ltd, 80 Strand, London WC2R 0RL, England

Penguin Group (USA) Inc., 375 Hudson Street, New York, New York 10014, USA

Penguin Group (Canada), 90 Eglinton Avenue East, Suite 700, Toronto, Ontario, Canada M4P 2YR
(a division of Pearson Penguin Canada Inc.)

Penguin Ireland, 25 St Stephen's Green, Dublin 2, Ireland (a division of Penguin Books Ltd)

Penguin Group (Australia), 250 Camberwell Road, Camberwell, Victoria 3124, Australia
(a division of Pearson Australia Group Pty Ltd)

Penguin Books India Pvt Ltd, 11 Community Centre, Panchsheel Park, New Delhi – 110 017, India

Penguin Group (NZ), 67 Apollo Drive, Rosedale, Auckland 0632, New Zealand
(a division of Pearson New Zealand Ltd)

Penguin Books (South Africa) (Pty) Ltd, 24 Sturdee Avenue, Rosebank, Johannesburg 2196, South Africa

Penguin Books Ltd, Registered Offices: 80 Strand, London WC2R 0RL England

www.penguin.com

First published 2011

1

Copyright © 4 Ventures Ltd and Red House Television Ltd, 2011
Photography copyright © Mark Read, Tricia de Courcy Ling and Jamie Simonds, 2011

The moral right of the author has been asserted

Set in Arial and Chalet

Printed and bound by Fimengruppe APPL, aprinta druck, Wemding, Germany

Colour reproduction by Altaimage

A CIP catalogue record for this book is available from the British Library

978–0–718–15806–4

CONTENTS

MEAT

PUDDINGS

SUPER ADVANCED

SKILLS

Gizzi Erskine and Richard Corrigan

INTRODUCTION

WELCOME TO °COOKERY SCHOOL, the place where anyone can learn how to cook. Whether a complete beginner or a more experienced cook, this is the place to learn new skills or to improve on what you already know. The one thing that can be guaranteed is that ordinary cooks will be transformed into extraordinary cooks. If you are determined to become a better home cook then this is definitely the environment for you. The idea behind the television show and this book is simple – it's that you can learn to cook, and then you can keep on learning. As the students did on the show, everyone brings their own personal motivations for wanting to cook better, and everyone takes away their own rewards.

Don't think you'll simply be learning the basics. Yes, there are skills included throughout the book, complete with step-by-step photographs to show you exactly what to do, but you'll also be learning how to cook aspirational and exciting recipes from the start. Why not learn how to fillet a fish or joint a chicken alongside how to fry an egg? It's about mixing it up and making it exciting. I want the recipes to test you but I don't want you to be out of your comfort zone too much as you progress through Cookery School, so you will find sections for Basic, Intermediate and Advanced recipes in each chapter.

Once you have mastered them all you will find a chapter at the end of the book called Super Advanced. This will really test your skills, featuring some fantastic recipes, suitable for cooking at home, from chefs who are at the top of their game. Get these right and you will be up there with the greats! These guest chefs appear on the television show to teach recipes from their own areas of expertise. Arun Kapil joined us in the semi-finals to look at a popular world cuisine. He is a specialist in Indian food, and gives us two very delicious recipes. In the final round, three chefs taught recipes from the three main areas featured on the show and in the book – meat, fish and puddings. Mark Edwards, the man behind Nobu, lets us in on some of his recipe secrets, Michelin-starred chef Martin Blunos

shows two very different ways to cook game and master pâtissier Eric Lanlard produces a couple of amazing puddings. These recipes are all very challenging and require some unusual ingredients, but if you feel you are ready to have a go alongside the finalists then do! The recipes I produced for this chapter were themed as 'ultimate' dishes: ultimate luxury (Fruits de mer and Roe deer venison fillet), my ultimate three-course meal (Salmon tartare, Roasted pork belly and Rhubarb crumble soufflé) and ultimate luxury on a budget (Classic roast chicken and Tipsy trifle). I hope you enjoy them!

Throughout the book you will also find notes on all sorts of cookery-related subjects by Gizzi Erskine. A great cook and food writer, she fronts the Cookery School television show as a mentor to the students and as a judge. Offering up tips and information, she will tell you about many things, including marinading, herbs, and how to put together a balanced cheeseboard. Look for her pieces called 'Gizzi's notes on…'

As well as learning great cooking skills I also want the Cookery School experience to get you thinking about the broader benefits of learning to cook better, like wastage, the amount of food you buy and the money you spend on your weekly shop. There's a frugal aspect to home cooks that I admire because great food costs a lot of money and if you're not frugal then you can end up wasting a lot. If you can cut down on this, whilst also spending 10% less on your food shopping, you will learn how to run your household better – that can only be a good thing! A lot of the recipes in this book are inexpensive so this should help you with your budgeting.

It's also about sitting down and making time – time to read the recipes, time to cook and time to sit down with your family to share the food you've created. It's this sharing that makes eating so enjoyable – rarely does a good cook enjoy eating on their own. I also want you to be aware of the ethics behind your food shopping too, so you come to understand where your food has come from and the hard work that's gone into the growing, fishing or farming of it. I've expanded on my thoughts around this in the section about food production on page 13.

Hygiene in the kitchen is also important. If cooking for yourself you can be a bit more relaxed, but when you're cooking for others you need to make sure that, for example, you don't place raw chicken down on another board being used for something else. Don't place half-eaten food in the fridge with cling film over it either. It's always best to strip down a chicken carcass and mix the meat with a little mayonnaise to make a sandwich filling for the next day or use the meat to make a chicken noodle soup. You can do these things really quickly and it will make all the difference. The whole chicken you started out with suddenly starts to look a lot more economical when you think you can get three meals out of it! Start thinking like this and you'll be thinking like a chef.

So I hope you enjoy watching the first series of Cookery School on Channel 4 and that it gets you in the mood for wanting to expand on your culinary repertoire and learn new skills. You'll see the students, from novices to more experienced cooks, being taught – and tested on – three recipes a day, rising from basic to advanced level. Each day focuses on a different area: starters, fish, meat and puddings. Those that make the grade move on to the super advanced recipes that will really challenge them. You will be able to cook all of the same things at home, as this book provides the whole curriculum, covering all the recipes and skills as demonstrated on the show.

The winning student each week goes on to compete for a place in the grand final, where one of them will be crowned the winner of Cookery School. You will see the students being pushed as much as possible to gain results, and discipline is a big part of that. With only a week to teach each set of students I had to remove all democracy to get them to learn the basics quickly. I hope you will benefit from this in the book as well, but you have the added luxury of being able to take your time, and you won't be eliminated from your own kitchen! What I loved most was seeing the enjoyment on the students' faces when they realized that they'd cracked a new skill. Cookery School will definitely teach you those skills and provide you with the motivation to keep practising until you can move on to the next challenge. Once you know how to switch on your oven and you've got your basic kit to hand in the kitchen you can prepare anything from scratch. And you will love it!

Richard Corrigan, 2011

A NOTE ABOUT KITCHEN EQUIPMENT

Don't think you have to go out and buy a whole new set of kitchen equipment in order to be able to cook well. However, there are some items which it just makes sense to have to hand as they make life easier. The minimum kit list I would suggest is this:

- a food processor
- a liquidizer or hand blender (great for making soups)
- a sieve
- a decent set of knives – treat them as you would a new car, with huge respect. Don't put beautiful knives in the dishwasher, wash them by hand and don't pile them up on top of one another. Sharpen them after every use so when you next need them they're sharp – get yourself a sandstone or a steel with your set.
- cast-iron, heavy-duty pots – great for making things like stews. Le Creuset is a fantastic brand. Historically, I've always failed to burn things in my Le Creuset pots because the lids are so heavy that they trap the moisture inside, meaning things end up being pot-steamed or pot-roasted. A wonderful situation to be in! So don't buy things because they may seem like a fashion statement, you want things that will work brilliantly for you.

- decent pots and frying pans – non-stick is good and you want them to be heavy because weight distribution means heat distribution. If you want the ultimate luxury then invest in some copper-lined pots.
- a little salt spoon – I usually use my hand for seasoning as I go by instinct but you should measure out the amount of salt you are adding to things, so it's worth getting a salt spoon until you feel confident enough to gauge the amount yourself.
- good chopping boards – it's important to have separate boards for meat and vegetables, as well as a good wooden board. Always wash them down thoroughly after use and look after them as they are indispensable bits of kit.

THOUGHTS ON FOOD PRODUCTION

I have very strong ethics surrounding food production. I want to know that the environment where animals are housed and fed is a good one. Without question, the basic minimum level for all meat production should be free-range. Yes, there's a need for industrial farming but I do question whether we need to eat as much meat. I think we have proved with Cookery School that a casserole or a cheese soufflé can be a substantial main course without the need for meat to play a big part.

People are more and more willing to question the standards of animal husbandry, so that can only be a good thing. I'd also rather see everyone eating animals from the British Isles and Ireland. We don't need to be importing food from all over the world when we have such great produce on our doorstep. The same goes for seasonal fruit and veg. I don't want to eat something that has been imported, like asparagus, out of season as it doesn't taste of anything. When you've tasted something so beautiful during its 6-week season, why would you want to eat it at any other time of the year when it's not going to be the same?

STARTERS

BASIC

- À la minute vegetable soup with bacon dumplings
- Griddled leeks with a honey and mustard dressing
- Deep-fried oysters with a honey and black pepper glaze
- Halloumi, tomato and green bean salad
- Sticky red onions with a poached egg and herb butter
- Heritage tomatoes with toasted bread salad
- Field mushroom salad
- Smoked garlic aioli with root vegetable crisps

INTERMEDIATE

- Cream of celeriac soup with chicken and girolles
- Citrus and herb roasted vegetable couscous
- Sautéed prawns with chickpea mayonnaise
- Blue cheese and bacon tarts with baby gem leaves
- Cream of onion soup with cheese and ham toasties
- Stuffed beef tomatoes with spinach purée
- Mushroom crêpe gratin
- Chicken kiev with tenderstem broccoli

ADVANCED

- Cornish red mullet soup with crispy croutons and rouille
- Mussel risotto
- Crispy duck, bok choi and black beans with a lime and ginger dressing
- Twice-baked goat's cheese soufflés with leeks and walnuts
- Onion, spinach and ricotta ravioli with a lemon-cream sauce
- Clear tomato soup with an aubergine, courgette and tomato ratatouille
- Mushroom tortellini with chicken consommé
- Garlic custard with snails

SKILLS
- Using a food processor
- Knife skills: chopping an onion; chopping vegetables neatly to the same size; chopping herbs

À LA MINUTE VEGETABLE SOUP WITH BACON DUMPLINGS serves 4

FOR THE DUMPLINGS

6 rashers dry-cured bacon

1 garlic clove, peeled and finely chopped

3 tablespoons finely chopped flat-leaf parsley

3 tablespoons grated Parmesan cheese

salt and freshly ground black pepper

FOR THE SOUP

2 tablespoons rapeseed oil

1 small onion, peeled and chopped

1 carrot, peeled and chopped

½ bulb fennel, chopped

200g celeriac, peeled and chopped

1 celery stick, chopped

a few thyme sprigs

1¼ litres vegetable stock

extra picked or chopped flat-leaf parsley, celery leaves and Parmesan cheese, to serve

This soup captures in one pot the delicate flavour of fresh vegetables straight from the garden. The dumplings are like mini bacon burgers – I would recommend buying free-range or organic British or Irish bacon because it is of a higher quality. You can make a vegetarian version of these dumplings using chestnuts instead of bacon for an autumnal flavour.

1 First make the dumplings. Cut off any rind from the bacon and keep to add to the soup for extra flavour. Finely mince the bacon in a food processor (if it is too coarse, the dumplings will fall apart). Mix the bacon together with the garlic, parsley and cheese in a bowl and season with salt and pepper. Divide the mixture into 12 and shape into small balls about the size of a walnut, pressing them together firmly with your hands. Cover with cling film and put in the fridge until needed.

2 To make the soup, heat the rapeseed oil in a large saucepan. Put in the onion and the reserved bacon rind and fry over a low heat until soft. Add the carrot and fry for 2 minutes. Add the fennel and fry for another 2 minutes, adding more oil if needed. Next add the celeriac and celery to the saucepan and fry for 1–2 minutes.

3 Add the thyme sprigs, then pour in the stock and bring to the boil. Next drop in the dumplings and gently simmer, without boiling, for about 4 minutes. Remove the thyme sprigs and the bacon rind to serve. Check the seasoning.

4 Garnish the soup with more picked or chopped flat-leaf parsley, some celery leaves and a grating of Parmesan cheese. Delicious served with some crusty bread.

SKILLS
- How to clean leeks
- Knife skills: preparing the leeks
- Correct timing to boil a duck's egg
- How to use a griddle pan
- How to make a salad dressing

GRIDDLED LEEKS WITH A HONEY AND MUSTARD DRESSING serves 4

2 duck's eggs

4 small leeks, trimmed and cut in half lengthways and rinsed thoroughly

1 tablespoon olive oil

knob of unsalted butter

4 tablespoons fresh wholemeal breadcrumbs

1 teaspoon English mustard powder

1 tablespoon runny honey

juice of 1 lemon

50ml rapeseed oil

1 tablespoon roughly chopped tarragon

When making the dressing it is important to taste, taste and taste again. Listen to your palate and season it to your taste. See the steps on pages 22–3 for how to make a dressing.

1 Bring a small pan of water to the boil and put in the duck's eggs. Boil for around 10–12 minutes. When cooked, remove the eggs and cool under cold running water, to prevent a black ring from appearing around the yolk, and set aside.

2 Bring another saucepan of water to the boil and place the trimmed and rinsed leeks in the water, then boil for 4–5 minutes until the leeks are tender. Once cooked, remove from the water and, once cool enough to handle, slice in half again lengthways.

3 Place a griddle pan over a high heat. While it is heating up, put the leeks on a plate and drizzle with the olive oil. Then place the leeks on to the hot griddle pan, turning them over after 2 minutes, until they have grill marks on both sides.

4 Meanwhile, heat a small frying pan over a low heat and put in the butter. Once it has melted, add the breadcrumbs and toss them in the butter to coat all over. Once golden brown and toasted, remove from the pan and set aside.

5 To make the dressing, put the mustard powder, honey, lemon juice, rapeseed oil and tarragon into a small bowl and whisk until combined.

6 Place some griddled leeks on each serving plate, drizzle the dressing over the leeks and sprinkle on the toasted breadcrumbs. Peel the duck's eggs and grate over the top of the breadcrumbs, then serve.

HOW TO MAKE A DRESSING

Very simple. My vinaigrette is three parts oil to one part vinegar or lemon juice with mustard powder and a bit of seasoning. The honey and tarragon give extra flavour to the basic vinaigrette. This specifically relates to Griddled Leeks with a Honey and Mustard Dressing (page 21).

1 Put the mustard powder and honey into a little bowl.

2 Add lemon juice.

3 Whisk with a small whisk, adding more honey for sweetness if necessary, but being careful not to mask the heat of the mustard and the sharpness of the lemon. You need to keep tasting and if you're not happy, taste again and again and again.

4 I like to add a neutral-tasting oil like rapeseed oil.

5 Whisk until the oil and lemon juice come together, thickening into an emulsion. The dried mustard will help the oil and vinegar blend.

6 I look for the smallest, most delicious tarragon leaves. Just pick and add to the dressing.

SKILLS
- Preparing oysters: how to take them out of their shells in one piece
- How to make a glaze: reducing vinegar and honey
- How to make the perfect tempura batter – the key is not to over-mix
- How to deep-fry oysters in tempura batter – see the steps on pages 26-7

DEEP-FRIED OYSTERS WITH A HONEY AND BLACK PEPPER GLAZE serves 4

vegetable, sunflower
  or groundnut oil,
  for deep-frying
12 Irish rock oysters
125ml white wine vinegar
165ml cider
120ml runny honey
10g black peppercorns,
  crushed
50g plain flour
50g cornflour
pinch bicarbonate of soda
pinch salt
150ml sparkling water
250g salt, to serve
optional: sea spaghetti
  (seaweed), to serve

This is one of my favourite ways of eating cooked oysters – an American craze, from New Orleans, which came to Bentley's restaurant in London in the 1930s. You should eat them straight away once you've cooked them. This recipe has a really good sharpness from the vinegar – what you want is a lovely sweet and sour flavour.

Pour in the oil and preheat the deep-fat fryer to 180ºC/350ºF, according to the manufacturer's instructions.

1   Using an oyster knife, carefully remove the oysters from their shells and keep them aside in a small bowl. Place the curved oyster shells in a pan of boiling water and boil for 6 minutes. Remove from the heat and rinse them under cold water, then leave the shells to one side until required for serving.

2   Put the white wine vinegar and cider in a small saucepan and bring to the boil. Simmer for 10 minutes until the liquid is reduced by a third. Add the honey and crushed peppercorns and stir until you have a glaze the consistency of runny honey. It will thicken on cooling.

3   Place the plain flour, cornflour, bicarbonate of soda and pinch of salt in a medium-sized bowl and stir. Gradually whisk in the sparkling water. Don't worry about lumps in the batter because these will add some crunch to the oysters.

4   Dip all the oysters in the batter, then carefully place them one by one into the deep-fat fryer for 2–3 minutes, turning them over halfway through cooking. Do not overcrowd the fryer, but cook the oysters in batches, so they crisp up.

5   Either mix 2 tablespoons of water with the salt to moisten it, then divide the salt between the serving plates and form a 'bed' on each one, or arrange the seaweed on the plates instead. Put 3 washed oyster shells on top of each bed of salt, and sit the fried oysters in their shells. Drizzle the cooled glaze over the oysters.

HOW TO MAKE TEMPURA BATTER

A Japanese-style tempura batter is made with fizzy water and cornflour and should be very light and crispy. This specifically refers to Deep-fried Oysters with a Honey and Black Pepper Glaze (page 25).

1 Add plain flour to a bowl.

2 Pour in the cornflour.

3 Add a pinch of bicarbonate of soda and a touch of seasoning.

4 Pour in cold sparkling water. The coldness of the water shrinks the gluten in the flour for a really crisp batter, while the fizz will make the batter puff up when it hits the fryer.

5 Whisk with a balloon whisk, but don't worry about a few lumps.

HOW TO BATTER AND DEEP-FRY OYSTERS

1 Pat dry the shelled oysters and add to the batter with a little of the well-seasoned oyster juices.

2 Spoon a few oysters out of the batter and into the deep-fat fryer.

3 Cook for a minute and a half to 3 minutes to create a really crisp batter around the oysters.

4 Tip the oysters out on to paper towels to dry.

SKILLS
● Knife skills: slicing the Halloumi and tomatoes
● Making a vinaigrette – using the right amount of oil to vinegar

HALLOUMI, TOMATO AND GREEN BEAN SALAD serves 4

200g fine green beans

400g Halloumi cheese, cut into 8 thick slices

8 purple basil leaves

4 tablespoons olive oil

salt and freshly ground black pepper

50g Kalamata olives, stones removed

125g red cherry tomatoes, halved

125g yellow cherry tomatoes, halved

1 tablespoon red wine vinegar

2 tablespoons finely chopped mint

extra virgin olive oil

Halloumi is a Cypriot cheese made from a blend of sheep's milk and goat's milk. It's like mozzarella but a little bit saltier, so be careful with the seasoning. When it's cooked, Halloumi goes deliciously soft. This salad should be served at room temperature, which is the best temperature for your palate to appreciate all the lovely flavours.

1 Place the green beans in a pan of boiling water and blanch them for 2 minutes. Drain in a colander and refresh under cold water.

2 Place the sliced Halloumi on the chopping board. Top each piece with a purple basil leaf, drizzle with 1 tablespoon of the olive oil and season with salt and pepper.

3 Heat a medium-sized frying pan and once hot put in the slices of Halloumi, basil-leaf side down and cook over a medium heat for 2 minutes. Turn the pieces over and cook on the other side for 2 more minutes, then add the olives to warm through. Remove the cheese and olives from the pan and set aside.

4 Put the two types of tomatoes and the beans in a large bowl. In a separate bowl, mix together the remaining 3 tablespoons of olive oil, the vinegar, mint and some salt and pepper, then pour the dressing over the salad and stir through.

5 Place the salad on the plates and top with the Halloumi cheese slices and the olives, then drizzle with a little extra virgin olive oil.

SKILLS
- Knife skills: slicing onions and chopping herbs
- Making a balsamic vinegar reduction
- Cracking an egg into simmering water
- Poaching an egg (see page 33)
- Using a griddle pan

STICKY RED ONIONS WITH A POACHED EGG AND HERB BUTTER serves 4

100g butter

3 red onions, peeled and sliced into rounds

150ml balsamic vinegar

150ml red wine

1 tablespoon roughly chopped sage

4 eggs

2 tablespoons olive oil

4 thick slices sourdough bread

salt and freshly ground black pepper

1 tablespoon finely chopped flat-leaf parsley

1 tablespoon finely chopped dill

This is a very simple recipe, and poaching an egg is a good skill to have (see page 33 for step-by-step photographs). Sage is a very strong flavour, so be careful how much you add. Try to get balsamic vinegar that has been aged for a minimum of ten years. And remember, when it comes to the reduction, you're not making a marmalade; you're just cooking the red onions down. Delicious!

1   Put a medium-sized sauté pan on the heat and put in half the butter. Once it has melted, add the red onion rounds. Cook for 10 minutes over a low to medium heat until soft, then add the vinegar, red wine and sage and cook over a high heat until the liquid has almost gone and the onions are sticky.

2   Bring a deep saucepan of salted water to simmering point and poach the eggs in it – this can be done one by one or all 4 eggs at the same time. Stir the water to create a whirlpool and crack the egg into the centre of the whirlpool, then simmer in the water for 3 minutes. Remove the egg from the pan with a slotted spoon. Repeat with the other 3 eggs.

3   Place a griddle pan on a medium heat. Drizzle the olive oil on to the slices of sourdough and season with salt and pepper, then place the bread on the hot griddle. Cook each side for 2 minutes or until golden and crisp.

4   Place the remaining 50g of butter in a small saucepan on the heat to melt. Add the chopped herbs just before serving to prevent them from turning grey.

5   Place a piece of griddled sourdough on each plate, cover with the sticky onions and then place a poached egg on the top. Spoon the herb butter over the egg.

HOW TO POACH AN EGG

Use an organic or really fresh farmyard egg because the older the egg, the weaker the albumen in the white and the more likely the egg will spread out in the water. The idea of putting vinegar in the egg-poaching water is to help keep an old egg together as it cooks. Just a dash is needed if you don't have fresh eggs. This specifically refers to Sticky Red Onions with a Poached Egg and Herb Butter (page 31).

1 Break your super-fresh egg into a ramekin or cup. The water in the pot needs to be just simmering. Stir the water to encourage the egg to swirl round and set compactly.

2 As the whirlpool subsides, add the egg. You're aiming for the white to wrap itself around the yolk with the stirring motion. Leave the egg to cook for a few minutes.

3 Remove the egg from the water using a slotted spoon to check if it's done. If it's not cooked to your liking, just pop the egg back into the pot. When done, drain on a paper or tea towel.

SKILLS
- Knife skills: slicing and chopping the red onion, bread, peppers, tomatoes and cucumber
- Frying the bread to make croutons
- Making a dressing in a food processor

HERITAGE TOMATOES WITH TOASTED BREAD SALAD serves 4

FOR THE SALAD

1 red onion, peeled and sliced into rounds

2 tablespoons olive oil

1 garlic clove, peeled and smashed

½ ciabatta loaf, sliced into 1½cm cubes

75g jar roasted red peppers, drained and cut into 2cm squares or strips

400g heritage tomatoes, cut into quarters

1 Lebanese or baby cucumber, peeled, seeds removed and cut into chunks

25g caper berries, rinsed

25g baby capers, rinsed

12 basil leaves

FOR THE DRESSING

3 tablespoons red wine vinegar

9 tablespoons extra virgin olive oil

12 anchovies, chopped

3 garlic cloves, peeled and finely chopped

This dish is known in Italy as *panzanella* – a bread and tomato salad. In the past, Italians would make this to use up stale bread, which would have otherwise gone into the bin. This is a wonderful salad to serve on its own on a nice sunny day or else as an accompaniment to cured meats or a piece of grilled fish. How simple and how delicious!

1   Place the red onion rounds in a small bowl and cover with boiling water, then set aside for 5 minutes.

2   Meanwhile, heat a large frying pan over a low to medium heat and put in the olive oil. Once the oil is hot, add the garlic. Then add the ciabatta cubes and fry for 3–4 minutes, until golden brown and crispy. Remove from the pan and set aside, discarding the garlic.

3   Drain the onion rounds and place them in a large bowl, along with the peppers, tomatoes, cucumber, caper berries, capers, basil leaves and toasted ciabatta cubes.

4   To make the dressing, put the red wine vinegar, olive oil, anchovies and garlic into a small food processor and blitz until emulsified.

5   Pour the dressing over the salad and toss together well.

6   Place a pile of the dressed salad in the centre of each serving plate.

SKILLS
- Preparing the mushrooms
- Knife skills: chopping the parsley
- Making a baking parcel out of greaseproof paper
- Griddling the focaccia

FIELD MUSHROOM SALAD serves 4

8 field mushrooms, stalks trimmed

6 tablespoons olive oil

2 garlic cloves, peeled and thinly sliced

2 teaspoons chopped thyme leaves

salt and freshly ground black pepper

1 focaccia loaf (approximately 18cm x 12cm)

100g dandelion leaves

3 tablespoons extra virgin olive oil

1 tablespoon finely chopped flat-leaf parsley

The field or meadow mushroom is the equivalent of a sirloin steak in the vegetarian world – it is ideal for people who are looking to cut down on their meat consumption. The dressed mushrooms are wrapped and baked *en papillote* (French for 'in parchment' or, in this case, within a parcel made from greaseproof paper) and the natural aromas of the mushrooms after baking are phenomenal! The salad uses a slightly obscure leaf, the dandelion, which you can buy from organic fruit and vegetable markets and shops, and you just need to drizzle over extra virgin olive oil and the wonderfully rich mushroom juices. Serve with grilled focaccia bread to soak up all the incredible juices.

*Preheat the oven to 200°C/fan 180°C/gas 6.

1   Place the mushrooms, 2 tablespoons of the olive oil, the garlic and thyme in a medium-sized bowl, season with salt and pepper and toss together well.

2   Lay a large square of greaseproof paper on top of a baking sheet and tip the herby oiled mushrooms into the centre. Then make a parcel by bringing up the sides of the greaseproof paper, folding over the top and twisting the edges to seal. Place the baking sheet with the parcel in the preheated oven for 5–10 minutes.

3   Slice the focaccia into 4 long rectangles about 18cm x 3cm, and drizzle them with the remaining 4 tablespoons of olive oil. Put a griddle pan over a medium heat. Place the focaccia rectangles on to the hot griddle and cook each side for about 1–2 minutes, until char marks appear.

4   Remove the baking sheet from the oven and unwrap the parcel. You can leave the mushrooms whole or slice any of the larger ones if you wish.

5   Put the dandelion leaves in another medium-sized bowl, season with salt and pepper and drizzle over the extra virgin olive oil. Then spoon on some of the warm juices from the mushrooms and toss.

6   To serve, place a piece of griddled focaccia in the centre of each plate and top with, or serve alongside, the mushrooms. Sprinkle with chopped parsley and place the dressed leaves to the side.

SMOKED GARLIC AIOLI WITH ROOT VEGETABLE CRISPS serves 4

vegetable, sunflower
 or groundnut oil, for
 deep-frying
2 cloves smoked garlic,
 peeled and finely grated
2 egg yolks
juice of ½ lemon
50ml mild olive oil
2 large Jerusalem
 artichokes, peeled
1 large carrot, peeled
1 large parsnip, peeled
1 large beetroot, peeled
sea salt
½ teaspoon paprika

Aioli is very simple to make, tastes delicious and is an incredibly versatile dip or sauce that can be served with numerous meat and fish dishes. It's also great when eaten with chips! Egg yolks and garlic – the key ingredients – are blended together with lemon juice and an emulsion is made by very slowly and carefully whisking in oil. If the mixture becomes too stiff, a dash of boiled water can be used to soften it – but be careful not to add too much. The consistency of the aioli should be stiff enough that it can stand up on its own. For the vegetables, simply wash and slice them and wait for a few minutes as they turn crispy in the deep-fat fryer. Serve with a sprinkling of paprika to give an extra kick.

Pour in the oil and preheat the deep-fat fryer to 180°C/350°F, according to the manufacturer's instructions

1   Place the garlic, egg yolks and lemon juice in a large bowl and whisk together using an electric beater or by hand until they form a smooth paste. Gradually pour in the olive oil little by little, whisking all the time, until the aioli thickens. If it becomes too stiff, soften with a little boiling water. Spoon the aioli into 4 small serving bowls, cover with cling film and put in the fridge.

2   Using a vegetable peeler, slice the artichokes, carrot and parsnip lengthways into wafer-thin vegetable crisps. Use a knife to slice the beetroot as thinly as possible. Leave the beetroot slices to one side for a few minutes on a plate with kitchen paper, to leach out the colour and any excess moisture.

3   Put all the vegetables, except the beetroot, in the preheated deep-fat fryer and cook for 2–3 minutes until they turn a light golden colour. Remove the cooked vegetable crisps from the fryer and place on kitchen paper. Season with salt and a pinch of paprika.

4   Next, put the beetroot slices into the deep-fat fryer and cook for 5 minutes. Remove, lay out for a few moments on kitchen paper to soak up the excess oil and season with salt and paprika.

5   To serve, place a pile of mixed vegetable crisps on each plate with individual bowls of aioli on the side.

SKILLS
● Grating garlic
● Whisking the egg
  yolks and lemon juice
● Peeling the root
  vegetables into
  thin slices
● Deep-frying the
  vegetables

The 'week one' students

SKILLS

- Sweating vegetables without colouring
- Using a bouquet garni
- Puréeing the soup using a stick blender, electric blender, food processor, food mill or sieve

CREAM OF CELERIAC SOUP WITH CHICKEN AND GIROLLES serves 4

FOR THE SOUP

2 tablespoons mild olive oil

30g unsalted butter

1 onion, peeled and chopped into 1cm pieces

1 head celery, trimmed and chopped into 1cm cubes

600g celeriac, peeled and chopped into 1cm cubes

1 bouquet garni (peppercorns, thyme, parsley stalks and bay leaf tied in a small muslin bag)

4 chicken drumsticks

about 1 litre chicken stock

150ml double cream (optional)

salt and freshly ground black pepper

FOR THE GARNISH

150g celeriac, peeled and cut into small dice

100g girolles, larger ones halved or torn in two

extra virgin olive oil

2 sprigs tarragon, leaves picked

Classic soups are almost forgotten about in kitchens these days. But for me, great eating starts with great basics and this dish is one of those. Warm and hearty, this soup will get you going in the winter. Cream is optional, but it adds gorgeous richness and decadence.

1 Heat the oil and butter in a large saucepan. Add the chopped vegetables and the bouquet garni. Sweat gently over a low heat until softened but not coloured, then add the chicken drumsticks and pour in enough chicken stock to cover. Bring to the boil, then lower the heat and poach gently for about 25–30 minutes until the chicken and vegetables are tender.

2 Take out the chicken drumsticks and leave on a plate until cool enough to handle. Remove the skin and cut the chicken meat into small pieces.

3 Meanwhile, discard the bouquet garni and then purée the contents of the saucepan until smooth, using any of the blenders listed in the skills section above. You could also pass the soup through a sieve for an extra-velvety finish.

4 Pour the puréed soup into a clean pan, stir in the cream if desired, season to taste with salt and pepper and keep warm.

5 Make the garnish by sautéing the celeriac and girolles in extra virgin olive oil in a frying pan over a medium heat until lightly coloured. Add the chicken meat and picked tarragon to the pan, toss together and heat through. Ladle the soup into bowls and top with the sautéed celeriac, girolles and chicken.

SKILLS
- Steaming the couscous
- Zesting and juicing a lemon
- Using the roasting method
- Knife skills: preparing the vegetables

CITRUS AND HERB ROASTED VEGETABLE COUSCOUS serves 4

FOR THE ROASTED VEGETABLES

1 red onion, peeled and cut into wedges

1 red pepper, deseeded and cut into 1½cm pieces

2 small courgettes, cut into 1½cm cubes

250g butternut squash, peeled, deseeded and cut into 1cm dice

3 garlic cloves, peeled and finely chopped

2 tablespoons thyme leaves

2 tablespoons olive oil

salt and freshly ground black pepper

FOR THE COUSCOUS

350g couscous

½ teaspoon turmeric

1 teaspoon ground cumin

450ml hot vegetable stock

3 tablespoons finely chopped mint

3 tablespoons finely chopped flat-leaf parsley

1 tablespoon olive oil

juice and zest of 1½ unwaxed lemons

50g pine nuts, lightly toasted

I love the fluffiness and versatility of couscous. People forget that different types have different absorbencies, so you need to keep an eye on the amount of liquid added. Like seasoning, you can always add more liquid, but you can never take it away. Putting it in the oven makes it just that bit more fluffy and also gives it a bit of a crunch.

Preheat the oven to 200°C/fan 180°C/gas 6.

1 Roast the vegetables first. Place all the chopped vegetables on to an oven tray, sprinkle over the garlic, thyme and olive oil and season with salt and pepper. Mix well, making sure all the ingredients are coated and cook for 20–25 minutes, or until slightly browned on the edges. Remove the tray from the oven and allow the vegetables to cool a little. Leave the oven turned on.

2 Place the couscous in a medium-sized bowl. Add the spices, season with salt and pepper and stir well. Pour over the hot vegetable stock, stir once more and cover the bowl with cling film for the couscous to steam and the water to be absorbed.

3 After 5 minutes, remove the cling film and fluff up the mixture with a fork. Spread the couscous out on an oven tray and place back in the oven for 5 minutes to dry out a little.

4 Combine the couscous and the roasted vegetables together in a large bowl. Add the herbs, olive oil, lemon juice and zest and mix well. Taste and season with salt and pepper again if needed.

5 Place on a large plate or in a large bowl, perfect for sharing, and sprinkle over the toasted pine nuts.

SKILLS

- Preparing the prawns – see page 48 for the step-by-step instructions and photographs
- Making crostini
- Making the flavoured oil – important not to overheat or cook the shells in the oil
- Cooking the chickpeas without them becoming mushy
- Blending the chickpeas to a purée
- Cooking the prawns – important not to overcook so they go tough

SAUTÉED PRAWNS WITH CHICKPEA MAYONNAISE serves 4

200ml mild olive oil, plus 2 tablespoons

3 shallots, peeled and finely chopped

2 garlic cloves, peeled and sliced

4 teaspoons ground cumin

2 x 410g tins chickpeas, drained

400ml water or vegetable stock

12 raw tiger prawns, shells, tails and heads removed (and retained), de-veined

100ml extra virgin olive oil, plus extra for drizzling

salt and freshly ground black pepper

juice of 1 lemon

4 thin slices sourdough bread

chopped coriander cress (baby coriander) or coriander, to garnish

The best prawns to use are organic tiger prawns, which are a really sweet, flavourful variety. If you have any leftover chickpea mayonnaise it works really well as a spread on fresh bread.

1   Place a large saucepan on the heat, and add 2 tablespoons of mild olive oil and the shallots. Cook for 2 minutes over a medium heat, then add the garlic and cook for a further 2 minutes. Add the cumin and chickpeas, cover with 400ml of water and simmer for 5 minutes.

2   Meanwhile, place the shells, tails and heads from the prawns in a medium-sized saucepan and pour in the mild olive oil. Turn up the heat, smash up the shells to release their colour and flavour and cook for 2 minutes, then remove from the heat and pour the mixture through a sieve, retaining the flavoured oil and discarding the shells.

3   Remove the pan of chickpeas from the heat. Drain the chickpeas in a colander, keeping the cooking liquid, and place them in a food processor. Blend together, adding the reserved cooking liquid a little at a time, until smooth. Gradually pour in the extra virgin olive oil and continue to process until you have a smooth purée. Season to taste with salt and pepper.

4   Put a large frying pan on the heat and add some of the prawn oil. When hot, add the prawns and sauté over a medium heat for 3 minutes, turning them over, until they have turned pink and are cooked through. Remove the prawns from the heat and squeeze over the lemon juice.

5   Drizzle the sourdough slices with a little extra virgin olive oil and place on a hot griddle for 1 minute on each side until well toasted.

6   Spoon the chickpea purée into the centre of each plate and top with the prawns. Garnish with the chopped coriander cress or coriander and a piece of sourdough toast to the side.

HOW TO PEEL A PRAWN

If your recipe involves cooking prawns, buy uncooked ones and shell them yourself. The tail is usually left on for an attractive presentation. This specifically refers to Sautéed Prawns with Chickpea Mayonnaise (page 47).

1 Pull the head off each prawn.

2 Peel the shells away from the body of each prawn, keeping the tails in place.

3 Cut each prawn very gently along its curved back with a sharp knife and take the thin, black intestinal tract out. The prawns can be really gritty if you leave this in.

HOW TO MAKE MAYONNAISE

1 Put your egg yolks, white wine vinegar and mustard (just a small bit to start with, you can always add some more) in a bowl.

3 When you have added all the oil, what you should have is a smooth, thick emulsion, but this will have no personality. What we do to give it personality is to add a little more mustard, vinegar, salt, lime juice and herbs or other flavourings.

2 Whisk with a balloon whisk, electric beater or in a small food processor.

Now, very slowly, start dripping in a room-temperature light, mild olive oil and rape-seed oil. If you add them too fast, the oil will separate from the egg yolk and the mayonnaise will split and won't thicken.

Tip: If the mayonnaise gets really thick and seems in danger of separating, add a dash of hot, just off the boil, water from the kettle to stop it splitting on you. This will help pin down the emulsion and allow you to add the rest of the oil.

BLUE CHEESE AND BACON TARTS
WITH BABY GEM LEAVES serves 4

FOR THE BLUE CHEESE AND BACON TARTS

20 sheets of filo pastry (13cm x 13cm)

25g unsalted butter, melted

1 tablespoon olive oil

4 rashers back bacon, cut into lardons

1 egg

150ml double cream

80g British blue cheese, crumbled into pieces

8 spring onions, trimmed and thinly sliced on an angle

salt and freshly ground black pepper

FOR THE BABY GEM DRESSING

3 tablespoons rapeseed oil

1 tablespoon white wine vinegar

1 teaspoon Dijon mustard

½ teaspoon sugar

leaves from 2 baby gem lettuces

SKILLS

- Using filo pastry: cutting the pastry to size, layering with melted butter, baking long enough so it does not burn
- Making a savoury custard using eggs, milk and any extra fillings, e.g. bacon and blue cheese
- Cooking the tart until it is just done in the centre, with a slight wobble
- Making a dressing: the balance of oil to vinegar

I love filo pastry, it's so simple and goes lovely and crispy when cooked. Having less butter than other pastry also makes it healthier. I chose baby gem for the salad because its sweet, delicate leaves really complement the tarts.

Preheat the oven to 180°C/fan 160°C/gas 4.

1 Brush a sheet of filo pastry with a little melted butter and carefully lay it over the outside of an upturned 6cm tart tin, making sure the pastry overlaps the sides. Repeat this process with 4 more sheets of filo pastry, laying each one at a slight angle to the last so they are fanned out, with the points of each piece making a star shaped pastry case. Then repeat and make three more pastry cases. See page 52 for step-by-step instructions and photographs.

2 Place the four upturned pastry-covered tart tins on a baking sheet and put in the preheated oven for 10 minutes until slightly coloured and starting to turn crisp. Remove from the oven and set aside to cool. Remove the tart cases from the tins and place the right side up so they can be filled.

3 Heat a small frying pan and put in the olive oil. Once the oil is hot, add the bacon lardons and cook for 3 minutes over a high heat until crisp, then set aside.

4 Crack the egg into a large bowl and whisk in the cream. Then add the cooked bacon, the cheese and spring onions and season with salt and pepper. Mix well. Using a ladle pour the mixture into the filo cases. Alternatively, place the bacon into the tart cases, topped with the spring onions. Crumble over the cheese and ladle over the egg mixture. (See pictures on page 53.)

5 Put the filled tart cases back in the preheated oven for 10–12 minutes until just cooked in the centre.

6 To make the dressing, place the rapeseed oil, vinegar, mustard, sugar and some salt and pepper in a small bowl and whisk.

7 Put the baby gem leaves in a medium-sized bowl and pour on the dressing to coat all the leaves.

8 Remove the tarts from their tins and place each on a serving plate. Serve the dressed baby gem lettuce leaves on the side.

HOW TO USE FILO PASTRY

I honestly love filo pastry – it's really simple to work with and it's healthy for you too. Just remember always to keep the pastry covered with a damp cloth as it has a terrible habit of drying out, becoming brittle and then breaking on you while you're working with it. This specifically refers to Blue Cheese and Bacon Tarts with Baby Gem Leaves (page 51).

1 Place a sheet of filo pastry on your board.

2 Brush the sheet with melted butter. This is the glue that will help the sheets stick together to give that flaky filo texture.

3 Stack the next sheet on top diagonally. Brush again with melted butter, but don't over-do it – if the pastry absorbs too much butter, it will be heavy.

4 Carry on stacking up the layers until you have used five or six sheets.

5 You don't want any air pockets whatsoever, so run your brush over the pastry to squash them out. The melted butter helps crisp the pastry as well as keeping it all together. Using a knife, pick up the pastry and place it on top of one of your small tart tins or moulds.

6 Now, make sure you wrap it around the mould to form a tart case, otherwise it will be just a flat disc and won't be able to hold the custard filling.

HOW TO MAKE A SAVOURY CUSTARD TART FILLING

There are two kinds of custards – the kind you pour over a delicious steamed pudding and a baked custard you cook in the oven until set. Here, the pastry cases enclose the custard, which must be thick enough to hold the bacon and cheese from the recipe on page 51.

2 Whisk together with a balloon whisk.

3 Cut up some delicious blue cheese.

1 Pour the cream into a large bowl. Crack in an egg.

4 Crumble the bacon, cheese and spring onion into the cases.

5 Carefully ladle the custard into the tarts, filling them almost to the top – you don't want the mixture to spill out. The pastry cases give a bit of protection from the heat to stop the custard overcooking.

6 As the egg slowly cooks, the filling should set just like a crème brûlée. Watch it carefully as overcooked custard can be rubbery.

SKILLS
- Caramelizing the onions with no colour
- Cooking the toastie so it is golden brown and melted in the middle
- Using a liquidizer

CREAM OF ONION SOUP
WITH CHEESE AND HAM TOASTIES serves 4

FOR THE CREAM OF ONION SOUP

50g unsalted butter

2 tablespoons olive oil

1kg white onions, peeled and thinly sliced

1 tablespoon marjoram leaves

2 tablespoons thyme leaves

900ml chicken stock

150ml double cream

salt and freshly ground black pepper

FOR THE CHEESE AND HAM TOASTIES

8 slices white bread

1 egg, beaten

40g sliced honey-roast ham

40g gruyère cheese, grated

40g unsalted butter

2 tablespoons vegetable oil

This is a delicious, simple winter soup. Sweating the onions without any colour, so that they just melt down, is really important to this dish. Straining a soup through a sieve after it's been blended will give you a silkier, more refined soup. To serve this at your dinner table, you could drop the cheese and ham toastie into the soup, like a big crouton, at the last moment.

1   Heat a large saucepan and add the butter and half the olive oil. Once the butter has melted, add the onions, marjoram and 1 tablespoon of the thyme. Soften the onions for 10–15 minutes over a medium heat.

2   Add the chicken stock and simmer for 10–15 minutes.

3   For the toasties, roll out the bread slices to 2mm thick and brush one side of each with beaten egg. Place a quarter of the ham and cheese in the middle. Lay another slice of bread on top and again brush with egg. Press together and pinch closed around the edges, then cut into a circle shape using an 8cm round pastry cutter. Repeat to make 3 more sandwich rounds.

4   Place a large frying pan on the heat, add the butter and oil. When melted, fry the toastie rounds over a low to medium heat until golden brown and toasted on each side. Keep warm in a low oven, 120°C/fan100°C/gas½. If you have a large pan you can do them all at the same time; if not, fry in batches, using a little of the butter and oil each time.

5   Meanwhile, pour the soup into a blender and blitz until smooth. Remove and pass through a fine sieve into a clean pan. Stir in the cream and season with salt and pepper.

6   Heat the remaining 1 tablespoon of olive oil in a small pan until hot. Add the remaining 1 tablespoon of thyme and cook for a minute then set aside.

7   Warm the soup through and pour into individual serving bowls. Drizzle with a little thyme oil and serve a warm toastie on the side.

SKILLS
- Knife skills: chopping onion, garlic, anchovies and herbs
- Pan-frying mince
- Deglazing the pan with the red wine and red wine vinegar
- Preparing and stuffing the tomatoes

STUFFED BEEF TOMATOES WITH SPINACH PURÉE serves 4

FOR THE STUFFED TOMATOES

2 tablespoons olive oil

250g lamb mince

1 onion, peeled and finely chopped

2 garlic cloves, peeled and finely chopped

4 anchovies, finely chopped

2 tablespoons finely chopped oregano

2 tablespoons finely chopped rosemary leaves

100ml red wine

50ml red wine vinegar

200ml passata

400ml lamb stock

200g orzo pasta

4 beef tomatoes

100ml double cream

zest of 1 unwaxed lemon

FOR THE SPINACH PURÉE

1 tablespoon extra virgin olive oil

200g baby spinach leaves

100ml double cream

Stuffing tomatoes seems an old-fashioned idea that has been lost, but we are going to bring it back again because I love big, meaty stuffed tomatoes. This Greek-style recipe sees them stuffed with lamb for the ultimate comfort food. What a lovely suppertime dish! And if you put this dish in front of any child, I know they will enjoy it.

Preheat the oven to 180°C/fan 160°C/gas 4.

1   Heat the olive oil in a large frying pan over high heat, and add the mince broken into small chunks. Brown the lamb without moving it for 1–2 minutes.

2   Add the onion, garlic, anchovies and herbs to the pan, and continue to fry until the onions start to brown.

3   Deglaze the pan with the red wine and the red wine vinegar and cook further to reduce the liquid by half.

4   Add the passata and stock to the pan, bring to the boil, then put in the orzo. Cook for about 10 minutes, or until most of the liquid has been absorbed and the orzo is cooked, then take the pan off the heat.

5   Cut the top off each beef tomato, retaining the top for a lid, and scoop out the seeds and most of the flesh.

6   Finish off the stuffing in the pan by stirring in the cream and lemon zest, and spoon the mixture into the 4 hollowed-out tomatoes. Place the tomatoes on a baking tray and put in the preheated oven for 10–12 minutes.

7   Meanwhile, to make the spinach purée, put the extra virgin olive oil in a medium-sized frying pan over a medium heat. When it is hot, throw in the baby spinach and cook until the leaves have wilted, which will take about a minute. When cooked, place in a sieve to remove any extra liquid. Return to the pan along with the cream, heat through, season, then blend in the food processor.

8   To serve, remove the tomatoes from the oven. Place a large spoon of spinach purée in the centre of each plate and then serve a tomato on top.

MUSHROOM CRÊPE GRATIN serves 4

FOR THE CRÊPES
250g plain flour, sifted
300ml whole milk
2 eggs
2 tablespoons melted unsalted butter
2 tablespoons vegetable oil
50g Parmesan cheese, grated

FOR THE MUSHROOM DUXELLE FILLING
75g unsalted butter
2 banana shallots, peeled and finely chopped
1 garlic clove, peeled and finely chopped
1kg button mushrooms, finely chopped
2 teaspoons finely chopped thyme leaves
2 teaspoons finely chopped flat-leaf parsley

FOR THE BÉCHAMEL SAUCE
400ml whole milk
1 bay leaf
8 black peppercorns
½ onion, peeled
40g unsalted butter
20g plain flour, sifted
salt
½ teaspoon cayenne pepper
½ teaspoon freshly grated nutmeg

FOR THE SPINACH
500g baby spinach leaves
1 tablespoon extra virgin olive oil

In this dish, the crêpes are filled with a comforting mushroom stuffing (called a 'duxelle') and topped with a wonderful béchamel sauce and a sprinkling of Parmesan cheese before being gratinated. A mound of chopped, wilted spinach makes the perfect bed on which to serve the crêpes. There are four elements that make up this recipe: the duxelle, the crêpes, the sauce and the garnish. If you break it down into these components, you won't go too far wrong. You need to cook down the duxelle so that the mixture left in the pan is almost dry – but don't let it burn! At the same time, you can have the milk infusing with the onion, bay leaf and peppercorns, which will then be added to the roux for the béchamel sauce, along with a touch of cayenne and nutmeg. This gratin dish makes a lovely family supper.

Preheat the oven to 200°C/fan 180°C/gas 6.

1   To make the crêpes, sieve the flour into a large bowl and gradually mix in the milk, 300ml of water, eggs and butter, then whisk until smooth.

2   Heat a medium-sized non-stick frying pan over a medium heat. Once the pan is hot, add a little of the vegetable oil. Then pour in a ladleful of the crêpe batter and swirl the pan to spread out the batter and form a thin crêpe. Cook for 2 minutes, flip the crêpe over using a spatula, fish slice or palette knife and cook for a further minute on the other side. Slide the crêpe out of the pan on to a plate to one side and place a sheet of kitchen paper on top to stop the crêpes from sticking together.

3   Repeat with the rest of the batter, one ladleful at a time and adding a little more oil to the pan between cooking each crêpe, until you end up with a pile of 8 cooked crêpes interleaved with sheets of kitchen paper.

4   To make the mushroom filling, place the butter in a medium-sized sauté pan over a medium heat. Once the butter has melted, add the shallots and cook for 2 minutes until they are soft, then add the garlic, mushrooms and thyme and cook for a further 8–10 minutes, until the moisture from the mushrooms has evaporated. Remove the pan from the heat, season with salt and pepper and sprinkle on the chopped parsley. Set aside.

5   To make the béchamel sauce, place the milk, bay leaf, peppercorns and onion in a medium-sized saucepan and warm over a low heat but do not let the milk boil.

6   In a separate medium-sized saucepan, melt the butter over a medium heat then add the flour to make a roux. Cook, stirring, for 2–3 minutes.

7   Strain the warmed milk, discarding the aromatics, and gradually pour the milk into the roux, whisking all the time. Cook for a further 5 minutes until you have a smooth, thickened béchamel sauce, then season with salt, cayenne pepper and nutmeg. Take 2 tablespoons of the sauce and mix into the mushroom filling to bind that together.

8   On a clean work surface, lay 2 crêpes overlapping one another to give a large surface area and spread a quarter of the mushroom filling evenly over the crêpes. Taking the end nearest to you, roll up into a Swiss roll shape. Cut the roll into 2cm-thick pieces. Repeat with the remaining 6 crêpes and the rest of the filling.

9   Heat a medium-sized frying pan over a low to medium heat, throw in the baby spinach and drizzle over the extra virgin olive oil. Cook for 2 minutes until the spinach leaves have wilted.

10 Place the wilted spinach in the bottom of 4 x 5 inch/13cm round or oval individual gratin dishes, or use one large dish. Pour a little béchamel sauce over the top and then place a quarter of the slices of filled crêpe roll on top, overlapping the slices slightly. Pour the remaining béchamel sauce over the top and sprinkle on the grated Parmesan.

11 Place the 4 gratin dishes on a baking tray and put in the preheated oven for 8–10 minutes until the gratins are golden brown on top.

HOW TO MAKE CRÊPES

This specifically refers to Mushroom Crêpe Gratin (page 59).

1 Add plain flour to a bowl. Pour in the milk and whisk to make a batter, but don't beat it too much as this can make the pancakes tough.

2 Add an egg, some melted butter and a pinch of seasoning and mix again.

3 Pour the batter through a sieve to remove any lumps.

4 Pour a ladleful of batter into a heated, oiled crêpe pan and tip the pan around to spread the batter evenly across the base. Return the pan to a medium heat.

When the crêpe has cooked through and is golden brown underneath, carefully turn it over to finish the other side. Then tip it onto a plate and keep warm until you have completed the remainder of the crêpes.

5

HOW TO MAKE BÉCHAMEL SAUCE

Begin by infusing the milk with the onion, pepper-corns and bay leaf over a low flame.

Melt the butter in a pan over a gentle heat, then add the plain flour. Continue to stir over a low heat for a few minutes to cook out the rawness of the flour.

1

2 Pour a small amount of the infused milk through a sieve into the flour mixture, then stir vigorously to amalgamate it. Continue to add small amounts of milk in this way until it has all been incorporated. Use the back of the spoon against the side of the saucepan to press out any lumps. This helps to release the gluten in the flour and will make the béchamel sauce really smooth and silky.

3 Once the sauce is smooth, remove it from the heat. Adding a little melted butter to the surface will prevent a skin forming on the top.

CHICKEN KIEV
WITH TENDERSTEM BROCCOLI serves 4

FOR THE GARLIC HERB BUTTER

120g unsalted butter (at room temperature)

3 garlic cloves, peeled and finely grated

2 tablespoons finely chopped flat-leaf parsley

3 tablespoons white breadcrumbs

salt and freshly ground black pepper

FOR THE CHICKEN KIEV

vegetable, sunflower or groundnut oil, for deep-frying

2 chicken breasts

50g plain flour

2 eggs, beaten

100g white breadcrumbs

FOR THE TENDERSTEM BROCCOLI

200g tenderstem broccoli, trimmed

juice of 1 lemon

2 tablespoons olive oil

SKILLS

- Making garlic butter
- Preparing the chicken
- Knife skills: chopping parsley
- Panéing (breadcrumbing) the chicken breast
- Deep-frying the chicken kiev
- Cooking the tenderstem broccoli

My tips for making these chicken kievs are to make sure you seal over the openings after the garlic butter has been added using pieces of the mini fillets. And be sure to use one hand when dipping the chicken in the flour and egg and the other for dipping the chicken in the breadcrumbs. This will ensure you get a beautiful, golden-brown soft crumb on the chicken with no lumps. As it cooks, the chicken is basted from the inside by the melted garlic-butter sauce. Don't worry if you make too much garlic butter – it is easily frozen and can be added to another dish at a later date.

Pour in the oil and preheat the deep-fat fryer to 170°C/325°F, according to the manufacturer's instructions.

1   First make the garlic herb butter. Place the butter, garlic, parsley and breadcrumbs in a medium-sized bowl. Season with salt and pepper and beat with a wooden spoon until all the ingredients are completely combined.

2   Prepare the chicken by removing the mini fillet from each breast and put these to one side. Then make a diagonal cut through the breasts, cutting them each in half on an angle, so you end up with 4 mini chicken breasts. Make as long an incision as possible in the thickest part of each mini breast through the centre, to form a wide pocket, but making sure not to pierce the flesh all the way through. Carefully use your finger to open up the pocket. See the step-by-step photographs on pages 66–7.

3   Spoon a quarter of the garlic butter into the pocket of each mini chicken breast, pushing it in using your fingers.

4   Slice the 2 mini chicken fillets in half and place each piece over the pocket opening for the butter in each mini breast and press to seal it. You can also trim the fillet halves and use to cover any thinner areas if necessary.

5   Put the flour, beaten egg and breadcrumbs into 3 separate bowls. Coat each stuffed chicken mini breast by first dipping it in the flour, shaking off any excess, then dipping it in the egg and finally in the breadcrumbs. Place the kievs in the fridge for 15–20 minutes to help them set. Then carefully place them in the preheated deep-fat fryer and cook for 5–6 minutes.

6   Meanwhile, put a saucepan of salted water on to boil. Add the tenderstem broccoli to the pan and blanch it for 2–4 minutes, then refresh under cold water. Place in a bowl and dress with the lemon juice and olive oil.

7   To serve, remove the chicken kievs from the fryer and drain on kitchen paper. Then place them on serving plates with the dressed tenderstem broccoli.

HOW TO MAKE A CHICKEN KIEV

This specifically refers to Chicken Kiev with Tenderstem Broccoli (page 65).

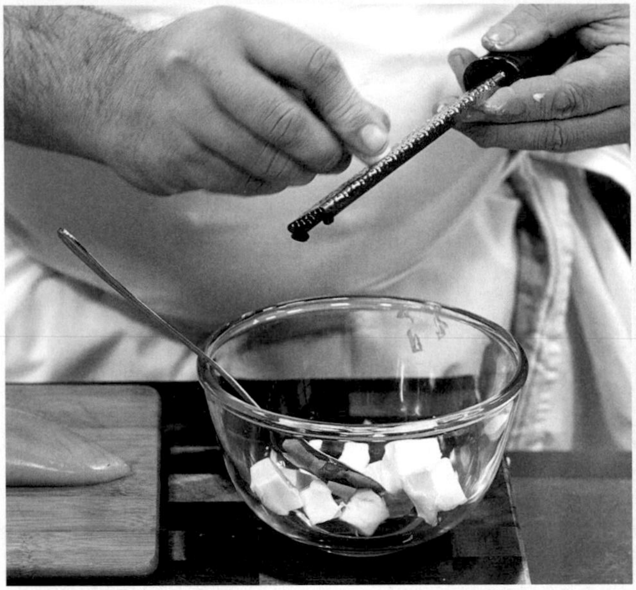

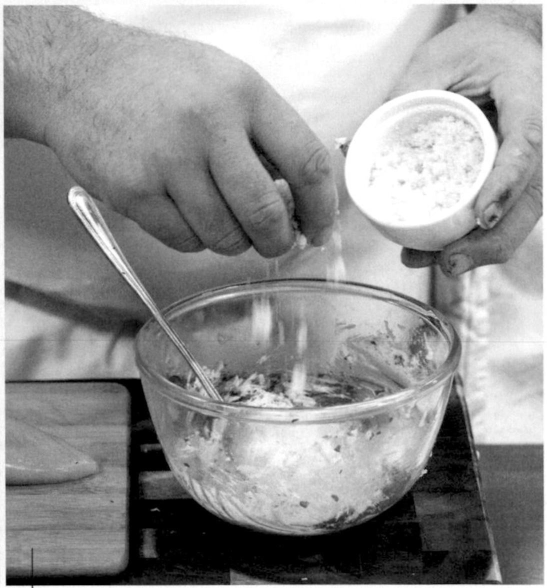

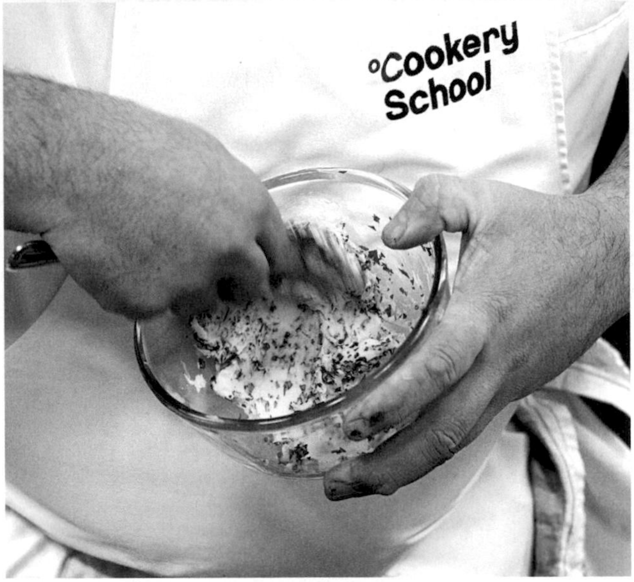

1 First, prepare the garlic butter. Place the butter in a bowl and grate in the garlic cloves. Add the finely chopped parsley, breadcrumbs and a good pinch of seasoning, then mix well.

2 Trim any excess sinew and fat from the chicken breasts, then remove the small mini fillet from the underside of each. Cut each chicken breast in half on the diagonal, so that you now have four pieces. Using a small, sharp knife, cut a pocket in the side of each, being careful not to cut all the way through. Divide the garlic butter mixture between the four pieces, pushing it well into the pockets you have made. Next, cut each mini fillet into two and use one to plug the pocket in each breast.

To cover the chicken in breadcrumbs, (a technique known as panéing, see also page 128), coat each piece of chicken in seasoned flour, shake off the excess, then dip in the egg and finally give it a covering of breadcrumbs. A good tip, which will make this less messy, is to use one hand for the first two stages, leaving your other hand clean and dry for the crumbs.

3

Put the chicken kievs in the fridge to firm up for about 20 minutes, then carefully place them in the deep-fat fryer and cook for about 5–6 minutes. Tip them out on to kitchen paper to dry, then serve.

4

SKILLS

- Filleting and removing the heads of the fish
- Pinboning the fish using fish tweezers
- Browning bones and making fish stock from them
- Dealing with chillies and saffron
- Puréeing in a blender and sieving
- How to co-ordinate several elements to a dish and have them ready at the same time

CORNISH RED MULLET SOUP
WITH CRISPY CROUTONS AND ROUILLE serves 4

FOR THE SOUP

4 whole small red mullet (120g each)

5 tablespoons rapeseed oil

1 onion, peeled and chopped

1 carrot, peeled and chopped

½ fennel bulb, chopped

1 celery stick, trimmed and chopped

1 leek, trimmed and chopped

2 garlic cloves, peeled and chopped

1 red chilli, deseeded and chopped

2 tablespoons tomato purée

large pinch saffron threads

2 tablespoons Pernod

salt and freshly ground black pepper

chopped flat-leaf parsley, to garnish

FOR THE CROUTONS

2 thick slices of white bread, each cut into 4 triangles, crusts removed

2 tablespoons rapeseed oil

2 tablespoons melted butter

chopped flat-leaf parsley, to garnish

FOR THE ROUILLE

4 tablespoons mayonnaise

1 garlic clove, peeled and finely grated

small pinch saffron threads, infused in 1 teaspoon warm water for a couple of minutes

few drops Tabasco sauce

lemon juice, to taste

Despite the origin of the fish, this soup is Mediterranean inspired. There are different layers of flavour and texture here that mean it can also be served as a main course. When shopping, look for fish that have full, not sunken, eyes and that don't smell 'fishy'; fresh fish never smells.

Preheat the oven to 200°C/fan 180°C/gas 6.

1 Prepare the red mullet by removing the heads and filleting each one. See the step-by-step photographs on pages 70-71. (You will get 2 fillets from each fish.) Remove any small bones with fish tweezers. Cut the fish heads and the bodies in half. Reserve the fillets for cooking later on. Heat 2 tablespoons of the oil in a large pan and fry all the fish bones and heads over a medium to high heat until golden brown.

2 Heat 2 more tablespoons of the oil in a separate large saucepan. Add the onion, carrot, fennel, celery and leek and cook over a medium heat until softened. Stir in the garlic and chilli and cook for a few more minutes. Add the tomato purée and cook for a further 2 minutes. Stir in the saffron threads and browned fish bones. Pour in about 1 litre of water and bring to the boil, then lower the heat and simmer gently for about 30 minutes.

3 While the stock is simmering, make the croutons and rouille. For the croutons (see page 72), lay the bread triangles on a baking sheet, drizzle over the oil and melted butter and toss together so the bread triangles are evenly coated. Toast in the preheated oven for about 10 minutes until golden and crisp. Take them out of the oven, sprinkle with parsley and cut each triangle into two smaller triangles.

4 Make the rouille by mixing the mayonnaise with the garlic and the infused saffron and water. Add a few drops of Tabasco, then add lemon juice and salt to taste.

5 Next put the soup in a jug blender in batches and pulse for a few seconds to help break up the bones. Strain the soup through a large sieve into a saucepan, pressing with the back of a spoon to encourage all the flavour out. Add the Pernod and keep the soup warm.

6 Lastly heat up a small frying pan with the remaining 1 tablespoon of oil. Season each red mullet fillet with salt and pepper and fry for 1½ minutes, skin-side down, then flip over and cook for a further 30 seconds. Remove from the heat and leave in the pan.

7 To serve, ladle the soup into individual bowls. Place 2 fillets of red mullet in each bowl, skin side up. Thickly spread the crouton triangles with the rouille and lay 1 in each bowl. Sprinkle with chopped parsley.

HOW TO FILLET A ROUND FISH

This specifically refers to Cornish Red Mullet Soup with Crispy Croutons and Rouille (page 69).

1 It is important to start with very fresh fish. Take a good look and check that the eyes are bright, not sunken. There should be no fishy smell whatsoever.

2 Take a sharp paring or filleting knife and slip the blade under the fin.

3 Now cut off the fish's head with a simple, strong cut.

4 Holding the fish firmly with your left hand, position your knife just below the back bone and run it down the back of the fish towards and beneath the tail to release the under fillet first. Be very gentle with the fish, just cutting and stroking, not tearing the flesh.

Gently remove the under fillet and then run your knife just above the backbone to take off the top fillet.

5 You will be left with the backbone, tail and head. Chop up into pieces to add to the stock later to flavour the soup.

7 Grasping a fillet at the tail end, scrape off all the fish scales from there to the head end using the back of your knife.

8 Remove any small pin-bones from the flesh of the fish with tweezers.

6 Trim around the fillets to remove any bits of fin or membrane.

9 It's now worth really taking your time, rubbing your finger down the back of the fish to check that there are no bones left in.

HOW TO MAKE CROUTONS

Croutons provide a crisp contrast in texture for a soup, so add them just before serving to keep them from becoming soggy. This specifically refers to Cornish Red Mullet Soup with Crispy Croutons (page 69).

1 Remove the crusts from a thick slice of white bread and lay the bread square on a baking tray. Brush melted butter over both sides of the bread slice. Then drizzle with oil.

2 Take the bread slice off the baking tray and slice into two triangles on a chopping board.

3 Place the crouton triangles back on the baking tray and toast in a preheated oven.

4 Take the croutons out of the oven. What we're looking for here is crisp, golden bread, not over oiled or buttered.

5 Sprinkle the chopped parsley over the croutons.

6 Cut each triangle into two smaller triangles and they're now ready to use.

PREPARING MUSSELS

Wild mussels are best avoided in the summer, but cultivated mussels can be eaten year round. Pick mussels that smell as fresh and salty as the sea. This specifically refers to Mussel Risotto (page 75).

1 Discard any mussels that have broken or cracked shells.

2 Pull off the wispy beards of your mussels.

3 Scrape off any barnacles and blemishes with a knife. Give them a quick wash and drain.

4 Discard any mussels that are open and refuse to close as they could be bad. It's important to be safe when handling shellfish.

5 Tip the mussels into a large heated pan. Add a dash of water, cover and bring to the boil and they will open in a matter of 4 or 5 minutes. Drain through muslin to get rid of the grit and discard any that haven't opened. Remove the mussels from the shells and give them another wash as they can still be a little bit grainy.

6 Set the mussel meat aside in a little bowl until you're ready to use it. Discard the shells if you don't need them.

SKILLS

• Preparing the mussels (see page 73), cooking and removing them from their shells
• Knife skills: preparing the shallots and garlic
• Making the risotto by gradually adding the stock
• Making sure the risotto has a loose consistency while keeping the grains *al dente*

MUSSEL RISOTTO   serves 4

400g live mussels, debearded, cleaned and scrubbed (discard any that are open but do not close when tapped)

50g unsalted butter

2 shallots, peeled and finely chopped

300g Arborio rice

100ml white wine

1 litre fish stock, kept hot in a pan

50g cold unsalted butter, cubed

2 tablespoons fresh dill, roughly chopped

2 tablespoons fresh chervil, roughly chopped

rapeseed oil, to drizzle

In Italy, risotto is never served as a main course, but as a starter. Cooking a good risotto is all about having a good technique. It requires patience and organisation. By the end the rice should be creamy but with a bite.

Before you cook your mussels, go through them and discard any that are open and refuse to close as they may be bad. It's best to err on the side of caution when cooking with shellfish.

1 Place a large saucepan on the heat, add 100ml water and the cleaned mussels and cover with a lid. Bring to the boil and steam the mussels for 4–5 minutes. Once the mussels have opened, drain through a sieve covered with muslin (for catching any grit), or a very fine sieve, but retain their juices. Discard any that have not opened and remove all the mussel meat from the rest of the shells, keeping 8 intact for garnishing. Set the meat aside in a small bowl and discard the shells.

2 Heat a large sauté pan and put in the butter. Once it has melted, add the shallots and cook over a medium heat for 4 minutes until they are soft but not coloured, then add the rice. Coat the rice in the butter and shallots and turn up the heat. Add the white wine and the reserved juices from the mussels and let the liquid reduce by a third.

3 Start to add the hot stock to the rice, a ladleful at a time, and continue stirring. Once the moisture has been absorbed and the mixture starts to look creamy, add another ladleful of stock. Continue to cook for 10 to 15 minutes, adding the stock gradually, until the rice grains are *al dente* and the risotto has a loose consistency that would drop off a spoon easily.

4 Stir in the cooked mussels and the cold cubed butter and warm through.

5 Spoon the risotto into the centre of 4 serving plates and garnish with the dill, chervil and 2 mussels in their shells on each risotto. Finish with a drizzle of rapeseed oil.

SKILLS
- Scoring the duck skin
- Preparation of ginger, garlic and chilli
- How to make a dressing
- Rendering the fat off the duck
- Roasting meat in the oven
- Using a wok – high heat, quick cooking
- Making a sugar syrup
- Segmenting, zesting and juicing the limes
- The art of resting meat

CRISPY DUCK, BOK CHOI AND BLACK BEANS WITH A LIME AND GINGER DRESSING serves 4

FOR THE DUCK

4 duck breasts, skin very thinly scored at an angle

2cm piece fresh ginger, peeled and finely chopped

1 garlic clove, peeled and thinly sliced

1 red chilli, deseeded and thinly sliced

4 baby bok choi, cut in half lengthways

20g fermented black beans

1 tablespoon roughly torn Thai basil

FOR THE LIME AND GINGER DRESSING

2cm piece fresh ginger, peeled and julienned

2 tablespoons caster sugar

3 tablespoons soy sauce

juice and zest of 1 unwaxed lime

1 lime, peeled, halved and flesh cut into segments

6 spring onions, trimmed and thinly cut on an angle

This is a dish that's all about the balance between sweetness, acidity and spiciness. Lime and ginger is a delicious combination that works really well with the duck. You won't need any oil in the pan because scoring the meat lets the fat out and crisps up the outside so all you're left with at the end is crispy skin and succulent meat, no fat.

Preheat the oven to 200°C/fan 180°C/gas 6.

1 Place a large ovenproof frying pan over a low heat and lay the scored duck breasts, skin side down, in the pan. Slowly turn the heat up under the pan to render off the fat – keeping this aside in a small jug or bowl – and make sure the skin is crispy.

2 Once the skin is crispy, either keep the duck breasts in the pan or transfer them to an oven dish, skin side down. Put the pan or dish in the preheated oven for 6–8 minutes. You want them to still be pink in the middle. Once cooked, remove from the oven and rest for a further 6–8 minutes, retaining the juices that have come out of the duck breasts.

3 Pour the reserved rendered duck fat into a hot frying pan or wok, then add the ginger, garlic and chilli and cook for 2 minutes over a high heat. Put the bok choi into the pan, and when it has wilted remove the pan from the heat and stir in the black beans, mashing them with a spoon, and the Thai basil. If the pan becomes too dry, add a little water.

4 To make the lime and ginger dressing, place the ginger, sugar and 50ml of water in a small saucepan. Bring to the boil and add the soy sauce, lime juice and zest, plus the reserved duck roasting juices. Remove the pan from the heat and add the lime segments.

5 Cut the duck breasts into slices on an angle and arrange with the bok choi on each plate. Drizzle over the lime and ginger dressing and garnish with the spring onions.

SKILLS

- Lining the moulds with butter, breadcrumbs and walnuts
- Making a roux and turning it into a white sauce
- Whisking egg whites
- Baking the soufflés in a bain-marie for the correct time
- Making a dressing
- Blanching the leeks

TWICE-BAKED GOAT'S CHEESE SOUFFLÉS WITH LEEKS AND WALNUTS serves 6

20g unsalted butter, melted

25g wholemeal breadcrumbs

25g walnuts, finely crushed

400ml whole milk

1 onion, peeled and cut in half

1 bay leaf

4 cloves

40g unsalted butter

40g plain flour

150g soft goat's cheese

4 eggs, separated

½ teaspoon freshly grated nutmeg

salt and freshly ground black pepper

150g hard goat's cheese, cut into 1cm fingers

3 leeks, trimmed

2 tablespoons finely chopped chives

walnut oil, to drizzle

9 walnuts, halved and then broken into quarters

A roux is the base for all white sauces – get it right and the rest of the recipe is easy. This one needs a thick consistency because when you add the goat's cheese it will become more runny and sauce-like. The reason this recipe calls for twice-baking (also known as a pudding soufflé) is for convenience: the soufflé can be made in advance and baked again just before serving. Step-by-step photographs for how to make a soufflé are on pages 80–81.

*Preheat the oven to 180°C/fan 160°C/gas 4.

1 Brush the insides of 8cm soufflé moulds with the melted butter. Mix the breadcrumbs and crushed walnuts together and put a heaped tablespoon in each of the moulds. Gently shake and move each mould around to coat the whole of the inside with the mixture and set aside in the fridge.

2 Place 300ml of the milk, the onion, bay leaf and cloves in a medium-sized saucepan and warm through. Do not let the milk boil till scalding.

3 Place the butter in another medium saucepan and melt over a medium heat, then add the flour, stir and cook for 4 minutes until the raw taste of the flour has gone. This is your roux. Gradually strain the warm milk into the roux while it is still on the heat, throwing away the aromatics left in the sieve, and whisking all the time. Add the soft goat's cheese and stir, then remove one quarter of the sauce to a small saucepan and set aside to cool for 10 minutes.

4 Stir the egg yolks into the sauce in the medium-sized saucepan, then add the nutmeg and seasoning. Transfer the mix to a bowl. In a separate bowl whisk the egg whites until firm. Off the heat, roughly fold in one tablespoon of the egg whites into the sauce, then gently fold in the rest, keeping the mixture airy.

5 Fill the moulds to the top with the mixture and run your finger around the edge to clean the lip – this will help the soufflés rise. Add the fingers of hard goat's cheese in the centre of each soufflé. Place the filled moulds in an oven dish and pour boiling water into the dish to a level halfway up the sides of the moulds (this is a bain-marie). Cook in the oven for 20 minutes.

6 Meanwhile plunge the whole trimmed leeks into boiling salted water and cook for 3 minutes until soft. Remove and slice the green part into thin rounds. Put the small saucepan that was set aside with the cooled sauce back on a low heat. Add the remaining 100ml of milk to make a thinner sauce. Then add the chives and keep warm until heated through.

7 Remove the soufflés from the oven and turn the oven up to 200°C/fan 180°C/gas 6. Use a knife to loosen the edges of the soufflés, then tip them out on to a baking tray lined with greaseproof paper and place back in the oven for 5 minutes.

8 Place 6 thin leek rounds in a circle on each plate. Place a soufflé on top of the leeks, drizzle with the remaining goat's cheese sauce and scatter the walnuts over.

HOW TO MAKE A SOUFFLÉ

A soufflé starts with a sauce made from equal quantities of fat and flour that thickens whatever liquid you add to it. This is called a roux and is the base for all white sauces. Get this part right and the soufflé is easy peasy. This specifically refers to Twice-baked Goat's Cheese Soufflés with Leeks and Walnuts (page 79).

1 Pour the milk into a saucepan with the onion, spices and any other flavourings and allow to just warm through to infuse. Melt the butter in another saucepan, add your flour and stir to cook and get rid of its rawness. Don't put any colour on the roux as it can change to a brown paste very easily. When the flour starts to bubble and the grains dance around in the pan, start adding the strained warm milk, bit by bit, whisking all the time. It will start to form a dough as you add the milk, so keep whisking until smooth, taking it on and off the heat to regulate the temperature. Use the back of a spoon to work the roux so you end up with an absolutely smooth sauce.

2 To prepare the moulds, use a little pastry brush to thoroughly line them with melted butter, trying not to use the milky residue, just the oily butter part.

Now line the moulds with the breadcrumb and nut mixture, not being afraid to put a little bit more on. By lining the moulds really well like this, you'll get the soufflés out much more easily. Set in the fridge.

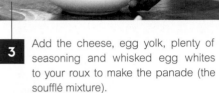

3 Add the cheese, egg yolk, plenty of seasoning and whisked egg whites to your roux to make the panade (the soufflé mixture).

4 Spoon in the soufflé mixture right to the top of the moulds. Run your finger around the edges to scrape off any excess mixture to help them rise.

5 Put the moulds in an oven dish and pour in hot water to make a bain-marie. What this does is to stop the soufflés cooking too fast.

Pop the soufflés in the oven. With these twice-baked, or pudding, soufflés, the advantage is that you can bake them in advance and then serve later by putting them back in the oven.

7 Turn out on to the baking tray and pop back in a hotter oven for 5 minutes before pouring over the cheese sauce.

6 The puddings should not have risen too much. Go round very gently with a knife to loosen them.

ONION, SPINACH AND RICOTTA RAVIOLI WITH A LEMON-CREAM SAUCE serves 4

FOR THE PASTA DOUGH

250g '00' flour, plus extra to dust

5 eggs (2 whole eggs, 3 egg yolks)

optional: 1 tablespoon olive oil

FOR THE RAVIOLI FILLING

knob unsalted butter

4 banana shallots, peeled and sliced

150g baby spinach leaves

pinch freshly grated nutmeg

125g ricotta cheese

salt and freshly ground black pepper

1 egg, beaten

Spinach and ricotta is a classic pasta filling, but adding onion creates an extra dimension of texture and flavour. When you drain the water from your spinach, instead of throwing it away you could use it in a vegetable stock, to cook pulses or even drink it! It is extremely good for you, with a high iron content.

Preheat the oven to 200°C/fan 180°C/gas 6.

1 To make the pasta dough, put the flour and eggs in a food processor with a standard blade attachment and pulse until the mixture comes together. Add 1 tablespoon of olive oil if a little extra moisture is needed.

2 Remove the dough from the processor to a board and knead until smooth, being careful not to overwork the dough. If the dough is too wet, add a little extra flour.

3 Cover the dough with cling film and leave to rest in the fridge for 30 minutes.

4 Remove the dough from the fridge and cut in half. Lightly dust the pasta and the pasta machine with some extra flour.

5 Feed the first half of the dough through the pasta machine, gradually reducing the setting each time, starting from the thickest and finishing with the thinnest setting, so you end up with a thin sheet of dough. Cover with a tea towel until ready to use. Repeat with the second piece of dough.

6 Next make the ravioli filling. Heat a medium-sized sauté pan and put in the butter. Once it is foaming, add the shallots and fry for 2–3 minutes over a medium heat until soft. Add the spinach and grated nutmeg and cook until the spinach has wilted. Transfer the mixture to a sieve and press down on it with a spoon, to get rid of the water.

SKILLS
- Making the pasta dough
- Rolling out and putting the pasta dough through the machine
- Making ravioli and cooking it
- Knife skills: chopping the shallots and red onion

FOR THE ONIONS AND SAGE LEAVES

4 red onions, peeled and thickly sliced
4 tablespoons olive oil
50g caster sugar
juice of 1 lemon
8 whole sage leaves

FOR THE LEMON-CREAM SAUCE

300ml single cream
peel of 2 unwaxed lemons
4 garlic cloves, peeled and smashed
2 whole sage leaves
juice of 1 lemon
knob unsalted butter

7 Remove the shallots and spinach from the sieve and roughly chop. Place in a bowl with the ricotta, season with salt and pepper, mix and set aside.

8 Lay the pasta sheets on a floured surface and cut out circles using a 6cm round pastry cutter.

9 Lay a teaspoon of the spinach and ricotta mix in the centre of one pasta circle and brush the beaten egg wash around the edge of the circle. Place another pasta circle on top and press to seal the edges. Repeat with all the pasta dough and filling, to make 8 ravioli.

10 For the griddled onions, place the sliced onions in an ovenproof dish and brush with 2 tablespoons of the oil. Sprinkle on the sugar and put in the preheated oven for 15 minutes. Remove from the oven and squeeze over the lemon juice.

11 Heat a large pan of salted water. Once it's boiling, carefully add the ravioli. They will take 3–4 minutes to cook and will float to the top when ready.

12 For the sauce, put the cream, lemon peel, garlic and 2 sage leaves into a medium-sized saucepan and slowly bring to the boil. Reduce the heat and simmer for 1 minute. Pass through a sieve then pour the flavoured cream back into the pan, add the lemon juice and season with salt and pepper. Gently warm through, adding the butter gradually.

13 Fry the sage leaves off in a small pan in the remaining 2 tablespoons of oil until crisp and drain on kitchen paper.

14 Place the griddled red onions in the centre of each plate and put 2 ravioli on top. Drizzle the lemon-cream sauce over and finish with 2 crispy sage leaves.

HOW TO MAKE FRESH PASTA

These instructions specifically refer to Onion, Spinach and Ricotta Ravioli with a Lemon-cream Sauce (page 82) and Mushroom Tortellini with Chicken Consommé (page 91).

1 Add the Italian '00' flour to a food processor. Using '00' flour will give you a higher concentration of gluten than plain flour and makes the pasta stringy with an *al dente* texture. Add the eggs, olive oil and salt, breaking it up in your fingers to disperse.

2 Pulse in a food processor to mix all the ingredients together, then flour your hands, not the dough, and take the dough out of the food processor.

3 Knead the dough until smooth to encourage the gluten to become elastic. The texture changes really fast, so work quickly, adding a little extra flour if it's too moist.

Wrap the dough in cling film to stop it becoming hard on the surface and leave to rest for half an hour.

4 When you're ready to work with the pasta, unwrap from the cling film. Cut the pasta dough in half, keeping the piece you're not working with covered.

If you look at your pasta machine, the settings start at six and go down to zero. The idea when making pasta sheets is to bring them down from six to zero, working the pasta a little bit each time to make it more elastic.

5

Flatten your pasta dough and pass through the machine at the widest setting. This is another form of kneading and gets the gluten working and becoming really elastic. You need a pass or two passes of the pasta at each setting and you must work at speed. This is really important as you don't want the pasta to dry out.

After you've passed the pasta through a setting a few times, take it out of the machine and flour if needed.

6 Fold the pasta in half, then fold it over again.

7 Keep passing the pasta through the machine, gradually reducing the setting each time until the pasta gets thinner and thinner. Don't bring it down too quickly through the settings or it will become like a wet sheet.

Flour the pasta if needed, but don't over flour it as this can make it tough. The pasta is ready when you start to see your hand underneath it. You want it really thin if you're making a filled pasta like ravioli as it will be doubled over the filling.

Tip: Get a damp cloth ready, fold it up and lay it gently on top of your sheets of pasta to keep them moist while you cut them into shape.

8 When the pasta is thin enough, cut into equal-size pieces as you bring it out of the machine.

HOW TO MAKE RAVIOLI

1 Lay a couple of pasta sheets on a floured surface and, working quickly, cut into squares.

2 Brush around the outside of the squares with egg to help the pasta sheets stick together.

3 Make sure the filling is not too wet: imagine what this will do to the pasta. We're going to do the ravioli in rounds, so not too much filling in each one.

4 Making sure your hands aren't wet, take another square of pasta and place over the top. Work your hands around the pasta, making sure you get rid of any air bubbles as air expands as it heats and you don't want the ravioli to become balloon-like or burst open.

5 If I was making these at home for myself, I wouldn't cut them out, but this is Cookery School, so I'm going to make you cut them out with a round pastry cutter.

6 Then snip, snip, snip around the outside to neaten them up.

The filling is already cooked, so you only need to warm it up and make sure the pasta is cooked. Just 3 or 4 minutes in boiled salted water should do it.

7 Filled pastas tend to sink, then bounce to the top when they're cooked. Take out with a slotted spoon to drain.

HOW TO MAKE TORTELLINI

1 Lay a couple of pasta sheets on a floured surface and, working quickly, cut into squares.

2 Using a round cookie cutter, cut out discs from your pasta squares.

3 Using a pastry brush, carefully brush whisked egg yolk around the edges of the discs and then place a small amount of filling into the centre of each.

4 Fold the pasta in half, over the top of the filling, and crimp the edges sealed with your fingers.

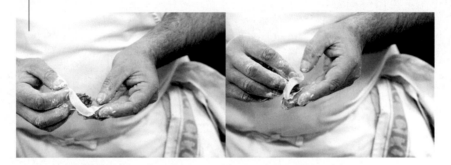

5 Once sealed, bend the pasta around your finger and press each end in towards the middle to form a parcel.

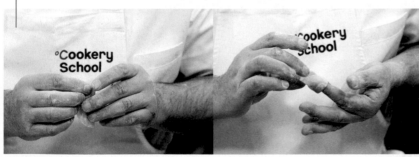

Bring a large saucepan of water to a rolling boil, and cook the tortellini for 2–3 minutes.

6

CLEAR TOMATO SOUP WITH AN AUBERGINE, COURGETTE AND TOMATO RATATOUILLE serves 4

1¼kg overripe cherry tomatoes, halved

1 garlic clove, peeled and finely chopped

8 basil leaves

½ teaspoon sea salt

1 medium aubergine

1 medium courgette

4 ripe plum tomatoes, peeled

2 tablespoons olive oil

salt and freshly ground black pepper

basil cress (baby basil), to garnish

extra virgin olive oil, to drizzle

This clear tomato consommé is not cooked at all. Try to start the day before, straining the tomatoes through muslin over a bowl, to produce delicious, clear tomato water. It is the perfect dish to make when you have a glut of summer tomatoes, or as a feel-good dish when you're a bit under the weather.

1 Put the cherry tomatoes, garlic, basil leaves and salt in a small food processer and pulse, just until you release the tomato juices. If you blend it too much, your soup won't be clear.

2 Place a sieve over a large bowl and put a piece of muslin inside the sieve. Pour the tomato mixture into the muslin and let the juices drain through into the bowl. Leave for 20–30 minutes.

3 Next cut the vegetables for the ratatouille into brunoise (small dice). Cut the aubergine into julienne batons. Then turn the batons through a quarter turn and cut again, to form tiny 3mm-sided dice. Do the same with the courgette and 1 of the peeled tomatoes – deseed the tomato first.

4 With the remaining 3 tomatoes, simply cut these into tomato petals by quartering them and removing the seeds.

5 Put a large sauté pan over a medium heat and pour in the olive oil. Once the oil is hot, add the aubergine brunoise and fry until they are cooked but still holding their shape; this will take 2–3 minutes. Then add the courgette and tomato brunoise and cook for another 1–2 minutes. Season with salt and pepper and remove from the heat.

6 To serve, place a 5cm-diameter pastry ring in the centre of the first serving bowl and line the ring with tomato petals, making sure they overlap. Fill the tomato ring with ratatouille. Remove the ring and repeat for the other 3 serving bowls.

7 Gently squeeze the muslin with the tomato pulp over the large bowl, but not too tightly since some tomato pulp could go into the soup and this will make it cloudy. Then carefully pour the clear tomato soup around the ratatouille in each serving bowl.

8 Garnish with the basil cress and drizzle a few droplets of extra virgin olive oil into the soup.

SKILLS

- Knife skills: cutting the tomatoes, aubergine and courgettes into brunoise (small dice)
- Making the clear tomato water
- Making the ratatouille, by frying the vegetables

MUSHROOM TORTELLINI WITH CHICKEN CONSOMMÉ serves 4

FOR THE PASTA DOUGH

250g '00' flour, plus extra to dust

5 eggs (2 whole eggs, 3 yolks, reserving 2 egg whites for the consommé)

1 tablespoon olive oil (if needed)

FOR THE CHICKEN CONSOMMÉ

2 deboned chicken legs, skinned

½ onion, peeled and roughly chopped

2 sprigs tarragon, roughly chopped

salt and freshly ground black pepper

2 egg whites (reserved from the pasta dough ingredients)

1¼ litres chicken stock

2 tablespoons fino sherry

FOR THE TORTELLINI

2 tablespoons olive oil

50g pancetta, cut into small dice

1 shallot, peeled and finely chopped

1 garlic clove, peeled and crushed

125g oyster mushrooms, finely chopped

125g chanterelle mushrooms, finely chopped

2 tablespoons double cream

2 sprigs tarragon, finely chopped

juice of 1 lemon

½ teaspoon truffle oil

1 egg, beaten

baby tarragon leaves, to garnish

Consommé is a clear, highly flavoured stock. As you cook the chicken mixture in it the stock clarifies, lifting all the impurities out of it. The strained consommé is probably one of the healthiest things you could ever imagine and is a joy to eat. The home-made tortellini, with fresh egg pasta and a rich chanterelle and oyster mushroom filling, perfectly matches the lightness of the consommé.

1 Start by making and rolling the pasta dough. (See pages 84–5.)

2 To make the chicken consommé, place the raw chicken meat in a food processor with the onion and tarragon and season with salt and pepper. Pulse to finely chop the mixture, then add the egg white and pulse again.

3 Pour the stock into a large saucepan, add the chicken mixture and slowly bring to the boil over a low to medium heat. Leave to simmer for 30 minutes.

4 Remove the saucepan from the heat and strain the consommé into a clean saucepan by pouring it through a piece of muslin placed in a sieve. Do not squeeze or stir the liquid. When it has all drained through, add the fino sherry to the consommé and return to a low heat to keep warm.

5 To make the tortellini filling, heat a medium-sized sauté pan over a medium heat and pour in the olive oil. Once the oil is hot, add the diced pancetta and cook for 2 minutes, add the shallot and cook for 2–3 minutes until soft, then add the garlic and cook for a further minute.

6 Add both types of mushrooms to the pan and cook until all their liquid has evaporated. Take the pan off the heat and, when the filling has cooled, pour in the cream and stir in the chopped tarragon, lemon juice and truffle oil.

7 Lay the pasta sheets out on a floured work surface and cut out 12 circles in the pasta dough using a 5cm round pastry cutter.

8 Place a teaspoon of the mushroom filling mixture in the centre of one circle and brush the beaten egg wash around the edge. Fold the circle over to form a half moon shape and press down gently around the edges to seal the filling in. Holding both ends of the pasta moon, twist slightly to form a shell-like shape. Repeat with the remaining pasta circles and filling.

9 Bring a large saucepan of salted water to the boil, drop in the tortellini and cook for 2 minutes.

10 To serve, remove the tortellini from the pan with a slotted spoon and place in 4 serving bowls, then pour the chicken consommé around the pasta. Garnish with the baby tarragon leaves.

GARLIC CUSTARD WITH SNAILS serves 4

2 eggs
  (1 whole egg, 1 yolk)
120ml whole milk
70ml double cream
12 garlic cloves, peeled
1 bunch flat-leaf parsley,
  roughly chopped
50g baby spinach leaves,
  plus 50g for serving
1 tablespoons olive oil
20 snails (buy boiled
  snails as these will be
  pre-cleaned and shelled,
  if you use tinned snails
  these need to be
  drained and washed)
4 rashers unsmoked
  bacon, cut into lardons

Custard is an incredibly delicate mixture and should be cooked evenly over time – there is no rush. The eggs must be added off the heat and the custard is warmed gently until slightly thickened. The baked custards are ready when they have a very slight wobble like a lightly set jelly. You can pop a tiny knob of butter on top of each custard when they come out of the oven to stop a skin forming as they start to cool. Make sure the snails you use are sterile and not just picked up from the garden!

Preheat the oven to 150°C/fan 130°C/gas 3.

1 Line the insides of 4 x 60ml ramekins or small moulds with cling film.

2 Place the whole egg and the egg yolk in a medium-sized bowl and whisk together by hand.

3 Put the milk and cream in a medium-sized saucepan, add 10 of the garlic cloves and bring to a gentle simmer. Reduce the heat and simmer for 14 minutes, then add the parsley and 50g of spinach leaves, leaving 20 leaves to one side.

4 Cook for another minute, then pour the mixture into a blender and liquidize until smooth. Pass through a fine sieve into a jug and then pour into the bowl with the eggs. Whisk well together. Wipe the saucepan, then return the flavoured custard to it and stir over a low heat until thickened slightly.

5 Pour the thickened custard into the lined ramekins. Place the ramekins in a deep roasting tin or oven dish and pour boiling water into the tin to about two thirds of the way up the sides of the ramekins (this is a bain-marie). Put the roasting tin in the preheated oven and cook for 25 minutes, until the custards have just set but there is still a slight wobble in the centre.

6 Meanwhile, slice the remaining 2 garlic cloves. Put them in a small frying pan with the olive oil and fry over a medium heat for 1–2 minutes until crisp. Remove the garlic from the pan and set aside on kitchen paper to soak up the excess oil.

7 Fry the bacon over a medium heat for about 5 minutes until crispy, then add the snails to the pan and cook for another 2 minutes. When they are cooked, remove the pan from the heat, add the remaining 20 spinach leaves to the pan and toss until wilted.

8 Remove the custards from the oven and allow to cool slightly.

9 To serve, carefully turn out a garlic custard upside down on to each plate, removing the cling film from around it. Wrap each snail in a wilted spinach leaf and arrange 5 on each plate, sitting each snail on 2 leaves of baby spinach. Top with the crispy bacon lardons and garlic slices.

SKILLS

• Knife skills: cutting
  the bacon
• Making the custard
• Wilting the spinach
• Cooking the bacon
• Liquidizing the spinach

GIZZI'S NOTES ON GARNISHING

Garnishing is not just about making something pretty – it has to contribute to the taste of the dish.

A classic example of bad garnishing is the restaurant-ordered pudding topped with a sprig of mint. What is the mint doing there? Nothing! All you want to do before tucking into the pudding is remove it. The thing to remember is that everything on the plate has to be relevant to the dish.

So, when you garnish, don't be tempted to think with your eyes, but with your mouth; always garnish food with herbs and foods that complement the flavours of the dish. Using basil as a garnish for some smoked salmon, for instance, will look pretty but it won't work, because the subtle aniseed flavour will be too aromatic for the salmon, which needs something more herbal like dill or chives. There is a tendency for people to put chopped parsley on everything, but raw parsley has a very aggressive flavour that can take over a dish. It's best when stirred in at the end of cooking, unless it's being used as a salad leaf. You can also deep-fry herbs as a garnish; flat-leaf parsley and sage leaves both work well.

The Japanese herb shiso is one of my favourites and it looks spectacular. It works brilliantly on Asian-inspired cold dishes like sashimis and tatakis, which are seared, dressed salads (see page 300). Crushed peanuts and fresh coriander are also used to garnish Asian dishes. Coriander cress (baby coriander) looks even more delicate and stylish. In the same context, fresh basil leaves work well as a final garnish for Italian dishes.

Classic pairings work best when garnishing – roast beef with horseradish and watercress, fried sage with veal, or a good grating of Parmesan over pasta or risotto dishes. These extra layers of flavour are a great way of elevating a dish from the everyday to the superb. What a difference a scattering of bacon lardons and sprigs of peashoots can make to a humble bowl of pea soup, for instance.

GIZZI'S NOTES ON BREAD

Bread has changed so much in the last few years. Just think of all the different varieties we enjoy now thanks to the rebirth of artisan bakeries. When my mum was growing up, all bakeries made their own bread on the premises, but then supermarket sliced bread took over the market. Nowadays we have come full circle and are starting to look back to how bread used to be made and finding inspiration there. Artisan breads taste phenomenal and contain only as many ingredients as you can count on the fingers of one hand. Compare that with the supermarket breads, which are packed full of numerous disconcerting additives.

Sourdough bread in particular is enjoying something of a renaissance. Naturally occurring yeasts from the air make sourdough bread denser and far more flavourful than regular bread. Because it is made from such natural ingredients and lacks artificial fillers, sourdough doesn't have the unnatural sponginess of overly processed bread. The result is a really tasty bread that has a nice, crispy texture.

Rye bread is another delicious variety, with a strong and malty flavour. It originates from Scandinavia and goes really well with northern delicacies like smoked salmon and gravadlax. Rye flour is a wheat-free grain, making 100% rye bread an ideal option for people who are allergic to wheat. It's not OK for people with gluten intolerances, though.

British and French breads are traditionally made to be eaten with butter, but Italian breads contain a lot of olive oil in the dough itself, creating chewy and stringy-textured breads. For this reason I prefer to serve them with olive oil and some balsamic vinegar to dip the bread into, rather than butter. Focaccia is a light but heavily oiled Italian bread that is very chewy. If you are cooking an Italian meal, focaccia or ciabatta would make the perfect accompaniment, served with olive oil and balsamic vinegar for plunging.

When cooking for a dinner party, you could have a bread board or basket at the beginning of a meal, or you could match the bread with your starter. Some dishes call for bread – like soup – and just think of how well brown, wholemeal or even soda bread goes with smoked salmon.

Leftover bread is very often just thrown away, but there's no need to waste it. Simply blitz it in the food processor to make breadcrumbs – you can always freeze them. Or why not use slightly stale bread to make bread sauce or a bread and butter pudding?

FISH

BASIC

- Wild salmon wrapped in lardo
  with fennel purée and fennel salad
- Sea bass with wilted spinach
  and mushrooms
- Smoked salmon with duck egg omelette
- Salt-and-pepper squid with dipping sauce
- Crab and orange salad
- Tuna burgers with wasabi mayonnaise
- Moules marinière
- Carpaccio of smoked haddock
  with a vegetable vinaigrette

INTERMEDIATE

- Sardines with pine nut and feta stuffing
  and a parsley-caper salad
- Pollock goujons with home-made tartare
  sauce and crispy parsley
- Chip-smoked scallops with sweetcorn
  and bacon salad
- Baby squid stuffed with chorizo and feta
  and a tomato and roasted garlic sauce
- Dressed crab with seasonal vegetables
- Tuna niçoise
- Razor clams with a tomato sauce
- Poached haddock with salsify fricassée
  and a salmon egg and chive sauce

ADVANCED

- Mackerel with gingered-rhubarb
  hollandaise and pickled rhubarb
- Stuffed lemon sole with scampi
  and tenderstem broccoli
- Tea-smoked mackerel with beetroot stew
  and fresh curd
- Squid-ink gnocchi with Brussels sprouts
  and chilli
- Crab bisque with sesame crab toasts
- Pepper-crusted tuna with carpaccio
  of mushrooms and chestnut beignets
- Clam chowder with mini garlic loaves
- Haddock and parsnip fish cakes with
  a spiced parsnip cream

SKILLS
- Pin-boning a fish with fish tweezers
- Pan-frying salmon and finishing it off in the oven

WILD SALMON WRAPPED IN LARDO WITH FENNEL PURÉE AND FENNEL SALAD serves 4

FOR THE FENNEL PURÉE

4 bulbs fennel, with feathery fronds reserved

salt and freshly ground black pepper

75g unsalted butter

100ml double cream, plus up to an extra 100ml if needed

2 tablespoons Pernod

FOR THE WILD SALMON

4 x 180g wild salmon fillets

8 strips very thinly sliced lardo

1 tablespoon mild olive oil

1 lemon, cut into wedges

FOR THE FENNEL SALAD

1 bulb fennel

1 tablespoon extra virgin olive oil

juice of 1 lemon

This is one of my favourite recipes. It was one of the first reviewed in my restaurant so it always brings a smile to my face. Personally I don't favour farmed salmon. As a minimum requirement it's worth eating organic, but wild salmon is the king of fish. Delicious, beautiful and there's no taste like it.

Preheat the oven to 180°C/fan 160°C/gas 5.

1   First make the purée. Chop the fennel into small, even dice to help it cook quickly and evenly. Season with salt and pepper, then sweat it in the butter in a frying pan over a low to medium heat until softened. Add 125ml of water and the 100ml of cream, and cook gently with the lid on for 20 minutes until softened but not coloured.

2   Once the fennel is cooked, add the Pernod and purée in a blender until thick and smooth, adding the extra cream if needed.

3   Remove the skin from the salmon and any dark grey bits. Cut each fillet in half lengthways. Pin-bone the fillets by running your finger down, along the line of the bone. If you feel a bone, pull it out with fish tweezers. Season with salt and pepper and form a circle by curving the two pieces round. Place a piece of the reserved fennel fronds in the middle of each and then wrap 2 strips of lardo around the sides. Secure the lardo with butcher's string.

4   Over a medium heat, pan-fry the fish fillet parcels in the olive oil in a large non-stick ovenproof frying pan for 1 minute on each side. Place them in the preheated oven for 5–8 minutes, until the salmon is cooked but still pink in the middle and the lardo has crisped up nicely.

5   Next prepare the salad by thinly slicing the fennel. Place in a bowl, pour over boiling water to cover and leave for 1–2 minutes. Drain the water and dress the fennel with the olive oil and lemon juice and season with salt and pepper.

6   Serve by spooning some fennel purée on to each plate, top it with the salmon fillets, place some fennel salad on the side and garnish with more of the reserved fennel fronds and a wedge of lemon.

SKILLS
● How to make a basic cream sauce
● How to wilt leaves in a pan

SEA BASS WITH WILTED SPINACH AND MUSHROOMS serves 4

50g unsalted butter

2 tablespoons olive oil

2 shallots, peeled and finely chopped

2 garlic cloves, peeled and crushed

4 x 180g sea bass fillets, skin on and scored

150g button mushrooms, sliced

50–100ml fresh fish stock

250g baby spinach leaves

4–5 tablespoons crème fraîche

salt and freshly ground black pepper

1 lemon, cut into wedges

This is such a delicious and flavoursome yet simple dish. Crème fraîche, garlic and lemon are all favourites of mine. You may wonder why the skin of the fish needs to be scored and the answer is that it ensures even cooking all the way through. With fish, though, undercooking is more acceptable than overcooking.

1 Heat a large frying pan and put in 30g butter and 1 tablespoon of the oil. Once hot, add the shallots and cook over a low to medium heat for 3 minutes until softened, then add the garlic and cook for a further 2 minutes.

2 Meanwhile heat another large frying pan and add the remaining oil and butter. Once the oil is hot put in the sea bass fillets and cook over a medium heat for 2–3 minutes on each side. Always cook fish presentation-side down first. In this instance it should be skin-side down first.

3 Add the mushrooms to the pan of shallots and cook for a further 2 minutes. Add the fish stock and allow to reduce for 1 minute before adding the baby spinach. If the liquid evaporates, add some more stock. Once the spinach has wilted, remove the pan from the heat and stir in the crème fraîche. Taste and season with salt and pepper if necessary.

4 Place the wilted spinach and mushrooms in the centre of each plate and put the sea bass fillets on top. Serve with the lemon wedges.

SKILLS
- Knowing when butter foams so it does not burn
- Making the perfect omelette, drawing the egg in from the sides of the pan
- Rolling the omelette in the pan
- Piping the crème fraîche mix into the omelette

SMOKED SALMON WITH DUCK EGG OMELETTE *serves 4*

40g unsalted butter

6 duck's eggs, beaten with a fork and seasoned with salt and freshly ground black pepper

2 shallots, peeled and finely chopped

200g crème fraîche

salt and freshly ground black pepper

150g smoked salmon

2 tablespoons finely chopped chives

40g fresh horseradish, finely grated

piping bag, or ziplock bag with the corner snipped off, for piping the filling

As far as I am concerned, this should be everyone's favourite supper! Salmon and chives are a marriage made in heaven and fresh horseradish lights up your palate like a Christmas tree. It's a cheap dish too, by the way. Try to stay away from using mass-produced smoked salmon. The best smoked salmon is first cured, then dried and cold smoked.

1 Heat a 20cm frying pan and put in a small knob of the butter. When it begins to foam, add a quarter of the beaten eggs.

2 With your fork, draw the egg continuously from the outside of the pan towards the centre, moving the pan so the base is always covered with uncooked egg. Once the omelette starts to set, roll it up so it resembles a thick spring roll.

3 Transfer the omelette roll to a warm plate and cook three more with the remaining butter and beaten eggs.

4 Combine the shallots and crème fraîche in a bowl and season with salt and pepper. Cut a slit along the top of each omelette roll with a sharp knife, and pipe a quarter of the crème fraîche mixture into each slit.

5 To serve, tear the smoked salmon into strips and drape over the top of the filled omelette rolls, then sprinkle with the chives and finely grated horseradish and serve any remaining mixture on the side.

SKILLS
- Preparing the squid: cleaning it and cutting it (see pages 108–109)
- Coating the squid in cornflour, salt and pepper
- Frying the squid until crispy
- Knife skills: preparing all the vegetables; julienning

SALT-AND-PEPPER SQUID WITH DIPPING SAUCE serves 4

FOR THE SQUID

vegetable, sunflower or groundnut oil, for frying

4 teaspoons black peppercorns, crushed

4 teaspoons sea salt

6 tablespoons cornflour

2 large whole squid, cleaned and prepared, flesh cut into triangles and scored in a diamond shape plus the tentacles (buy ready prepared or see page 108)

FOR THE DIPPING SAUCE

½ carrot, peeled and cut into small dice

1 shallot, peeled and cut into small dice

⅓ cucumber, deseeded and cut into small dice

1 red Thai chilli, cut into small dice

4 tablespoons fish sauce

4 tablespoons rice vinegar

1½ tablespoons tomato ketchup

2 tablespoons caster sugar

juice of 2 limes

FOR THE GARNISH

6 spring onions, trimmed and thinly cut on an angle

1 lime, cut into wedges

1 red Thai chilli, thinly sliced

Cooked squid has such a clean taste and soft texture. You might be surprised to see ketchup in this recipe but, believe it or not, when used in a dipping sauce it helps to bring all the flavours together really quickly. The mixture of vinegar, sugar and salt acts as a flavour enhancer. For further instructions on how to clean and prepare squid, see pages 108–9.

Pour in the oil and preheat the deep-fat fryer to 180ºC/350°F, according to the manufacturer's instructions.

1   In a large bowl, mix together the crushed peppercorns, salt and cornflour. Place the prepared squid pieces and tentacles in the bowl and mix well to coat.

2   To make the sauce, place the diced carrot, shallot, cucumber and chilli (remove the seeds if you don't want it too hot) in a medium-sized bowl and add the fish sauce, rice vinegar, ketchup, sugar and lime juice. Stir well and set aside while you fry the squid.

3   Put the seasoned squid in the preheated deep-fat fryer, a few pieces at a time so as not to overcrowd the fryer (otherwise the squid will not crisp up), and fry for 3–5 minutes, until browned and crisp.

4   Remove the squid from the fryer and place on a piece of kitchen paper to soak up the excess oil.

5   To serve, place the squid on plates and put the dipping sauce in small individual dishes on the side. Garnish with the spring onions, lime wedges and sliced chilli.

HOW TO CLEAN AND PREPARE SQUID

When you buy a squid that has not been prepared, you will need to clean it – a messy, but not too difficult, business. This specifically refers to Salt-and-Pepper Squid with Dipping Sauce (page 107).

1 Very fresh squid looks shiny and slippery with clear eyes. First of all, cut the head and tentacles from the body.

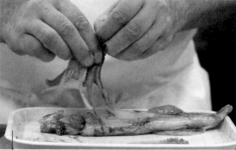

2 Now, peel the squid (the skin should come off quite easily).

3 Hold the squid up and give it a squeeze to remove all the entrails from inside.

4 There's a piece of plastic-like cartilage in the back that you need to pull out and remove.

5 Put the squid in a bowl of cold water to clean it.

6 Cut through and remove any tentacles. Don't throw them away, they are delicious too.

7 Cut the squid into pieces. I like to keep them as large as possible. When you open the squid up, even if it has been cleaned, it's always a good idea to give it a scrape down the middle in case there's anything left in there.

8 Put the squid into the seasoned cornflour and mix together.

SKILLS
• Segmenting oranges
• Making a dressing: the correct balance
  between the orange juice and oil

CRAB AND ORANGE SALAD serves 4

4 green cardamom
  pods, split open
2 oranges
2 ruby grapefruit
juice of 1 lemon
1 head of frisée lettuce
1 small bag of lamb's
  lettuce
300g white crabmeat
3 tablespoons olive oil
salt and freshly ground
  black pepper

This salad is infused with the lovely flavour of cardamom. You want to have a light touch when seasoning it, so you don't destroy the subtle flavours. Frisée is a great lettuce. The outside leaves are strong and quite peppery, perfect for a bacon salad, but this recipe calls for something more delicate, so be sure to pick out the choicest leaves from the centre.

Preheat the oven to 180°C/fan 160°C/gas 4.

1   Place the cardamom pods on a small baking tray and place in the preheated oven for 5 minutes. Take the tray out of the oven and, using the end of a rolling pin, bash the pods to remove the seeds and then gently crush the seeds.

2   To segment the oranges and grapefruit, cut the top and the bottom off the fruit and remove the peel. Hold the fruit in your hand and, using a small sharp knife, cut in between the segments. The segments will drop out. Squeeze any remaining juice from the shell of the oranges and grapefruit, and retain the juices in a small bowl for the dressing. Add the lemon juice.

3   Place the orange and grapefruit segments in a large bowl and add the toasted and crushed cardamom seeds, the frisée and lamb's lettuce leaves and the crabmeat.

4   To the reserved citrus juice, add the olive oil and some salt and pepper and whisk. Pour this dressing over the salad and mix.

5   Place the dressed salad in the centre of each serving plate.

HOW TO PREPARE AND PICK CRABMEAT

I like to cook with a male (cock) crab as they're much bigger and have more meat in the claws. This specifically refers to Crab and Orange Salad (page 111).

1 Take your whole cooked crab and pop it on the board.

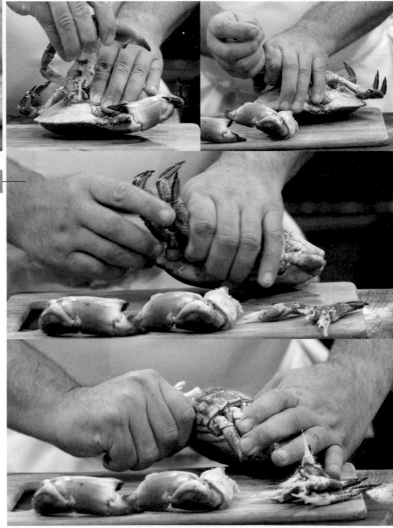

2 A crab has two claws and eight little legs. Lay the crab on its back and remove the claws, twisting and breaking them off.

Grab hold of all four legs on one side and pull them to the back, taking them out of their sockets together. Repeat on the other side.

3 Stand the crab up on the board and then place your two thumbs on its back.

Push the belly shell forward until it cracks off and discard.

Take out the small sac at the top of the body and the dead man's fingers (the lungs) that line the edge of the body.

Using the back of a knife, crack open the claws with one large crack, trying not to break and disintegrate the shell into pieces. Crab shell shatters like glass and you can never remove it all. Break the legs with the knife on the pointy side.

4

Using a lobster pick or the end of a teaspoon, open up the shells of the legs to scoop the white meat out.

5

6 Now take the white meat from the claws.

7 For the brown meat, I use a lobster pick or a tablespoon to scoop it out from the body.

Knife skills: cutting the spring onions
and tuna into brunoise (small dice)

TUNA BURGERS WITH WASABI MAYONNAISE

serves 4

FOR THE TUNA BURGERS

400g tuna steak

4 spring onions, trimmed

2cm piece fresh ginger, peeled and grated

salt and freshly ground black pepper

2 tablespoons vegetable oil

50g crispy seaweed

50g wasabi peas, crushed

1 lime, cut into wedges

FOR THE WASABI MAYONNAISE

2 egg yolks

3 teaspoons wasabi paste

2 tablespoons white wine vinegar

250ml mild olive oil

juice of 1 lime, to taste

The belly part of the yellowfin tuna is ideal to chop up finely and mix with spring onions and ginger to make lightly seasoned burgers. This fish is widely available and avoids using any tuna from over-fished areas, such as the Atlantic bluefin tuna and tuna from the Bay of Biscay.

Wasabi is an oriental wild horseradish. Added to a plump homemade mayonnaise, it's a fiery accompaniment that goes particularly well with fish. Flash-fry the burgers on both sides and serve them rare.

1 Cut the tuna and spring onions into julienne batons. Then turn the julienne batons through a quarter turn and cut again, to form tiny 3mm-sided dice (brunoise).

2 Place the tuna, spring onions and ginger in an ice-cold medium-sized bowl and season with salt and pepper, then mix well to combine.

3 Place a 7cm-diameter pastry ring on to a plate and fill with one quarter of the tuna mixture. Press to pack the mixture down. Remove the ring and set the burger aside. Repeat with the remaining tuna mixture to make 3 more burgers, then cover and place in the fridge until needed.

4 To make the wasabi mayonnaise, place the egg yolks in a small food processor and add the wasabi paste and white wine vinegar. Start the motor and gradually pour in the mild olive oil until you have a thick, smooth mayonnaise. Check the seasoning at this stage and add lime juice to taste.

5 Heat a large frying pan over a medium to high heat, and once it is hot add the vegetable oil. Carefully lift each tuna burger with a fish slice and gently place in the frying pan. Cook for 30 seconds on each side to seal the burgers.

6 Place each tuna burger on a serving plate with a dollop of the wasabi mayonnaise beside it. Top with the crispy seaweed, scatter the crushed wasabi peas around the burger and place a lime wedge on the side.

SKILLS
- Knife skills: cutting the shallots, garlic and parsley
- Cooking the mussels correctly

MOULES MARINIÈRE serves 4

2 tablespoons olive oil

2 shallots, peeled and finely chopped

1 garlic clove, peeled and crushed

1 bay leaf

200ml white wine

50g unsalted butter, diced

1½kg mussels, debearded, cleaned and scrubbed (discard any that are open but do not close when tapped)

1 handful flat-leaf parsley, finely chopped

1 country loaf, broken into large chunks

Moules marinière (mariners' mussels) is one of those dishes that everyone has eaten at some point – it's an all-time favourite. Mussels are incredibly environmentally friendly because stocks are plentiful. Wild mussels are delicious – buy them from a reputable supplier or fishmonger to make sure you are getting the freshest ones possible. It's important to know how to give them a really good clean, so see page 73 for some tips on how to prepare them. Moules marinière is a simple and delicious lunchtime dish, so get straight in there with some bread to dunk in! You can use an empty shell as your little knife and fork.

1   Heat a large saucepan and pour in the olive oil. Once the oil is hot, add the shallots and cook for 2 minutes over a medium to high heat. Add the garlic and bay leaf and cook for a further minute.

2   Pour the white wine into the saucepan and add the diced butter. Bring to the boil, then put in the mussels. Place a lid on the saucepan and cook for 3–4 minutes, giving the pan a good shake a few times during cooking.

3   Once the mussels have opened up during cooking, remove the pan from the heat and take the lid off. Pick out and discard any mussels that did not open and then sprinkle over the chopped parsley.

4   Ladle the mussels into 4 serving bowls along with the cooking liquor. Serve with the chunks of bread on the side.

SKILLS
- Skinning the haddock
- Knife skills: cutting the carrots and leeks into brunoise; chopping the herbs
- Frying the vegetables
- Making the vinaigrette
- Grilling the haddock

CARPACCIO OF SMOKED HADDOCK
WITH A VEGETABLE VINAIGRETTE serves 4

600g undyed smoked
 haddock fillets
2 carrots, peeled
1 leek, trimmed
120g unsalted butter
juice of 1 lemon
salt and freshly ground
 black pepper
2 tablespoons finely
 chopped chives
2 tablespoons finely
 chopped dill
2 tablespoons finely
 chopped chervil
2 tablespoons chervil
 leaves, to garnish

The word carpaccio is normally associated with thinly sliced raw beef, but this carpaccio is a delicious fish alternative where the haddock has been naturally salted and smoked beforehand to bring out the beautiful flavours and colours. The fish slices should be paper thin so be careful when cutting them! The finely chopped and cubed vegetables (technically called brunoise) are added to the buttered frying pan over a medium heat to make the dressing – if the pan gets too hot the butter will burn, so keep an eye on it. It is important here to remember that the dressing should accompany the fish, not take it over – a drop of lemon juice at the end is all it needs. The slices of haddock are laid out on a plate and warmed under the grill or with a cook's blow torch before the dressing is drizzled over. A final sprinkling of chervil enhances the flavour.

Preheat the grill to high.

1   Remove the skin from the haddock fillets and slice the fish very thinly – use a sharp knife and be careful not to break the flesh.

2   Cut the carrots and leek into brunoise. To do this, first cut them into julienne batons. Then turn the julienne batons through a quarter turn and cut again, to form tiny 3mm-sided dice.

3   Place a medium-sized frying pan over a medium heat. Put in half the butter, and once it has melted add the carrot and leek brunoise. Cook for 3–5 minutes until the vegetables are tender, then add 75ml of water and bring to the boil. Cut the remaining 60g of butter into dice and stir slowly into the vegetables.

4   Once the butter has melted, pour in the lemon juice and season with salt and pepper, then remove the frying pan from the heat. Finish the vinaigrette by adding the chopped chives, dill and chervil and stir.

5   Arrange the sliced haddock fanned out in flower shapes on 4 heatproof serving plates and place under the preheated grill for 1–2 minutes until the fish becomes opaque. Alternatively grill the haddock with a cook's blow torch.

6   Whilst the haddock slices are still warm, drizzle over the vegetable vinaigrette and sprinkle with the chervil leaves.

SARDINES WITH PINE NUT AND FETA STUFFING AND A PARSLEY-CAPER SALAD serves 4

FOR THE PARSLEY SALAD

40g raisins

1 small red onion, peeled and finely sliced

leaves from a small bunch of flat-leaf parsley

1–2 tablespoons small capers, drained

salt and freshly ground black pepper

2 tablespoons extra virgin olive oil

2 tablespoons sherry vinegar

FOR THE STUFFING

2 tablespoons pine nuts

25–50g fresh breadcrumbs

100g fermented feta, crumbled

4 tablespoons chopped flat-leaf parsley

1 garlic clove, peeled and crushed

2 teaspoons grated unwaxed lemon zest

FOR THE FISH

8 fresh sardines, about 150g each

SKILLS

- Butterflying and de-boning sardines
- Chopping herbs
- Toasting nuts in a dry pan
- Stuffing and securing the sardines

I usually love sardines just as they are, cooked on a grill or on a barbecue, but this is a great way to serve them, stuffed with pine nuts and feta cheese. It's not an ultra-refined dish for a fine-dining experience; it's a rustic dish for what I call an 'eating experience'. There are lots of strong, hearty flavours here that really complement each other: oily fish, salty cheese, sweet onions and sour capers. One tip for sardines is never squeeze lemon juice directly on to them as it can give you indigestion. Instead, put lemon zest in them.

Preheat the oven to 200°C/fan 180°C/gas 6.

1   Soak the raisins in enough boiling water to just cover them. Set aside for the salad.

2   Begin the stuffing by dry-toasting the pine nuts over a low to medium heat in a small heavy-based frying pan until evenly coloured. This will take just a couple of minutes.

3   While the pine nuts are toasting, butterfly the sardines and discard the backbone. To do this, open up the fish cavity and run your thumb down the centre of the spine to loosen it. Pull the spine out gently, from the head end, taking care not to tear the skin. Open each sardine out flat. See pages 124–5 for step by step photographs.

4   Finish off the stuffing by mixing the toasted pine nuts with the breadcrumbs, feta, parsley, garlic and lemon zest. Season to taste with salt and pepper. Spoon the stuffing evenly in the cavity down the middle of each sardine. Fold the opened-out sardine flesh back over like an envelope to enclose the stuffing. Tie with butcher's string to secure. Lay the sardines on a baking sheet lined with greaseproof paper, then bake in the preheated oven for 8–10 minutes.

5   Meanwhile, make the salad. Pour boiling water over the sliced red onion to soften it. Leave for a few minutes and then drain off the water. Drain the soaked raisins and mix them with the parsley leaves, capers and drained onion in a bowl. Season to taste with salt and pepper, dress with the extra virgin oilve oil and sherry vinegar and serve alongside the sardines.

HOW TO BUTTERFLY-BONE A ROUND FISH

This is the technique to use if you want to stuff a round fish, like the sardines in Sardines with Pine Nut and Feta Stuffing and Parsley-caper Salad (page 123).

1 Fresh sardines should not seem dry, but should look shiny and plump.

2 Slip a small, sharp knife under the fin and cut off the head in one clean chop. Use your knife to open up the abdominal cavity of the fish.

3 Place the sardine on a board and press down all along the backbone with your thumb.

4 Now use your knife to slice the backbone free at the head and tail end.

6 Using your knife, very, very carefully clean the fillet, removing the bony parts of the backbone and cage that remain on the outside of the belly.

7 The filleted fish are now ready to stuff.

5 Turn the fish over and grasp and pull the backbone out so that the cage and all the bones are fully removed, leaving the tail on the sardine.

SKILLS
- Preparing the goujons
- Making mayonnaise
- Knife skills: chopping the cornichons, shallots, capers and herbs

POLLOCK GOUJONS WITH HOME-MADE TARTARE SAUCE AND CRISPY PARSLEY serves 2

FOR THE POLLOCK GOUJONS

vegetable, sunflower or groundnut oil, for deep-frying

100g plain flour

salt and freshly ground black pepper

2 large eggs, beaten

150g fresh white breadcrumbs

4 x 150g pollock fillets, skin off and pin-boned, each fillet cut into 3 goujons

FOR THE TARTARE SAUCE AND CRISPY PARSLEY

2 egg yolks

2 teaspoons white wine vinegar

1 teaspoon Dijon mustard

150ml rapeseed oil

150ml mild olive oil

75g cornichons, drained and coarsely chopped

2 banana shallots, peeled and finely diced

75g small capers, drained

1 tablespoon finely chopped flat-leaf parsley

1 tablespoon finely chopped tarragon

1 tablespoon finely chopped chervil

1 tablespoon finely chopped chives

5g flat-leaf parsley leaves, washed, dried and left whole

1 lemon, cut into wedges

Pollock is a fish that you can eat with a special sense of satisfaction because, unlike cod, stocks are high and it is also great value for money. My tip for coating the goujons in the egg and breadcrumb mixture is to use only one hand for the egg, because otherwise both hands will get crumby and wet.

Pour in the oil and preheat the deep-fat fryer to 190°C/375°F, according to the manufacturer's instructions.

1   First prepare the goujons. Season the flour with salt and pepper. Place the seasoned flour, beaten eggs and breadcrumbs on separate plates in a row. Coat the pollock pieces in the flour first, then the egg and finally in the breadcrumbs. Make sure you coat the fish completely in the egg as the breadcrumbs will not stick otherwise.

2   You can place the coated goujons in the fridge for 20 minutes just to make sure the breadcrumbs stay on the fish once fried. Alternatively cook them straight away but try not to move the goujons around too much in the fryer.

3   Place the coated fish goujons in the preheated deep-fat fryer for 2–3 minutes until they turn golden brown. Then remove from the fryer and place on a piece of kitchen paper to soak up the excess oil.

4   To make the tartare sauce, put the egg yolks in a small food processor, add the white wine vinegar, mustard and a pinch of salt and start to process. With the motor on, gradually pour the two types of oil into the food processor until you are left with a thick creamy mayonnaise. (If the mayonnaise becomes too thick, loosen it with a tablespoon of warm water.)

5   Meanwhile place the cornichons, shallots, capers, chopped parsley, tarragon, chervil and chives in a medium-sized mixing bowl. Add the home-made mayonnaise and stir to mix.

6   Just before serving, dry the whole parsley leaves and place them in the deep-fat fryer for 5–10 seconds only, until they become crispy. Drain on kitchen paper.

7   Place the cooked pollock goujons on each plate with the tartare sauce and lemon wedges on the side and sprinkle with the crispy parsley.

HOW TO PANER

Paner is a lovely French term, meaning to coat delicate foods, like fish goujons, in a flour, egg and breadcrumb mixture before frying. This specifically refers to Pollack Goujons with Home-made Tartare Sauce and Crispy Parsley (page 127).

1 Cut your piece of pollock into fingers.

3 Dip the fish goujons in the flour.

2 Prepare three shallow plates of eggs, seasoned flour and white breadcrumbs.

4 Dip the goujons in the egg, making sure you completely cover as the egg is the glue that will stick the breadcrumbs.

5 Dip the goujons in the breadcrumbs.

Using a deep-fat fryer filled with vegetable oil, add the goujons (never just drop them in) and fry without moving them around too much.

6

Remove the fish after 2–3 minutes, when crisp and golden brown.

7

Tip: Make a delicious little garnish by deep-frying some parsley for just 5–10 seconds until crispy.

SKILLS
- How to make creamed corn
- Knife skills: removing the corn kernels from the cob
- How to make your own smoker (see pages 150–1)
- How to prepare scallops and remove the roe (see pages 132–3)
- How to cook scallops correctly

CHIP-SMOKED SCALLOPS WITH A SWEETCORN AND BACON SALAD serves 4

30g butter

½ onion, peeled and finely chopped

kernels from 2 whole sweetcorn cobs

4 tablespoons double cream

4 rashers unsmoked streaky bacon, cut into lardons

12 scallops, removed from the shell and roe removed

200g pea shoots

1 lemon, cut into wedges

approx. 200g wood chips

Bacon and scallops is one of those combinations that just works so well. This dish packs in all the flavours of woody smokiness, zingy lemon and the saltiness of bacon to complement the subtle sweetness of the scallops. Make sure the scallops stay opaque in the middle and that the sweetcorn purée is creamy.

1 Heat a sauté pan over a low to medium heat and put in the butter. Once it has melted, add the onion and cook for 3–4 minutes until soft. Add half the sweetcorn kernels and cook for 2 minutes, then add the cream and simmer for 4–5 minutes until the sweetcorn is cooked. Place in a food processor and blitz until smooth.

2 Heat a small frying pan over a medium heat and put in the streaky bacon lardons and the rest of the sweetcorn. Cook for 3–4 minutes until the bacon is crispy. Add a dash of water to the pan to moisten if necessary.

3 Place some tin foil in the bottom of a wok and put the wood chips on top. Then place a metal rack on top of the chips and turn on the heat under the wok. Once the chips have begun to smoke, place the scallops on top of the rack, put a lid over the rack and smoke for 30 seconds to 1 minute. The scallops should be browned and coloured on the outside but not cooked through.

4 Transfer the smoked scallops to the bacon pan and sear over a high heat for 10–20 seconds on each side.

5 Using a spoon, place the creamed sweetcorn in 3 dollops on each plate to form the shape of a triangle, leaving a space in the middle. Then place a scallop on top of each dollop of creamed sweetcorn and scatter the fried sweetcorn and bacon around. Dress the pea shoots with some lemon juice and place them in the space in the middle of the plate.

PREPARING SCALLOPS

If money is no object, diver-caught scallops, bought live in the shell, are delicious. This specifically refers to Chip-smoked Scallops with a Sweetcorn and Bacon Salad (page 131).

1 To open the scallop, pick it up in your hand and insert a small knife between the two shells.

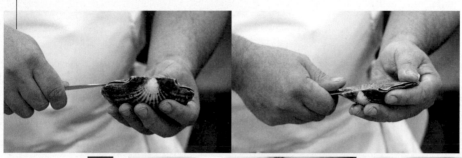

2
Run your knife around the top of the shell to detach it from the bottom and push down carefully to lever the shell open.

3
Cut any white muscle or membrane from the scallop and remove the orange coral (roe) if required by the recipe.

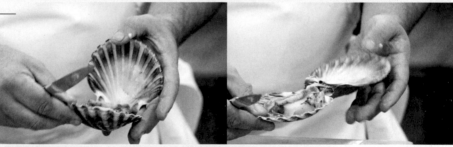

4 Gently scoop the scallop out of its shell.

5 Clean your scallops in a bowl of water before cooking as they can be very sandy.

BABY SQUID STUFFED WITH CHORIZO AND FETA AND A TOMATO AND ROASTED GARLIC SAUCE serves 4

FOR THE TOMATO AND ROASTED GARLIC SAUCE

1 bulb garlic

1 tablespoon olive oil

8 tomatoes, roughly chopped

½ loaf ciabatta bread, cut into rough slices then again into fingers

150g toasted almonds

100g roasted red peppers in olive oil, drained

salt and freshly ground black pepper

50ml extra virgin olive oil

FOR THE STUFFED SQUID

200g semi-cured chorizo

150ml white wine

200g feta cheese, finely diced

16 baby squid, including the tentacles, cleaned and prepared

2–3 tablespoons olive oil

FOR THE DRESSING AND GARNISH

4 tablespoons olive oil

1 tablespoon sherry vinegar

2 tablespoons picked flat-leaf parsley leaves

4 spring onions, trimmed and finely chopped

SKILLS

- Preparing the squid: cleaning it and removing the tentacles (see pages 108–9)
- Roasting garlic in the oven
- Using a liquidizer to blend the sauce
- Stuffing the baby squid
- Pan-frying the squid
- Making a dressing

I like to poach the chorizo in this recipe because it gives it an immense, beautiful flavour and takes out some of the fat. The idea of poaching chorizo in white wine is an old farmhouse technique. It preserves the meat for longer, which is ideal for chorizo as it is a raw meat. If you want to preserve normal sausages for longer, by the way, poach them in some water. That way, you can cook them at a later date and they don't go off so quickly. That is exactly what my mother used to do.

*Preheat the oven to 200°C/fan 180°C/gas 6.

1 Place the bulb of garlic on a baking tray and drizzle with the olive oil, then place in the preheated oven for 10–15 minutes. Take out and allow to cool enough to handle.

2 Put the tomatoes, bread, toasted almonds and peppers in a blender and liquidize. Squeeze out the roasted garlic from the cloves and add to the blender, along with some salt and pepper and the extra virgin oil. Pulse again to liquidize.

3 To make the stuffing, place the chorizo in a small saucepan with the white wine and cook over a medium heat for 5–8 minutes. Drain, discarding the wine (or use it to loosen the sauce if you think it needs it), and when the chorizo has cooled remove its skin and finely dice.

4 Put the diced feta cheese and chorizo into a small bowl and mix well. Stuff this mixture into the baby squid. Heat a large frying pan, put in the olive oil and pan-fry the squid over a medium heat for 2 minutes each side until golden brown. You will probably need to do this in two batches unless you have a very large pan.

5 Place the roasted garlic and tomato sauce in a small pan and warm through.

6 To make the dressing, put the olive oil and sherry vinegar in a small bowl and whisk together.

7 To serve, place the warm tomato sauce in serving bowls, top with the fried stuffed baby squid and drizzle the oil and vinegar dressing over the squid. Sprinkle with the flat-leaf parsley and spring onions.

SKILLS

- Removing the white and brown meat from the crab (see pages 112–13)
- Blanching vegetables
- Making mayonnaise
- Knife skills: chopping spring onions and tarragon

DRESSED CRAB
WITH SEASONAL VEGETABLES serves 4

120g tenderstem broccoli

80g fresh or frozen peas

80g broad beans

2 egg yolks

2 teaspoons Dijon mustard

1 tablespoon white wine vinegar

2 anchovies

4 x whole cooked hen crabs, brown and white meat picked, claws kept whole and the body shells retained

salt and freshly ground black pepper

125ml rapeseed oil

125ml mild olive oil

juice of ½ lime

1 tablespoon finely chopped tarragon

4 spring onions, trimmed and thinly sliced

Britain has some of the best crab in the world. It is very expensive, though, so when you are preparing it, make sure you get everything out of the shells. The rich, flavoursome brown meat is seasoned in the salad, while the white crab meat is left unseasoned. That way, you get a lovely contrast of flavours. Keep your crab shells: they can be turned into a delicious crab bisque (see page 157).

1 Bring a saucepan of salted water to the boil and blanch the broccoli, peas and broad beans for a couple of minutes. Remove the vegetables from the pan and refresh under cold water. Cut the broccoli into thin strips and leave the peas and broad beans whole. Set aside.

2 To make the mayonnaise, place the egg yolks in a small food processor and add the mustard, white wine vinegar, anchovies, brown crabmeat and pepper, to taste. Start the motor and gradually pour in the two types of oil until you have a thick and smooth mayonnaise. Check and adjust the seasoning at this stage.

3 Place the vegetables, lime juice, tarragon, spring onions and most of the home-made crab mayonnaise in a large bowl and mix together. Use just enough of the mayonnaise to bring everything together (any leftovers are delicious spread on toast).

4 To serve, place the vegetables in the centre of each crab shell and place the picked white crabmeat down the sides of the shells. Top with the crab claws.

SKILLS
- Making a dressing: the balance of vinegar and olive oil
- Cooking green beans
- Griddling tuna fish
- Knife skills: cutting new potatoes

TUNA NIÇOISE serves 4

FOR THE SALAD

8 quail's eggs

8 baby new potatoes

100g green beans, trimmed

4 tuna steaks, about 125g each

salt and freshly ground black pepper

2 tablespoons olive oil

outer leaves from 2 baby gem lettuces

12 baby plum tomatoes on the vine, cut in half

8 anchovy fillets, whole

FOR THE DRESSING

35ml white wine vinegar

1 garlic clove, peeled and finely sliced

2 teaspoons fennel seeds

3 sprigs tarragon

1 tablespoon Dijon mustard

2 anchovy fillets, chopped

100ml extra virgin olive oil

2 tablespoons olive tapenade

Here is a great-tasting variation on the classic French country salad, using quail's eggs instead of hen's eggs. The dressing, similar to a vinaigrette, is flavoured with a mixture of fennel seeds, garlic, anchovies, Dijon mustard and tarragon, which provides a sharpness to wake up the palate.

1 Soft-boil the quail's eggs by bringing a small pan of water to the boil. Gently drop in the eggs and boil for 2–3 minutes. Remove them immediately and plunge into cold water. When cooled, peel and halve the eggs.

2 To make the dressing, place the vinegar, garlic, fennel seeds and 2 sprigs of the tarragon in a small saucepan and heat gently for a couple of minutes. Remove from the heat, rest for 5 minutes to allow the mixture to infuse, then strain through a sieve into a bowl. Reserve the sliced garlic and add to the dressing. Add the mustard to the strained vinegar and whisk. Gradually whisk in the extra virgin olive oil and season with salt and pepper. Remove the leaves from the remaining sprig of tarragon and chop them, then add to the dressing with the olive tapenade and chopped anchovies and mix well.

3 Boil the potatoes in a medium-sized saucepan of salted water for 10 minutes. Drain and, once cool enough to handle, halve the potatoes.

4 Meanwhile, place another medium-sized saucepan of salted water on to heat. Once the water is boiling, add the green beans and cook for 2–4 minutes, until *al dente*, then drain and refresh in iced water.

5 Season the tuna steaks with salt and pepper. Heat the olive oil in a medium-sized griddle pan over a high heat, then cook the tuna on each side for 30 seconds. Leave the steaks to rest for 1 minute.

6 Just before serving, add the still-warm potatoes to the salad dressing in the bowl, so that the dressing is absorbed.

7 Divide the baby gem leaves, beans, potatoes and tomatoes, plus the remaining 8 anchovy fillets, amongst 4 plates, and top with 1 tuna steak and 2 halved quail's eggs per plate. Drizzle any extra dressing over the tuna and around the plate.

RAZOR CLAMS WITH A TOMATO SAUCE serves 4

FOR THE RAZOR CLAMS

5 tablespoons white breadcrumbs

2 tablespoons finely chopped flat-leaf parsley

1 garlic clove, peeled and grated

1½ tablespoons melted unsalted butter

16 razor clams, washed and scrubbed under cold running water, then drained

100ml white wine

FOR THE TOMATO SAUCE

50g unsalted butter

1 garlic clove, peeled and crushed

3 ripe plum tomatoes, roughly chopped

1 red chilli, finely chopped

1 anchovy fillet, diced

1 tablespoon chopped oregano

zest of ¼ unwaxed lemon

4 tablespoons double cream

One great thing about razor clams is that you can go out hunting for them yourself if you can get to a suitable sheltered sandy beach. Take a bucket of sea water with you and look for little marks in the wet sand where the clams are. Simply pour a little bit of water on top and then grab the clam when it comes to the surface. You don't want to be picking clams off contaminated seashore areas so make sure you only do this on beaches in areas with a small population.

This simple, light, delicious and uncomplicated dish only takes about 30 minutes to prepare. I call the tomato sauce here an instant tomato sauce. You can use any tomatoes in this recipe but plum tomatoes are especially good. Keep an eye on the clams when they are being gratinated – you want them to become golden and toasted on top but no more. When they are under the grill, the smell from the parsley, garlic, breadcrumbs and melted butter is just fantastic. This also makes a great dinner party starter.

Preheat the grill to high.

1   In a small bowl, mix together the breadcrumbs, parsley, garlic and melted butter, then set aside.

2   Next make the tomato sauce. Heat the butter in a medium-sized saucepan. Once it has melted, add the garlic, tomatoes, chilli, anchovy, oregano and lemon zest, and cook down over a low heat for 25 minutes. Stir in the cream and remove from the heat.

3   Meanwhile, put a large saucepan over a high heat. Place the razor clams and the white wine into the saucepan, put the lid on and steam for 2–3 minutes until the clams open.

4   Remove the saucepan from the heat and strain the clams through a piece of muslin placed in a sieve, retaining the cooking liquor. Discard any clams that have not opened and remove all the meat from the rest of the shells. Slice the meat into bite-sized pieces and pour the clam cooking liquor into the tomato sauce.

5   To serve, lay the empty shells on to a baking tray, spoon in some tomato sauce and divide the sliced clams between the shells. Top with the breadcrumb mix. Place the baking tray under the preheated grill for 1–2 minutes or until the breadcrumbs are toasted and golden brown.

POACHED HADDOCK WITH SALSIFY FRICASSÉE AND A SALMON EGG AND CHIVE SAUCE serves 4

4 x 120g haddock fillets
500ml fresh fish stock
2 sprigs dill, stalks separated and leaves chopped
120g unsalted butter
2 bay leaves
1 tablespoon finely chopped chives
1 leek leaf
a few parsley stalks
1 sprig thyme
150g salsify, peeled and cut into long batons
25g plain flour, sifted
juice of 1 lemon
salt and freshly ground black pepper
50g salmon caviar, rinsed

There is no need for waste when you make this tasty poached haddock dish – just keep all the remaining stock liquids when you have finished and use them to make a flavourful chowder (see page 161). The skin from the fish fillets is added along with the fish trimmings to give the stock even more flavour. Once you've added the butter to form the poaching liquid, this mixture must be whisked constantly until the fish fillets are placed in the pan. In order to preserve the oyster-like colour of the salsify (also known as oyster plant or goat's beard), you need to boil it in a blanc – a mixture made by adding a touch of flour and a light seasoning of lemon juice and herbs to cold water.

1 Trim the haddock fillets and remove the skin. Place the haddock trimmings, stock, dill stalks, 100g of the butter and 1 of the bay leaves in a large saucepan and bring to the boil. Simmer for 4–5 minutes, then strain the liquid through a sieve into a sauté pan and cook further over a medium heat to reduce slightly.

2 Place the fish fillets in the sauté pan with the stock, take the pan off the heat and leave to poach for 10 minutes.

3 When the fish is cooked through, remove the fillets from the pan with a fish slice and set aside on a plate. Keep warm. Add the chopped chives and dill leaves to the stock in the pan while it is still on the heat and then whisk in the remaining 20g of butter to form a sauce.

4 Make a bouquet garni by tying together the leek leaf, parsley stalks, thyme sprig and the remaining bay leaf with butcher's string.

5 Place the salsify batons in a medium-sized saucepan with 650ml of water, the flour, lemon juice (to stop the salsify discolouring) and the bouquet garni. Bring to the boil and simmer for 5 minutes until the salsify is tender. Strain the liquid into a sauté pan and season with salt and pepper. Discard the bouquet garni, then tip the salsify batons into the sauté pan and toss to cover in the sauce.

6 To serve, place the dressed salsify batons in a uniform line down one side of each serving plate and place a poached haddock fillet alongside or on top. Drizzle on the leftover sauce and spread the salmon caviar over the haddock fillets.

SKILLS
- Skinning the haddock
- Knife skills: cutting the fish and herbs
- Making the sauce
- Poaching the fish
- Cooking the salsify

SKILLS

- Cleaning and filleting mackerel and scoring the skin
- Knife skills: cutting ginger into julienne slices
- Making a hollandaise sauce over a bain-marie
- Griddling
- Testing when the fish is cooked

MACKEREL WITH GINGERED-RHUBARB HOLLANDAISE AND PICKLED RHUBARB serves 4

FOR THE MACKEREL

4 plump mackerel
rapeseed oil, for brushing
75g watercress,
  to garnish

FOR THE PICKLED RHUBARB

200g forced rhubarb,
  sliced on an angle
75g caster sugar
50ml white wine vinegar

FOR THE RHUBARB HOLLANDAISE

200g forced rhubarb,
  cut into 1cm dice
1 tablespoon caster sugar
2½cm piece fresh ginger,
  thinly sliced into
  julienne
115g unsalted butter
1 egg yolk
1½ teaspoons white
  wine vinegar
lemon juice, to taste
salt and freshly ground
  black pepper

The best time of year to make this dish is late summer, when both rhubarb and mackerel are in season. Hollandaise sauce is another summery classic. It is basically a thick, warm mayonnaise. Adding the clarified butter slowly at the beginning will ensure it reaches the right consistency.

Preheat the oven to 200°C/fan 180°C/gas 6.

1   Clean and fillet each mackerel, lifting the bone out in one piece. Set the fillets aside. (See page 70 for how to fillet the fish.)

2   Make the pickled rhubarb by scattering the rhubarb slices over a baking sheet in a single layer. Sprinkle over the sugar and drizzle on the white wine vinegar, then cover with foil. Place in the preheated oven to bake for about 12 minutes, until the rhubarb is just starting to soften but still keeping its shape. The exact time will depend on the size of the rhubarb pieces. Remove to a shallow dish and leave the rhubarb to cool in its marinade.

3   Next make the sauce. Put the rhubarb, sugar and ginger into a saucepan. Pour over 5 tablespoons of water and cook gently over a medium heat for about 10 minutes, or until the rhubarb has softened. Remove and purée in a blender or food processor.

4   Clarify the butter. Melt it slowly in a small pan. Carefully pour off the clear golden liquid and leave behind the milky part left at the bottom, which can be discarded. Beat the egg yolk and white wine vinegar in a bowl sitting over a pan of simmering water, making sure the water is not touching the bowl. (This is your bain-marie.) Then, whisking all the time, slowly pour the clarified butter into the egg yolk and vinegar. Keep whisking until you have a smooth, thick sauce. Check for seasoning, adding a little lemon juice and salt and pepper if needed. Gently fold in the rhubarb purée. Keep warm.

5   Brush the mackerel fillets with a little oil. Place on a griddle pan over a medium heat, skin side down, for 2 minutes, then turn over and cook for another 2 minutes or until just cooked.

6   Next take the watercress and dip it into the liquid of the pickled rhubarb. Serve alongside the griddled mackerel fillets, rhubarb hollandaise and pickled rhubarb.

SKILLS

• Filleting and skinning the sole
• Making a fish mousse and getting the right consistency
• How to make a classic fish sauce using the bones
• Cooking the tenderstem broccoli

STUFFED LEMON SOLE WITH SCAMPI
AND TENDERSTEM BROCCOLI serves 4

**FOR THE STUFFED
LEMON SOLE**

2 whole lemon sole
(approx. 800g each)

150g frozen scampi,
defrosted and drained

70ml double cream

1 teaspoon unwaxed
lemon zest

2 teaspoons finely
chopped dill

salt and freshly ground
black pepper

FOR THE BUTTER SAUCE

1 onion, peeled and
roughly chopped

1 stick celery, roughly
chopped

1 carrot, peeled and
roughly chopped

1 bay leaf

5 black peppercorns

90g unsalted butter, cut
into small cubes

2 tablespoons finely
chopped chives

**FOR THE TENDERSTEM
BROCCOLI**

250g tenderstem broccoli

large knob butter

In this recipe, the softness of the lemon sole and fish mousse is complemented perfectly by tenderstem broccoli that is cooked *al dente* – with a bit of bite. If you are filleting the lemon sole yourself, a tip to know whether you're doing it correctly is to listen for the sound of the bones being scraped. You want to use every bit of this beautiful fish to make sure that you waste nothing.

Preheat the oven to 120°C/fan 100°C/gas 1.

1 Remove the lemon sole fillets from the bone (4 per whole fish) and skin them, keeping the bones and the trimmings separately.

2 Clean the skin off the fish trimmings and place the trimmings in a food processor along with the scampi and the cream. Blitz until smooth.

3 Pass this fish mousse through a fine sieve into a medium-sized bowl and stir in the lemon zest and dill. Season with salt and pepper and place in the fridge until needed.

4 To make the sauce, place the fish bones, onion, celery, carrot, bay leaf and peppercorns into a saucepan. Cover with water and bring to the boil, then simmer for 10 minutes, skimming off the froth if necessary. Strain the stock into a clean saucepan and continue to simmer to reduce the liquid by half.

5 While the stock is simmering, lay the lemon sole fillets on a board. Divide the mousse between 4 of the fillets and spread evenly across each one. Top each of the covered fillets with one of the remaining uncovered fillets to form a sandwich. Place on a baking sheet lined with greaseproof paper and cook in the preheated oven for 10–12 minutes, or until the fish is cooked and the mousse is set.

6 Finish the sauce by adding the cubes of butter to the reduced fish stock a few at a time, whisking well with each addition. Taste and adjust the seasoning if necessary. Keep the sauce warm until needed, adding the chopped chives just before serving.

7 Place the tenderstem broccoli in boiling salted water for 2 minutes and then drain and transfer straight into a warm frying pan with the butter. Season well with salt and pepper, and toss to coat in the butter.

8 To serve, place the mousse-filled lemon sole fillets on the plates, with the broccoli on the side, and spoon over the butter sauce.

SKILLS
- The use of tea and sugar when smoking
- Boning and filleting a mackerel
- Knife skills: preparing the beetroot

TEA-SMOKED MACKEREL WITH BEETROOT STEW AND FRESH CURD serves 4

100g jasmine leaf tea
200g demerara sugar
200g long-grain white rice
4 whole mackerel, filleted and deboned, skin left on
2 tablespoons olive oil
1 onion, peeled and finely sliced
2 large cooked beetroots, 1 grated and 1 thinly sliced
4 tablespoons red wine vinegar
50ml red wine
about 1 teaspoon caster sugar
100g fresh goat's curd
4 tablespoons thinly sliced sorrel

Tea is less robust, more fragrant and more subtle for smoking than wood-chip, so it works really well with strong, oily fish. By smoking the fish, you keep all the oils inside it. The sugar in the smoking also creates a lovely caramelization that sits beautifully with the sourness of the beetroot. See the step-by-step photographs on pages 150–51 for how to make your own smoker for use in this recipe.

1 Put the tea leaves, demerara sugar and rice in a medium-sized bowl and stir to mix.

2 Place tin foil in the bottom of a wok, pour the tea mixture on to the foil and place a rack on top of that. Place the mackerel fillets on the rack, turn the heat up under the wok so the tea mixture starts to smoke and put a lid on top. Smoke the mackerel for 8 minutes over a low to medium heat, turning the fillets over once during cooking.

3 Meanwhile place a medium-sized sauté pan over a medium heat and pour in the oil. Once the oil is hot, add the onion and cook for 3–4 minutes until soft. Add the grated beetroot and cook for 2 minutes, then add the vinegar and wine and cook for a further 5–8 minutes until the liquid is reduced by half. Add sugar to taste, stir and set aside.

4 Using a 5cm pastry cutter, cut equal-sized rounds out of the cooked beetroot slices.

5 To serve, place a row of the beetroot rounds on one side of each plate. Then spoon some beetroot stew along the side and place the tea-smoked mackerel fillets on top. Garnish with the curd and sorrel.

HOW TO MAKE A SMOKER WITH TEA AND SUGAR

Smoking is a traditional way of preserving fish. Tea is more fragrant and lighter than wood-chips and it works really well with oily fish like mackerel. This refers to Tea-smoked Mackerel with Beetroot Stew and Fresh Curd (page 149). The scallops on page 131 are also smoked over wood-chips using this method.

1 Put the sugar in a bowl. This will create a nice caramelization from the smoke.

Add an equal quantity of rice. The rice is there to regulate the heat and stop everything burning.

2 Add the jasmine tea – this is for flavour.

4 Place some tin foil in the bottom of a wok and pour in the tea mixture.

3 Mix it all together and that's your smoking mixture.

5 Place a rack in the wok above the smoking mixture. Put the wok on the heat.

6 Place the mackerel fillets on greaseproof paper, just to stop them sticking, and put on the rack.

7 When it's just starting to smoke, put a foil lid over the smoker to keep all the heat in.

8 Add a plate to weight down the foil lid.

9 Smoke the mackerel for 8 minutes, turning the fillets over once during cooking.

10 The mackerel is ready when the flesh is firm, but still plump, not dry.

SKILLS

- Cleaning and preparing the squid, removing the ink sac
- Making the gnocchi dough, getting the right consistency (see pages 154–5)
- Rolling out the gnocchi dough and cutting it
- Boiling the gnocchi until cooked
- Frying the garlic without burning it

SQUID-INK GNOCCHI WITH BRUSSELS SPROUTS AND CHILLI serves 4

2 medium-sized squid, with ink pouches intact (if you can't find squid with the pouches still intact, you can buy the ink from fishmongers and speciality delis)

400g floury potatoes, freshly oven-baked in their skins

juice and zest of 1 unwaxed lemon

50g plain flour

1 egg yolk

salt and freshly ground black pepper

2 tablespoons olive oil

2 garlic cloves, peeled and finely chopped

2 red chillies, finely chopped (and deseeded if you prefer less heat)

leaves of 8 Brussels sprouts (cut the base off with a sharp knife and peel the leaves off with your fingers)

Gnocchi are basically Italian potato dumplings. The combination of the squid ink with gnocchi is dramatic and delicious. Squid ink is the animal's defence mechanism but also tastes very good! It has the salty flavour of the sea and because of this you won't need to add much salt to your gnocchi. But be careful to cook your squid quickly, so it doesn't become tough and chewy. This may not be the simplest recipe, but it is definitely fast food.

1   To clean the squid and retain the ink, gently pull the head away from the body. The ink sac will be in the innards. Puncture the ink sac and pour the contents into a small bowl.

2   Slice the tentacles away from the head just below the eyes, remove and discard the beak from the centre of the tentacles. (See pages 108–9.) Inside the body of the squid, remove the thin cuttlebone and discard. Wash the squid and tentacles under cold running water.

3   While they are still warm, remove the baked potatoes from their skins and mash with half the lemon zest in a large bowl using a ricer. Add the flour, egg yolk and ½ a teaspoon of the squid ink, and season with salt and pepper. Mix together well. Knead together to form gnocchi dough, then set aside. If the mixture is too wet, knead in a little more flour.

4   Roll out the dough between your hands into a long sausage shape approx. 2.5cm in diameter – you might find it easier to work with 2 or 3 sausage shapes than one very long one. Cut the dough sausage into 2cm lengths and pull a fork across the top of each gnocchi to make small ridges.

5   Bring a pan of salted water to the boil and put in the gnocchi. Once they float back to the top remove from the pan with a slotted spoon. This will take 2–3 minutes.

6   Meanwhile, put 1 tablespoon of the olive oil in a large frying pan and heat. Then add the chopped garlic and chillies and cook over a medium heat for 2 minutes.

7   Cut the washed squid into 2½cm squares and add to the frying pan along with the boiled gnocchi and the squid tentacles. Cook for 2 minutes before adding the Brussels sprout leaves and the lemon juice, to taste. Cook for a further minute or two. Garnish with the remaining lemon zest.

8   To serve, pour the gnocchi and squid into warmed serving bowls, placing the tentacles on the top.

HOW TO MAKE GNOCCHI

Gnocchi are little Italian potato dumplings. The squid ink in these gnocchi gives fantastic colour, lots of salty, treacle flavour and adds real drama to the dish. These instructions specifically refer to Squid-ink Gnocchi with Brussels Sprouts and Chilli (page 153).

1 Scrape the still-warm flesh out of the baked potatoes (the starch in the potato is easier to work with if it's warm). Put the flesh into a potato ricer and push through. This is a great utensil to have as it makes very fine potato mash.

Add the flour, egg yolk and squid ink. **2**

3 With floured hands, roll the dough out on a board into a long sausage shape, but don't work it too much as you want the gnocchi really light, not stodgy.

4 Don't spend too long cutting the gnocchi into pieces. Just chop quickly through the dough as you want quite rustic little dumplings.

5 Pull a fork quickly across the top of each dumpling to make ridges.

Take the gnocchi and immerse in salted boiling water. They will sink to the bottom and then float to the top (hopefully!) Remove with a slotted spoon.

SKILLS

- Knife skills: cutting the vegetables
- Dismantling the crab and retaining the meat and shells (see pages 112–13)
- Cutting the crab shell safely
- Making the stock for the bisque
- Liquidizing the bisque
- Whisking egg whites

CRAB BISQUE WITH SESAME CRAB TOASTS
serves 4

FOR THE CRAB BISQUE

2 tablespoons olive oil

1 onion, peeled and roughly chopped

2 carrots, peeled and roughly chopped

2 stalks celery, roughly chopped

¼ teaspoon cayenne pepper

2 sprigs thyme

2 bay leaves

2 sprigs tarragon

10 whole black peppercorns

1½kg crab, white and brown crabmeat removed and kept aside (keep the outer shell and claws whole; using a cleaver chop up the legs and body into small pieces)

1½ tablespoons tomato purée

150ml white wine

1½ litres fresh fish stock

100ml double cream

50ml brandy

salt and freshly ground black pepper

baby tarragon leaves, to garnish

FOR THE SESAME CRAB TOASTS

vegetable, sunflower or groundnut oil, for frying

4 raw king prawns, peeled

1 egg white

½ tablespoon finely chopped tarragon

zest of ½ unwaxed lime

pinch white pepper

2 slices white bread

4 tablespoons sesame seeds, to coat

A bisque is traditionally a thick and creamy fish soup made out of shellfish stock. The onion, celery and carrot make up the basis of the soup. The onion adds savoury flavour, celery adds aroma and carrot adds sweetness. Toasting the tomato purée off at the beginning of cooking ensures deep flavour and takes off any raw edge to the taste. The sesame crab toasts are delicious and they really lift the dish to a higher level, as does the addition of brandy, so be sure to include it at the end.

1   First make the bisque. Heat a large saucepan and pour in the olive oil. Once it is hot, add the onion, carrots, celery, cayenne pepper, thyme, bay leaves, tarragon and peppercorns. Cook over a medium to high heat for 3–4 minutes until the vegetables are soft.

2   Add the crab claws and shells, and the tomato purée, and cook for a further 2 minutes. Deglaze with the white wine and reduce the liquid by a third.

3   Add the fish stock to the saucepan and bring to the boil. Simmer for 30 minutes, then remove the crab claws and the outer shells.

4   Place the crab bisque in a blender with all but 1 tablespoon of the brown crabmeat and liquidize. Remove from the blender and pass the bisque through a fine sieve into a clean saucepan.

5   Add the cream and brandy to the bisque, warm through and season with salt and pepper.

* Pour in the oil and preheat the deep-fat fryer to 180°C/350°F, according to the manufacturer's instructions.

6   Next make the sesame crab toasts. Put the prawns, egg white, 1 tablespoon of the brown crabmeat and the tarragon in a small food processor and blend until smooth.

7   Transfer the mixture from the processor to a bowl and stir in the white crabmeat and lime zest. Season with salt and the white pepper.

8   Cut the white bread slices into 8cm x 3cm rectangles (each slice of bread should make two rectangles). Press the crab mixture on to the bread, to form a pyramid shape, and coat the top in sesame seeds.

9   Place the crab-coated bread pyramids in the preheated fryer for 2–3 minutes until golden brown.

10 To serve, ladle the bisque into small soup bowls and garnish with a few picked baby tarragon leaves. Serve the crab toasts on the side or on top of the bisque.

PEPPER-CRUSTED TUNA WITH CARPACCIO OF MUSHROOMS AND CHESTNUT BEIGNETS serves 4

vegetable, sunflower or groundnut oil for deep-frying

1 tablespoon black peppercorns, crushed

200g tuna loin (6cm in diameter)

2 tablespoons olive oil

juice of 1 lemon

salt and freshly ground black pepper

1 tablespoon thyme leaves

150g large chestnut mushrooms, thinly sliced

50g unsalted butter

75g plain flour, sifted

2 eggs

4 tablespoons unsweetened chestnut purée

A beignet is a deep-fried dumpling made from choux pastry, flavoured here with chestnuts. Carpaccio is an Italian word originating from the Cipriani Hotel in Venice, which is famous for serving paper-thin slices of beef dressed with lemon juice and olive oil.

Pour in the oil and preheat the deep-fat fryer to 180°C/350°F, according to the manufacturer's instructions.

1 Lay a piece of cling film on the work surface and sprinkle the crushed peppercorns over it. Roll the tuna loin in the peppercorns and wrap tightly in the cling film, then set aside in the fridge.

2 Lay a piece of greaseproof paper on a baking sheet and drizzle with 1 tablespoon of the olive oil, half the lemon juice and season with salt and pepper. Scatter over half the thyme leaves and place the sliced mushrooms on top. Drizzle on another 1 tablespoon of olive oil, the remaining lemon juice and season with salt and pepper. Scatter over the remaining thyme leaves and then place another sheet of greaseproof paper on top. Position a heavy weight, such as a saucepan filled with water, on top and set aside for 20 minutes.

3 Put a medium-sized frying pan over a high heat, add the remaining 1 tablespoon of olive oil, then seal the tuna loin for 10–20 seconds on all sides. Move the tuna to a plate and leave to rest in the fridge for 10 minutes.

4 To make the beignet mixture, place 125ml of water and the butter in a medium-sized saucepan and bring to the boil over a low heat. Quickly add the flour and beat until the mixture becomes smooth and comes away from the sides of the saucepan. Remove from the heat and then add the eggs one by one, beating in between each egg. Add the chestnut purée and stir well.

SKILLS

- Crusting the tuna loin with peppercorns
- Knife skills: thinly slicing the mushrooms
- Sealing the tuna loin
- Making the beignets and deep-frying them

5 Shape a portion of the beignet mixture between two teaspoons into a rugby ball-shaped quenelle and drop it into the preheated deep-fat fryer. The mixture should make 16 beignets. Cook for 1–2 minutes, then remove the and drain on kitchen paper. Meanwhile, continue shaping and cooking the remaining mixture into beignets.

6 To serve, lay the pressed mushrooms neatly on the plate. Thinly slice the tuna loin and lay the slices to one side of the mushrooms. Finish with three beignets and sprinkle with sea salt.

SKILLS
- Cleaning and preparing the clams
- Cooking the clams; knowing which are fresh
- Knife skills: cutting the potato and onion
- Making the chowder
- Making a bouquet garni

CLAM CHOWDER WITH MINI GARLIC LOAVES

serves 4

FOR THE MINI GARLIC LOAVES

1 garlic clove, peeled and finely chopped

2 teaspoons chopped flat-leaf parsley

50g unsalted butter, softened

125g wholemeal flour, sifted

125g strong white bread flour, sifted

4g dried active yeast

90ml tepid whole milk

85ml tepid water

FOR THE CLAM CHOWDER

70g smoked bacon, cut into lardons

olive oil, for frying

100ml white wine

24 Palourde clams

25g unsalted butter

1 onion, peeled and finely chopped

1 bouquet garni (parsley stalks, thyme sprig, bay leaf wrapped in a celery or leek leaf)

500ml fish stock

100ml whole milk

100g Desirée potatoes, peeled and diced into 1cm cubes

100g sweetcorn

salt and freshly ground black pepper

150ml double cream

2 tablespoons finely chopped flat-leaf parsley

Chowder is a soup and a great hangover cure, too! It is popularly supposed to be an American invention, from Boston, but in fact it arrived in the States with the French whalers and European fishermen working off the coasts of Newfoundland and Boston in the late 1700s and 1800s. The first chowders were tomato-based fish soups, but the recipe was adapted over time to accommodate what was in the larder: potatoes, corn, cured bacon and local clams.

For this recipe we have used Palourde clams and thinly sliced bacon. It's important to wash the clams properly to avoid any grit in the soup. A bouquet garni of thyme, parsley, bay leaf and leek adds extra flavour. This is a harmonious marriage of simple yet tasty food.

Home-made mini garlic loaves accompany this dish. It is crucial to make sure the water and milk are tepid to ensure that the yeast works properly – both should be blood temperature. A good tip for proving the loaves is to turn on the oven and open the oven door, then leave the bread sitting on the oven door for about 25 minutes.

Preheat the oven to 200°C/fan 180°C/gas 6.

1   First make the mini garlic loaves. Mix the garlic and parsley into the softened butter in a small bowl. Press the flavoured butter flat between two layers of cling film to form a rectangular block and leave to harden in the fridge.

2   Mix the two types of flour and the yeast together in a large bowl. Add the tepid milk and water to the bowl and mix well with your hands until the dough comes together.

3   Knead the dough on a floured surface for 2–3 minutes until it is smooth. Then divide the dough into 4 equal sized balls. Roll each ball into a log shape that will fit into a mini loaf tin.

4   Cut the chilled butter into quarters and push a piece into the base of each bread dough log. Place the dough logs into 4 non-stick mini loaf tins.

5   Leave the dough-filled loaf tins in a warm place for 25 minutes to prove the rolls.

6   Meanwhile, make the chowder. Fry the bacon lardons in a small non-stick frying pan in a little olive oil until crispy and then set aside on kitchen paper to drain the excess grease.

7   Place a large saucepan over a high heat and pour the white wine into the pan. Bring to the boil and add the clams. Place the lid on top and cook for 2–3 minutes until the clams have opened.

8   Remove the pan from the heat and strain the clams through a piece of muslin placed in a sieve to remove any grit from the cooking liquor. Reserve the liquor. Discard any clams that did not open, then set 4 clams aside and remove the remaining clam meat from the shells.

9   Heat the butter in a large sauté pan and once it has melted, add the onion and cook for 2 minutes. Add the bouquet garni, fish stock, milk, potatoes, sweetcorn and the strained clam cooking liquor to the sauté pan and season with salt and pepper. Bring to the boil and then simmer for 15–20 minutes until the potatoes are cooked.

10 While the chowder is cooking, bake the mini garlic loaves. Place the 4 mini loaf tins on a baking tray and put in the preheated oven for 12 minutes.

11 When the potatoes are done, pour the cream into the pan with the chowder, then stir in the clam meat and the bacon lardons and keep warm over a simmer.

12 To serve, ladle the chowder into 4 serving bowls and garnish with the chopped parsley and reserved clams in their shells. Take the mini garlic loaves out of the oven and serve alongside.

HOW TO COOK CLAMS

1   Before you begin, make sure you wash the clams very well in running water to remove any traces of grit. Add the washed clams to a large saucepan, and pour

2   over just enough boiling water to cover.
Cover the saucepan with a lid and simmer over a medium heat for 2–3 minutes

3   until the shells have opened and you can see the clams within.

4   Place a piece of muslin inside a sieve, and place over a clean bowl. Strain the clams and liquor through the muslin to catch any last traces of grit. Reserve the liquor to make a broth.

5   Discard any clams that did not open, and then carefully separate out the clam meat from the shells.

HADDOCK AND PARSNIP FISH CAKES WITH A SPICED PARSNIP CREAM serves 4

FOR THE FISH CAKES

vegetable, sunflower
or groundnut oil,
for deep-frying

1 parsnip (about 100g),
peeled

½ teaspoon red chilli
flakes, finely diced

1 teaspoon cumin seeds

1 teaspoon coriander
seeds

½ teaspoon ground
turmeric

160g haddock, skinned
and cut into 1½cm dice

1 tablespoon finely
chopped fresh coriander

about 50ml double cream

1kg Maris Piper potatoes

25g coriander cress

FOR THE PARSNIP PURÉE

25g unsalted butter, diced

2 parsnips (about 200g),
peeled and chopped
into 1cm dice

1 red chilli, deseeded
and finely chopped

1 garlic clove, peeled
and finely chopped

50g root ginger, peeled
and finely chopped

1 teaspoon curry powder

100ml fresh vegetable
stock

50ml single cream

SKILLS

- Boiling and steaming
  the parsnips
- Dry-frying the spices
- Mashing the parsnips
- Knife skills: chopping
  the parsnips, chilli,
  garlic and ginger
- Making the purée,
  using the liquidizer
- Grating the potatoes and
  forming the fish balls
- Deep-frying the fish
  balls

Thanks to the potato-based coating on these fish cakes, they are great for those with a wheat or gluten intolerance. They should have real texture so make sure they don't end up too mushy. Serve with the spiced parsnip cream and a little garnish of baby coriander.

Pour in the oil and preheat the deep-fat fryer to 170°C/325°F, according to the manufacturer's instructions.

1   To make the mixture for the fish cakes, place the parsnip in a saucepan of salted water, bring to the boil and cook for 5–8 minutes until tender. Drain, place a tea towel over the pan to steam the parsnip and set aside.

2   Put the chilli flakes, cumin seeds and coriander seeds in a small frying pan and dry-fry for 1 minute over a high heat. Then remove the pan from the heat, pour the spices into a pestle and mortar and grind them to a powder.

3   Place the cooked parsnip in a large bowl and add the roasted spices. Use a fork to mash together, then stir in the turmeric, diced haddock and fresh coriander, plus enough double cream to combine. Take a golf ball-sized lump of the fish mixture, gently roll it into a ball between your hands and place on a large plate or tray that will fit in the fridge. Repeat with the rest of the fish mixture to make 8 fish cakes. Place in the fridge.

4   For the parsnip purée, melt the butter in a medium-sized frying pan. Tip in the parsnip dice and add the fresh chilli, garlic and ginger. Fry for 2 minutes over a medium heat, then add the curry powder. Pour in the vegetable stock and simmer to reduce the liquid by a third. Pour the mixture into a blender, add the single cream and liquidize until smooth, then set aside.

5   Peel the potatoes and grate them using a fine grater. Wrap in a piece of muslin and squeeze out any excess water. Then place a sheet of cling film on the work surface and tip the grated potatoes on to it. Put another sheet of cling film on top and use a rolling pin to roll out until you have a very thin layer of grated potatoes. Remove the top sheet of cling film.

6   Remove the fish cakes from the fridge. Place one on to the layer of grated potatoes. Cut a circle into the potato about 3cm larger than the fish cake, then use your hands to wrap the potato up around the fish cake to form a thin shell. Place on a plate to one side. Repeat with the rest of the fish cakes.

7   Place the potato-coated fish cakes in the preheated deep-fat fryer for 10 minutes until golden brown, then remove to a plate with kitchen paper. To serve, warm the parsnip puree through gently in a saucepan over a low heat, then spoon the purée into 4 serving bowls and place 2 fish cakes on top. Garnish with the coriander cress.

GIZZI'S NOTES ON FISH AND SEAFOOD

A lot of people have trouble buying fish and seafood – firstly, knowing what they're buying and secondly, figuring out if it is fresh or not – so here are some guidelines.

Fish and seafood fall into different categories. First you have **round fish** like sea bream, cod, mackerel, snapper, salmon and sea bass. They are plump and rounded in shape with a backbone along their upper body and a fillet on each side. The eyes are located on each side of the head.

Bottom-ocean dwellers are called **flatfish**. Millions of years ago, they started off like the round fish but evolved to become thin and oval-shaped, as they ended up living on the seabed and flattened out to adapt to that environment. They swim horizontally and have both eyes on top, plus four fillets. Examples of this type of fish are Dover sole and plaice. Skate is another flatfish, but it's been overfished and stocks are low, so is best left alone for at least the next 20 years to allow numbers to replenish. Most flatfish have a mild-tasting flesh which is light in colour.

Sardines, salmon, mackerel and tuna (fresh, not tinned) are examples of **oily fish**. All fish are high in omega fatty acids but, as the name suggests, oily fish are particularly rich in these oils. You can even feel the oil on their skin. Once you have cut into an oily fish, it can spoil within an hour so freshness is essential.

Cod, tuna, swordfish and turbot are all classed as **sea fish** because they come from the depths of the sea. Sea fish are meaty and their flesh is quite durable. Monkfish is a great example, with monkfish tail being one of the best cuts of fish you can eat. As the flesh is so robust, it can be roasted like a joint of meat or served with a red wine sauce and it still maintains its strength of flavour. Alas, like skate, monkfish is in short supply so should only be eaten as an occasional treat.

Cephalopods are the squids, cuttlefish and octopuses. They either need fast cooking in a hot pan, or very long, slow cooking. Octopus, for instance, needs stewing to become tender.

Oysters, clams, scallops, mussels and cockles belong to the group known as **bivalves**, so named because they have two shells. They should be bought whilst still alive in order to be cooked as freshly as possible. If they're not alive, they could easily turn rancid and poisonous. Ask your fishmonger how fresh they are and put them in the fridge when you get home. Tap the bottom of their open shells and the shells should close up quickly. If they don't, throw them away because the meat inside is dead. Once you have cooked bivalves, discard any that have their shells clamped shut.

Crustaceans are animals with an exoskeleton, so that includes prawns, crabs, lobsters and langoustines. Like bivalves, you want your fishmonger to sell them to you as fresh as possible. As these types of seafood eat whatever surrounds them, try to buy from a fishmonger that sources his fish from areas with clean seas.

There are some easy rules to remember about figuring out how fresh fish is. Firstly, smell it. A fresh fish doesn't smell 'fishy', but should still smell of the sea. Other indications of freshness are that the fish has glossy eyes and red, clear gills. The body of the fish should be firm. If it is floppy or bendy, this means proteins have started to break down in the fish. The texture of the fish is also a giveaway – it shouldn't be too slimy to the touch.

All fish should be eaten within three days of being fished. Smoked fish has a longer shelf life because it is salted and, in some cases, cooked. You can often find fish in packets which have up to a ten-day shelf life. You have to ask yourself how. The reason is because this fish has had gases added to preserve it. If you want to buy a fish fillet, there is no need to reach for anything pre-packaged – a fishmonger can fillet a whole fish for you. All in all, I would really recommend finding your own good local fishmonger.

MEAT

- Steak tartare with quail's eggs, watercress salad and a simple vinaigrette
- Chicken schnitzel with crispy capers and a fried egg
- Spiced lamb koftas with minted yoghurt
- Lamb's kidneys with griddled sourdough
- Thai pork lettuce cups
- Crispy confit duck leg with celeriac remoulade
- Guinea fowl hash with fried quail's egg
- Veal carpaccio

INTERMEDIATE

- Pan-fried beef with a tarragon and chervil sauce and baked beetroot
- Baby chicken with puy lentil dahl
- Herb-crumbed Barnsley chop with quick mint sauce and flageolet beans
- Crispy chicken liver rolls with carrot and yoghurt slaw
- Pork chops with an apple and grain mustard sauce and colcannon
- Pan-fried guinea fowl breast with polenta and a chanterelle mushroom sauce
- Pan-roasted duck breasts with apples, Calvados and black pudding
- Poached veal with fennel salad and an anchovy and caper mayonnaise

ADVANCED

- Hand-cut burgers with hot pepper salsa and chunky chips
- Chicken chasseur with fresh tagliatelle
- Saffron and balsamic lamb rump studded with frozen anchovies and lardons
- Potted duck's liver with pickled mushrooms and Irish soda bread
- Pork and fruit Wellington
- Ballotine of guinea fowl with chard and Jerusalem artichokes
- Poached duck breast with beetroot purée and mooli
- Stuffed veal escalopes with aubergines and courgettes

STEAK TARTARE WITH QUAIL'S EGGS, WATERCRESS SALAD AND A SIMPLE VINAIGRETTE serves 4

FOR THE STEAK TARTARE

4 gherkins, finely chopped

2 teaspoons capers, finely chopped

1 teaspoon paprika

2 small shallots, peeled and finely chopped

a dash of Tabasco

2 tablespoons tomato ketchup

2 tablespoons Dijon mustard

350g sirloin steak, fat removed, finely chopped

4 quail's eggs, shells washed and dried

FOR THE WATERCRESS SALAD AND VINAIGRETTE

1 tablespoon white wine vinegar

1 teaspoon Dijon mustard

pinch caster sugar

2 tablespoons rapeseed oil

2 bunches watercress, stalks removed

This is one of those recipes that every cook should have on their list. If you're cooking a dinner party, this is a perfect starter; it can even be served as a main meal with *frites*. Although steak tartare originated in Russia and is now associated with French cookery, in my opinion British cooks, thanks to great British and Irish beef, do it particularly well. There's a trend in restaurants at the moment to put the beef through a mincer and serve the other ingredients on the side, but I think the classic recipe is so simple and looks so stunning that it cannot be bettered.

1   Put the gherkins, capers, paprika, shallots, Tabasco, ketchup and mustard in a small bowl and stir to mix well. Place the chopped steak in a separate bowl and add enough of the sauce to coat the meat.

2   To make the vinaigrette, whisk the vinegar, mustard, sugar and oil in a small bowl.

3   Place a 6–8cm chef's ring in the centre of the first plate and pack in the steak mixture. Remove the ring and make an indent in the centre of the steak. Crack open a quail's egg, remove the white and discard. Place the egg yolk back into half of the egg's shell and position in the indent in the steak. Repeat for 3 more plates.

4   Toss the watercress in the vinaigrette and place alongside the steak tartare.

SKILLS

- How to butterfly a chicken breast and bash it into a schnitzel shape
- How to breadcrumb (paner) a schnitzel
- How to shallow fry

CHICKEN SCHNITZEL WITH CRISPY CAPERS AND A FRIED EGG serves 4

FOR THE CHICKEN SCHNITZEL

4 boneless chicken breasts, butterflied
100g plain flour
2 large eggs, beaten
150g fresh white breadcrumbs
6 tablespoons olive oil

FOR THE CRISPY CAPERS AND FRIED EGGS

2 tablespoons olive oil
50g capers, drained
4 eggs
8 fresh anchovies
1 lemon, cut into wedges

This is such a great recipe. If you're bored of life, have a schnitzel; if you come in late from work and fancy a takeaway, have a schnitzel. It's fantastic food. Originating from the Austro-Hungarian Empire, the schnitzel was adopted by the Italians after the nineteenth-century Austrian invasion and given the name '*milanese*'. One last thing: always remember to wash your hands after handling raw chicken.

1   Place a piece of cling film on the chopping board and put the first chicken breast on it, then place another piece of cling film on top of that. Using a rolling pin, bash the chicken breast out to about 1¼cm thick and then remove it from the cling film. Repeat for the other 3 chicken breasts.

2   Put the flour, beaten egg and breadcrumbs on separate plates in a row. Dip the flattened chicken breasts first in the flour, then in the egg and then the breadcrumbs until well coated.

3   Heat a large frying pan. Once it is hot, put in 3 tablespoons of the oil and then add 2 of the coated chicken breasts at a time, so as not to overcrowd the pan. Fry the chicken for 2–3 minutes on each side over a medium heat until golden brown. Repeat with the remaining oil and the other 2 chicken breasts.

4   Meanwhile, make the crispy capers. Put a small frying pan over a medium heat and pour in 1 tablespoon of the oil. Once the oil is hot, add the capers and fry for 3–4 minutes until they become crispy.

5   Heat a second large frying pan and add the remaining 1 tablespoon of oil. Crack in the eggs and fry in the oil over a medium heat for 2–3 minutes. Remove the eggs from the pan and, using a 7–8cm round pastry cutter, cut the edges of the egg white off, leaving a neat circular finish.

6   To serve, place each chicken schnitzel on a plate and top with a fried egg. Sprinkle the crispy capers over and lay 2 anchovies on top of each egg. Lovely served with lemon wedges and a simple mixed leaf salad.

SKILLS
- Dry-frying and grinding spices
- Shaping and forming the koftas
- Threading the koftas on to the skewers
- Griddling
- Knife skills

SPICED LAMB KOFTAS WITH MINTED YOGHURT

serves 4

FOR THE LAMB KOFTAS

2 teaspoons cumin seeds

2 teaspoons coriander seeds

500g minced lamb

1 red chilli, deseeded and finely chopped

1 garlic clove, peeled and crushed

4 tablespoons finely chopped fresh coriander

salt and freshly ground black pepper

1 tablespoon olive oil

FOR THE MINTED YOGHURT

200g natural yoghurt

½ cucumber, grated then placed in a tea towel and squeezed to remove any liquid

3 tablespoons finely chopped fresh mint

juice of 1 lemon

1 teaspoon ground cumin

1 lemon, cut into wedges

8 wooden kebab skewers

Every country has its own mince dish, and this is Turkey's. It's a very simple technique and quick to make, but it's all in the taste. Toasting the spices first brings out an intense, warm flavour that goes well with the cool cucumber and yoghurt. A shoulder of lamb, minced by your butcher, is the best meat to use for this dish – and it's great value.

1 Soak 8 wooden kebab skewers in water so they don't burn when you cook them.

2 Put the cumin seeds and coriander seeds in a small dry frying pan without any oil and toast for 3 minutes over a medium heat, then remove from the heat and crush them in a pestle and mortar.

3 Place the minced lamb in a large bowl and add the crushed cumin and coriander seeds, the chilli and garlic. Mix with your hands to work all the aromatics into the meat. Lastly stir in the fresh coriander, season with salt and pepper and mix again.

4 Divide the lamb mixture into 8 balls and roll each ball between your hands to form a tube shape. Thread a tube on to each skewer and brush with the oil.

5 Heat a griddle pan over a medium heat and cook the koftas on it for 3–4 minutes on each side, until cooked through.

6 Meanwhile place the yoghurt, cucumber, mint, lemon juice and ground cumin in a medium-sized bowl and stir well.

7 To serve, place the koftas on a large serving plate with the minted yoghurt and lemon wedges on the side.

HOW TO MAKE KOFTAS

Every country has a mince dish: think Scottish mince and tatties, Swedish meatballs or Middle Eastern and Turkish lamb koftas. Making koftas is all about taste. The technique is simple, but getting the taste right requires skill. Here are some steps to show you how to make them. These instructions specifically refer to Spiced Lamb Koftas with Minted Yoghurt (page 177).

1 Place the mince in a large bowl, add the spices, seasoning and flavourings and work into the meat.

2 Divide the lamb into balls, then roll each one in your hands to form a tube shape.

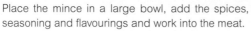

Tip: When you make koftas, before you put the mixture on to the sticks, break off a small piece and cook it, then if you want more spices, you can add more.

3 Soak the wooden kebab sticks so they don't burn and thread a kofta on to each skewer.

4 Continue to roll the meat into tubes on the skewers.

5 Heat a griddle pan and add the koftas, pouring a tiny bit of olive oil over them, which will give you a better colouration than adding the oil directly to the pan. Cook for 3–4 minutes each side until cooked through. It's always good to then rest your meat – even minced meat should be rested.

SKILLS
- How to prepare lamb's kidneys
- Frying whole spices before adding ground spices
- Griddling sourdough bread
- Cooking the kidneys so they are pink in the middle

LAMB'S KIDNEYS WITH GRIDDLED SOURDOUGH

serves 4

50g unsalted butter

1 teaspoon cloves

1 teaspoon green cardamom pods, broken open

8 curry leaves

1 red chilli, deseeded and finely chopped

1 teaspoon turmeric

1 teaspoon ground coriander

pinch ground cinnamon

10 lamb's kidneys, trimmed, membrane and core removed, and sliced in half (see page 182)

juice of 1 lime

2 tablespoons olive oil

4 slices sourdough bread

If you eat meat, you should eat offal because every meat-eater should eat every part of the animal. Out of every two animals killed for meat, one dies in vain because so many people just eat prime cuts. Enough statistics. The kidneys in this recipe are so delicious as they are flavoured with spices, curry leaves, lime juice and butter. Griddled sourdough is perfect to mop up the juices.

1   Heat a large frying pan over a medium heat and put in the butter. Once the butter has melted, add the cloves, smashed cardamom pods and curry leaves and cook for 1 minute or until the leaves begin to pop.

2   Add the chilli, turmeric, ground coriander and cinnamon and stir. Put in the prepared kidneys and cook for 3–5 minutes until golden brown. Squeeze over the lime juice and mix with the kidneys. Leave to rest in the pan.

3   Meanwhile heat a griddle pan over a medium heat. Brush oil over the sourdough bread slices and place them on the griddle for 2 minutes each side until the bar marks appear.

4   Place a griddled sourdough slice in the centre of each serving plate and top with the kidneys. Pour over the spiced buttery juices left in the pan, disregarding the whole spices.

HOW TO PREPARE AND COOK KIDNEYS

Lamb's kidneys are delicious. They cook very quickly, so be prepared as they can easily overcook. You can pan-fry them whole, as seen here, or you can slice them first – as in the Lamb's Kidneys with Griddled Sourdough (page 181).

1 Take off the membrane surrounding the kidneys. Usually kidneys come swathed in a huge amount of delicious white fat, the suet, and when you get rid of the fat, you'll see the membrane just below that.

2 Take out the little core in the middle that holds the fat in place.

3 Add the kidneys to a pan with the fried spices and a bit of foaming butter. Turn the kidneys to cook and coat with the spices. You want the high heat to give colour without overcooking them. Turn the heat down to make sure they don't burn. Kidneys are just a piece of muscle, so you want to keep them nice and moist.

4 Take the kidneys off the heat when they are just medium-rare and leave to rest on a plate.

5 Slice the kidneys into three or four slices. They should be beautifully pink inside. Put the kidneys back in the pan, off the heat, and bathe them in their own juices. Just leave them there briefly to absorb all the flavours.

HOW TO JULIENNE

'Julienne' is the name given to the way that vegetables (and sometimes other things like meat) are cut into long, equal-size matchsticks. Here is how to julienne a carrot.

1 Peel the carrot with a sharp knife or a vegetable peeler.

2 Top and tail the carrot and cut into pieces about 5cm long.

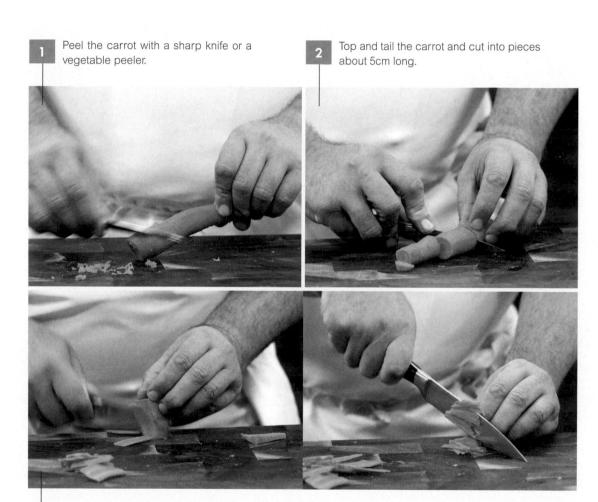

3 Place the carrot pieces on the board, flat side down. Square off the sides if necessary and then cut nice thin little strips of the carrot, just cutting down with your knife. Take a pile of the carrot rectangles and cut across into fine matchsticks about 1mm to 2mm thick.

SKILLS
- Knife skills: chopping garlic, ginger, chilli, carrots, mushrooms and water chestnuts
- Stir-frying mince and vegetables

THAI PORK LETTUCE CUPS serves 4

2 tablespoons vegetable oil

½ onion, peeled and finely sliced

2 garlic cloves, peeled and finely chopped

2cm piece fresh ginger, peeled and grated

1 red chilli, finely sliced

500g pork mince

1 large carrot, peeled and julienned (see page 183)

125g baby mushrooms, chopped

75g water chestnuts, drained and sliced

2 tablespoons soy sauce

2 tablespoons oyster sauce

2 tablespoons rice vinegar

125g bean sprouts

2 tablespoons roughly chopped coriander

outer leaves from 4 baby gem lettuces

6 spring onions, trimmed and finely sliced

70g toasted cashew nuts, roughly chopped

1 lime, cut into wedges

This dish is full of natural flavours from the chilli, garlic, ginger and soy so there is no need to add any salt unless, on tasting at the end, you feel it needs it. Scraping carrots is better than peeling them because there is less wastage and you conserve the vital nutrients found under the surface of the vegetable skin. You can buy water chestnuts either in tins or in pouches for using in this recipe.

1 Heat a large sauté pan over a medium heat and pour in the oil. Once the oil is hot, add the onion, garlic, ginger and chilli and cook for 2–3 minutes, then add the pork mince and turn up the heat to high. Cook, stirring, for 5–6 minutes until the pork is browned.

2 Add the carrot, mushrooms and water chestnuts to the pan and cook for a further 2 minutes.

3 Add the soy sauce, oyster sauce and rice vinegar and cook for another 2 minutes, or until some of the liquid evaporates. Mix in the bean sprouts and chopped coriander and take the pan off the heat immediately.

4 Place little gem leaves on 4 serving plates to form cups and spoon the pork mixture into them. Sprinkle over the spring onions and toasted cashew nuts. Serve each plate with a lime wedge.

SKILLS

- Making sugar syrup
- Deep-frying the walnuts
- Pan-frying the duck legs
- Knife skills: chopping celeriac
- Dressing the spinach

CRISPY CONFIT DUCK LEG
WITH CELERIAC REMOULADE serves 4

100g caster sugar

1 teaspoon white wine vinegar

50g whole walnuts

vegetable, sunflower or groundnut oil for frying

4 confit duck legs, skin on

½ celeriac, peeled and julienned (see page 183)

juice of 2 lemons

1 tablespoon Dijon mustard

4 tablespoons mayonnaise

25g baby spinach leaves

1 tablespoon olive oil

salt and freshly ground black pepper

Confit duck is a French bistro staple. Confit is a form of preserving whereby the meat is cooked for hours in its own fat. Prior to the use of fridges, farming communities would preserve meats such as pork and duck in this way to lay down provisions for the lean winter months. The meat would first be salted to draw out all the moisture before being cooked down in the fat from the same animal; the lard would then be reused for frying or cooking.

The duck legs need a bit of preparation for this dish: take the excess bone out first and then trim off some of the fat. You should use a heavy-duty cast-iron pan to crisp the duck. Very thinly sliced celeriac is mixed with lemon juice, mayonnaise, mustard, walnuts and seasoning to make a remoulade. This is a dish of delicious contrasts.

Preheat the oven to 200ºC/fan 180ºC/gas 6.

1 Pour 100ml of water, the sugar and white wine vinegar into a small saucepan and bring to the boil. Then place the walnuts in the pan and simmer for 1–2 minutes.

2 Half fill a small saucepan with vegetable oil and place over a medium heat. When the oil is hot, remove the walnuts from the pan with a slotted spoon, carefully shake off any excess sugar syrup and place them straight into the oil. Fry the walnuts for 1–2 minutes, then drain and set aside on a plate with kitchen paper to soak up the excess oil. Once cool, halve lengthways.

3 Meanwhile, heat a medium-sized ovenproof frying pan. Once the pan is hot, put the confit duck legs into the pan skin side down, and add the excess duck fat. Let the skin brown slightly, then put the pan in the preheated oven for 20 minutes until crispy.

4 While the duck is in the oven, make the celeriac remoulade. Place the julienned celeriac in a large bowl and stir in half the lemon juice, the Dijon mustard and mayonnaise.

5 Place the baby spinach in a medium-sized bowl with the halved walnuts, dress with the remaining lemon juice and the olive oil, and season with salt and pepper.

6 Remove the duck from the oven and leave to rest for a couple of minutes. To serve, place some celeriac remoulade on each plate, with the dressed baby spinach leaves and a duck leg.

SKILLS

- Mashing potatoes
- Removing the meat from the guinea fowl leg
- Crisping the skin in the oven
- Shaping the hash into a burger shape
- Frying a quail's egg

GUINEA FOWL HASH WITH FRIED QUAIL'S EGG

serves 4

300g floury potatoes
(for example,
Maris Piper)
2 guinea fowl legs
salt and freshly ground
black pepper
3 tablespoons olive oil
4 shallots, peeled and
finely diced
2 tablespoons finely
chopped rosemary
2 tablespoons finely
chopped flat-leaf
parsley
40g unsalted butter
4 quail's eggs

The great thing about a hash is that it not only provides a great fridge clear-out but is also good as a breakfast dish or light lunch with a salad. Save the skin from the guinea fowl and roast it until crisp in the oven – then serve it up with the finished dish.

Preheat the oven to 200°C/ fan 180°C/ gas 6.

1 Prick the potatoes and bake them in their skins in the preheated oven for 1½ hours.

2 Half an hour before the end of the cooking time, season the guinea fowl legs and cook in the oven for 20 minutes. Remove from the oven and set aside to cool, then flake the meat into a bowl.

3 Remove the potatoes from the oven and when they have cooled enough to handle, remove their skins and fork through to a rough mash. Leave the oven on.

4 Put 2 tablespoons of the olive oil in a medium-sized frying pan over a medium heat. Once the oil is hot, add the shallots and rosemary and cook for 3–4 minutes until soft. Turn off the heat and add the parsley to warm through.

5 Stir the flaked guinea fowl meat into the mashed potatoes and then add the cooked shallots, rosemary and parsley. This is your hash mixture.

6 Place the skin from the guinea fowl legs on a baking sheet lined with greaseproof paper and sandwich it flat by placing another sheet of greaseproof paper on top and then a second baking sheet. Cook in the preheated oven for 10 minutes until crisp, then remove.

7 Meanwhile, using your hands, take a quarter of the guinea fowl hash mixture and shape it into a burger patty. Repeat with the remaining hash mixture to make 3 more.

8 Put a large frying pan over a medium heat and add the butter and a further 1 tablespoon of the olive oil. Once the oil is hot and the butter has melted, use a fish slice to carefully lift the 4 hash patties into the pan and then fry them for 2 minutes on each side until crisp.

9 Meanwhile, put a small frying pan over a medium heat and add in the remaining tablespoon of olive oil. Once the oil is hot, crack the quail's eggs into the pan and fry for 1–2 minutes.

10 To serve, place a hash in the centre of each plate and top with a fried quail's egg and some crispy skin.

SKILLS
- Shaping the veal loin in cling film
- Dry-frying the almonds
- Frying the bacon
- Slicing the veal into very thin slices
- Making a vinaigrette

VEAL CARPACCIO serves 4

500g veal loin

50g flaked almonds

6 tablespoons extra virgin olive oil

4 rashers unsmoked streaky bacon, cut into lardons

20g runny honey

juice of 1 lemon

salt and freshly ground black pepper

2 handfuls pea shoots

50g Parmesan cheese

This delicate dish will melt on your tongue. First, the tender veal fillet is rolled and double wrapped in cling film and placed in the freezer to make it strong enough to cut into slices later. Keep the cling film on while slicing to help the veal keep its shape, but be sure to remove the film before serving. The wafer-thin veal slices are then dressed with toasted almonds, crispy lardons and sweet vinaigrette, and finished with a generous sprinkling of pea shoots and shaved Parmesan to create a symphony of flavours. Use a knife, not a peeler, to shave the cheese, as this will give it a feather-like consistency.

1   Trim the veal and then roll the loin tightly in cling film to form a sausage shape. Put it in the freezer for 20 minutes until nearly frozen.

2   Place the flaked almonds in a small non-stick frying pan without any oil and cook over a medium heat for 2–3 minutes until toasted, then tip out on to a plate and set aside. Add 1 tablespoon of the olive oil to the same frying pan and fry the bacon lardons for 3–5 minutes until crispy. Put the lardons on a plate with kitchen paper to soak up the excess oil.

3   Remove the veal from the freezer and slice into very thin slices. Arrange the veal slices over individual plates, then scatter over the almonds and lardons.

4   Make a vinaigrette by whisking together the honey, lemon juice and the remaining 5 tablespoons of the olive oil in a medium-sized bowl. Season with salt and pepper. Dip the pea shoots in the bowl to coat them in the vinaigrette.

5   Place the dressed pea shoots in the middle of the platter. Dress the veal, almonds and lardons with the leftover vinaigrette from the bowl and shave the Parmesan over the top.

HOW TO MAKE VEAL CARPACCIO

These instructions specifically refer to Veal Carpaccio (page 191).

2 It is important to make it as tight as possible, so twist the ends very firmly, like a cracker. Neatly trim the excess cling film from the ends.

1 Trim any excess fat off the veal loin, then roll it in a double layer of cling film.

Place the parcel of veal in a freezer, or a bowl of ice cubes, for 20 minutes, until it is very firm and almost frozen. This will make it possible to slice it very thinly.

4 When the veal is firm, put it on a chopping board and cut into wafer-thin slices using a very sharp knife. It is easier if you keep the cling film on while you do this; just remember to remove it from the slices before serving.

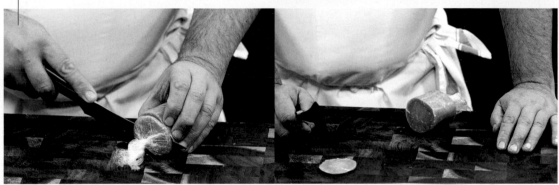

Lay the slices out on a serving plate, using your fingers to gently press and spread the meat out as thinly as possible. Dress the carpaccio just before you serve it, otherwise the lemon in the dressing will start to cook the meat.

PAN-FRIED BEEF WITH A TARRAGON AND CHERVIL SAUCE AND BAKED BEETROOT serves 4

FOR THE BAKED BEETROOT

4 large beetroot

50g unsalted butter, melted

2 tablespoons red wine vinegar

4 heaped teaspoons caster sugar

4 thyme sprigs

salt and freshly ground black pepper

FOR THE TARRAGON AND CHERVIL SAUCE

5 tablespoons white wine vinegar

1 sprig of tarragon

1 shallot, peeled and finely chopped

4 black peppercorns, lightly crushed

200g unsalted butter, clarified

2 large egg yolks

1 garlic clove, peeled and crushed

2 teaspoons roughly chopped tarragon

2 teaspoons roughly chopped chervil

2 teaspoons lemon juice

FOR THE STEAK

4 x 200g rump steaks, 2½cm thick, at room temperature

rapeseed oil, to coat

Rump steak has lots of flavour for a lower price than fillet or sirloin. Look for a good ratio in the marbling of fat to meat. The longer the beef is hung, the more its moisture disappears and the flavour develops. Remember to remove it from the fridge so it is at room temperature before cooking. (See pages 196–7 for how to cook the perfect steak.)

Preheat the oven to 200°C/ fan 180°C/ gas 6.

1   Trim off the tops and bottoms from the beetroot. Cut into 4cm-thick slices then, using a 7–8cm pastry cutter, cut the slices into rounds. Lay in the middle of a large piece of greaseproof paper (30cm x 50cm) on a baking sheet. Pour over the melted butter and red wine vinegar, and sprinkle with the sugar and thyme sprigs. Season with salt and pepper. Fold each edge of the greaseproof paper over to form an envelope and fold over the edges again to seal, then bake in the preheated oven for 30 minutes or until tender.

2   Place the vinegar, tarragon sprig, shallot and peppercorns in a small saucepan on a medium to high heat and reduce until you are left with a third of the original liquid. Remove the tarragon.

3   Clarify the butter by melting it slowly in a small pan. Skim off any froth then carefully pour off the clear golden liquid, discarding the milky solids at the bottom.

4   In a heatproof bowl, break down the egg yolks by beating with a fork and stir in the tarragon vinegar reduction. Place the bowl over a pan of simmering water making sure the bowl doesn't touch the water and, whisking all the time, slowly pour the clarified butter into the egg yolk mixture until you have a smooth, thick sauce. Stir in the garlic, chopped tarragon and chervil. Check for seasoning, adding salt, pepper and lemon juice if needed. Keep warm. Add a touch of warm water if the sauce becomes too thick.

5   Drizzle the steaks with rapeseed oil and use your fingers to coat well. Season with salt and pepper. Heat a large heavy-based frying pan. Once it is really hot, place the steaks in the pan, then sear over a high heat, without moving them, for 2–3 minutes, depending on how thick they are and how rare you want to serve them. Turn and cook on the other side. To test when done, use your finger or the back of a fork. Rare steaks will still feel springy, medium-rare steaks will still have a bit of give, and well-done steaks will feel firm, with no give to them.

6   Lift the steaks from the pan and let them rest for 5 minutes before serving with the baked beetroot and herb sauce.

HOW TO COOK THE PERFECT STEAK

Rump is one of my personal favourites for a steak. There's a little chewing, but it has lots of flavour and, most importantly, it is much cheaper than fillet or sirloin. How do you judge a really good piece of steak? Start by holding the steak up and looking for a nice ratio of marbling fat to meat. I also like my beef to be hung for at least 25 days, and even 35 days, to intensify the flavour, though the cost does go up the longer it hangs. These instructions specifically refer to Pan-fried Beef with Tarragon and Chervil Sauce and Baked Beetroot (page 195).

1 Make sure the steak is at room temperature. Add a nice sprinkling of seasoning and press it down into the steak.

2 Heat a large heavy-based griddle or frying pan. Get the pan really hot. Add a good dash of oil and put the piece of meat in the pan. Don't turn the steak or move it around – just sear it over a high heat, then turn down the heat and cook for 2 to 3 minutes, letting it brown beautifully.

3 Have a quick look to see that the steak's cooking OK. For medium-rare, you want a really good marking on the outside while keeping the inside pink, so press the steak down with a spoon.

Turn the steak and cook on the other side.

4 To test if the beef is done to your liking, use your finger. If the meat bounces back really quickly, it's too rare; the less spring there is in the meat, the more it's cooked. Rare steaks feel springy, medium-rare steaks still have a bit of give and well-done steaks feel firm, with no give to them. Personally, I think rump needs to be served medium-rare at the minimum because if you cook it medium or well done, it becomes that bit tougher. The outside should be nice and charred.

5 Lift the steak from the pan, wrap in foil to keep the heat in and let it rest and relax in a warm place for 5 minutes before serving.

SKILLS
- Spatchcocking a baby chicken
- Cooking lentils correctly
- Knowing which spices are good to combine
- Roasting the chicken for the correct cooking time so the juices run clear

BABY CHICKEN WITH PUY LENTIL DAHL   serves 4

4 baby chickens
(standard poussin size)

salt and freshly ground
black pepper

4 tablespoons olive oil

1 teaspoon cumin seeds

1 teaspoon coriander
seeds

2 tablespoons vegetable
oil

1 onion, peeled and finely
chopped

handful of curry leaves

2 garlic cloves, peeled
and finely chopped

2cm piece fresh ginger,
peeled and grated

1 red chilli, deseeded and
finely chopped

2 teaspoons turmeric
powder

300g dried puy lentils

100g passata

800ml chicken stock

150g natural yoghurt

2 tablespoons roughly
chopped fresh coriander

coriander cress or baby
coriander, to garnish

Spatchcock cooking is a great way to cook chicken quickly; grilled, fried or roasted. The greater surface area of the meat means it soaks up marinades really well. The most delicious flavours will be left in the pan after you cook the chicken so make sure you use them. Simply scrape them off the pan and add them to your dahl.

Preheat the oven to 200°C/fan 180°C/gas 6.

1   To spatchcock the baby chickens, place them on a chopping board breast side down and cut down either side of the spine of the chicken to remove it. Open the chicken out and push down. Cut each chicken in half lengthways, straight through the breast bone. Then slash the skin and season well with salt and pepper.

2   Heat the olive oil in a large ovenproof frying pan. Put the 8 chicken halves in the pan to brown over a medium heat, skin side down, for 2–3 minutes, then place the pan in the preheated oven for 10–15 minutes, or until the skin is crispy and the meat is cooked. If you don't have a pan big enough, cook them in two pans. Remove from the oven and rest for a few minutes.

3   Meanwhile make the lentil dahl. First, toast the cumin seeds and coriander seeds in a small frying pan over a medium heat until fragrant – this will take around 30 seconds to a minute. Grind to a powder in a pestle and mortar. Set aside.

4   Heat a large saucepan over a medium heat, add the vegetable oil and onion, and sauté until soft. Put in the curry leaves and, once they start to pop in the pan, add the garlic, ginger and chilli. Cook for 1 minute.

5   Add the turmeric and the ground cumin and coriander seeds. Cook for a further minute, then add the lentils, passata and stock. Bring to the boil and allow to simmer for 15 minutes. When ready to serve, stir in the yoghurt and the chopped coriander.

6   Place the lentils in the centre of a large serving plate and put the chickens on top, then pour the juices from the frying pan over the chickens. Garnish with coriander cress or baby coriander.

SKILLS

- Knife skills: chopping the herbs and shallots
- Making the crumb for the chop
- Coating the chop
- Browning the meat in a pan
- Cooking the beans, so as not to overcook them

HERB-CRUMBED BARNSLEY CHOP WITH QUICK MINT SAUCE AND FLAGEOLET BEANS serves 4

FOR THE MINT SAUCE

leaves from 1 bunch fresh mint, finely chopped

4 tablespoons white wine vinegar

1 tablespoon caster sugar

FOR THE HERB-CRUMBED BARNSLEY CHOPS

2 tablespoons finely chopped flat-leaf parsley

2 tablespoons finely chopped chervil

100g white breadcrumbs

2 tablespoons olive oil

4 Barnsley chops, kidney removed

salt and freshly ground black pepper

FOR THE FLAGEOLET BEANS

2 tablespoons olive oil

2 shallots, peeled and finely chopped

2 garlic cloves, peeled and finely chopped

2 x 400g tins flageolet beans, drained

100ml double cream

100ml fresh vegetable stock

2 tablespoons finely chopped flat-leaf parsley

A Barnsley lamb chop is a delicious cut of meat from the north of England, very much like a T-bone lamb steak. This dish is ideal for Sunday lunch; if you don't want the expense of a leg of lamb, four nice Barnsley chops will do you fine. Lamb and mint is a British institution. The slight fattiness of lamb is cut through beautifully by the delicious sweet and sour flavour of mint sauce.

*Preheat the oven to 200°C/fan 180°C/gas 6. If you have an internal grill element, turn this on too.

1 To make the mint sauce, place the mint in a medium-sized bowl and add 50ml boiling water, vinegar and sugar to taste. Stir well.

2 To make the herb crumb, put the parsley, chervil and breadcrumbs in another medium-sized bowl and mix, then transfer to a plate and set aside.

3 Heat a large frying pan over a high heat and add 1 tablespoon of the olive oil. When hot, season the chops with salt and pepper and place them into the pan, fat side down. This will allow the fat to render from the lamb so you don't have to add any further oil to the pan. Brown each chop well, turning them over. After about 5 minutes, when golden all over, remove the chops from the heat.

4 While they are still hot, so they absorb more flavour, dip each chop in the mint sauce, coating well on both sides, then dip into the breadcrumb mix and transfer to an oven tray lined with greaseproof paper. Drizzle with the remaining tablespoon of olive oil and transfer to the middle shelf of the preheated oven for 5–8 minutes. Once the breadcrumbs have toasted and turned golden brown, remove from the oven and allow to rest.

5 Meanwhile, prepare the flageolet beans. Heat a medium-sized sauté pan over a medium heat, pour in the olive oil and, once the oil is hot, add the shallots. Cook until they are soft, then add the garlic and cook for a further minute before adding the beans. Stir in the cream and stock and cook for 3 minutes. If the mixture becomes too thick, add a dash of warm water to thin it down.

6 Just before serving, stir the chopped parsley into the beans. Spoon the beans on to 4 serving plates and place the chops on top.

HOW TO CRUMB A CHOP

A Barnsley lamb chop is almost like a T-bone of lamb and is one of my favourite chops. A delicious cut with a great northern name, Barnsley chops make a perfect Sunday lunch alternative to a leg of lamb. These instructions specifically refer to Herb-crumbed Barnsley Chop with Quick Mint Sauce and Flageolet Beans (page 201).

1 Season the chop well and add to a hot pan with a very small amount of olive oil.

2 Render, or melt, the fat from your lamb chop simply by turning it in the pan.

3 Keep turning the chops so that the fat side is pressed against the pan. The idea is just to get a nice bit of golden, caramelized colour on the outside while keeping the lamb 'rose' (pink) within.

4 Add herbs to the breadcrumbs and mix together with a generous touch of seasoning before putting on a plate.

Put the browned chop into
the bowl of mint sauce and
coat well all over.

5

6 Take your chop and coat in the breadcrumbs,
making sure you have enough mint sauce for
them to stick.

7 Pile the herb crumb mixture up on
top, using as much as you can so it's
almost acting like a little stocking.

Add a tiny bit of olive oil to the pan and put the
chop in again, sprinkling any stray herb stuffing
back over it to give a loose, not compact, coating
on top.

8

Pop the chop in a nice hot oven to brown the
breadcrumbs on top, then let the meat rest for
another 4 minutes, either in a warm place or still
in the oven, with the door open and the oven
turned off.

9

SKILLS

- Preparing the chicken livers for cooking
- Making the dough, rolling it out and shaping it
- Frying the chicken liver rolls
- Knife skills: julienning the chilli and carrot

CRISPY CHICKEN LIVER ROLLS
WITH CARROT AND YOGHURT SLAW serves 4

FOR THE CHICKEN LIVER ROLLS

vegetable, groundnut or sunflower oil, for frying

250g plain flour, plus 50g extra to dust

salt and freshly ground black pepper

225ml dry white wine

1 shallot, peeled and finely chopped

30g unsalted butter

250g chicken livers, trimmed and core removed

1 teaspoon ground coriander

½ teaspoon chilli powder

1½ teaspoons ground cumin

1 egg, beaten

FOR THE CARROT AND YOGHURT SLAW

2 carrots, peeled and julienned

100g natural yoghurt

1 green chilli, deseeded and julienned

zest of 1 unwaxed lime

juice of ½ lime

1 teaspoon black onion seeds

2 tablespoons coriander cress or baby coriander, plus extra sprigs for garnishing

This dish is very refreshing and light. Chicken livers make a great, simple meal and, importantly, they are very economical. But be careful when handling them, as they are very delicate. For this reason, coat the livers lightly in flour before you cook them as this will protect them. Call it a Corrigan special to add wine to a pastry recipe but, I can tell you, this pastry mix will smell and taste amazing.

Pour in the oil and preheat the deep-fat fryer to 180°C/350°F, according to the manufacturer's instructions.

1 Place the flour and a pinch of salt in a large bowl and gradually pour in 125ml of wine. Mix together until a dough is formed and then knead until smooth. Cover the dough with a damp tea towel or some cling film and leave to rest at room temperature for 10–20 minutes.

2 Sweat the shallot in the butter in a medium-sized frying pan over a low to medium heat. Meanwhile dust the chicken livers in flour seasoned with salt and pepper. Add the livers to the frying pan and cook for 30 seconds on each side. Once they are sealed, add the spices and the rest of the wine and cook for 1–2 minutes until the wine has evaporated. Remove the livers from the pan and leave to cool. Once cooled, cut the livers into 1cm dice and return to the pan.

3 Sprinkle flour over the work surface and, using a floured rolling pin, roll out the rested dough as thin as you can. Cut the dough into 12cm x 12cm squares. You need 2 squares per portion, so roll out 8 squares in total.

4 Place the diced liver filling in a diagonal line across the middle of one square from corner to corner. Brush the beaten egg around the edges of the dough, around the filling. Fold the opposite corner over the line of filling, tuck the ends in and roll up to form a thin spring roll (see page 207). Repeat with the remaining dough squares and filling.

5 Carefully place the chicken liver rolls in the preheated deep-fat fryer for 3 minutes until golden brown and cooked.

6 Meanwhile combine the carrots, yoghurt, chilli, lime zest and juice, black onion seeds and coriander cress or baby coriander in a medium-sized bowl.

7 To serve, plate up the salad alongside the chicken liver rolls and garnish with a little extra coriander.

HOW TO MAKE FILLED PASTRY ROLLS

This is not your standard shop-bought wonton or filo pastry. I'm using my very own crispy pastry (made with wine!) to make these lovely little canapés. This specifically refers to Crispy Chicken Liver Rolls with Carrot and Yoghurt Slaw (page 205).

1 Your board and rolling pin need to be well-floured before putting down the pastry and rolling it out.

2 This pastry is almost like a pasta dough and you need it paper-thin and almost see-through to get it really crispy.

3 Cut the pastry into large (12cm x 12cm) squares.

4 Add the filling in a line diagonally across the pastry squares. Don't put in too much as you don't want to overfill them.

5 Brush the pastry with beaten egg. This will help to bind the rolls together.

6 Fold in the ends and roll again to make spring-roll-shaped pieces.

Use your knife to help you roll the pastry up from the corner, enclosing the filling. **7**

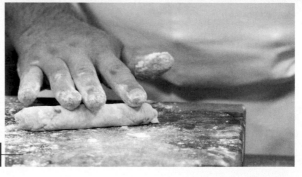

Fold in the ends and roll again to make perfect sealed rolls. **8**

PORK CHOPS WITH AN APPLE AND GRAIN MUSTARD SAUCE AND COLCANNON serves 4

FOR THE COLCANNON

600g floury potatoes

½ head of kale, finely chopped

100ml whole milk

8 spring onions, trimmed and thinly sliced

60g cold unsalted butter

FOR THE PORK CHOPS AND SAUCE

4 x 2½cm-thick pork chops, preferably a rare breed such as Gloucester Old Spot or Middle White

50g unsalted butter

2 Braeburn or Granny Smith apples, peeled, cored and diced into 1cm cubes

2 teaspoons wholegrain mustard

100ml fresh chicken stock

100ml single cream

1 tablespoon finely chopped dill

SKILLS

- Knife skills, peeling and chopping the apples, cutting kale and spring onions
- Cooking a pork chop so it is slightly pink in the middle
- Making a cream sauce
- Boiling and steaming potatoes, making the colcannon
- Presentation of the dish

Pork and apple go so well together – it was actually a Roman idea to pair up meat and fruit. The pork is fatty and the apple helps offset that, as does the mustard in this dish. I'm going to accompany this with colcannon, which is usually served around Hallowe'en time when brassicas – kale, cabbages, etc. – are aplenty in the fields. It's a wonderful way to make the potato more interesting. See pages 210–11 for more information on how to cook pork chops.

Preheat the oven to 180ºC/fan 160ºC/gas 4.

1 For the colcannon, peel and cut the potatoes into even-sized pieces. Bring a large saucepan of salted water to the boil, put in the potatoes and boil for 10 minutes. Once completely cooked, drain the potatoes, put them back in the pan then place a tea towel over to continue to steam them.

2 Scrape the bone clean using a knife. This is called French-trimming. (See pages 210–11.) Heat a medium-sized ovenproof frying pan over a high heat and place the chops in the pan skin side down until golden brown and crispy. Turn them over to brown on the other side and then place the pan in the preheated oven for 4–5 minutes. Remove and keep warm.

3 Meanwhile, to make the apple and mustard sauce, melt the butter in a large saucepan over a medium heat, then add the apples to the hot pan and cook for 4–5 minutes. When the apples start to go soft, add the mustard and stock and continue to cook. Once the liquid has reduced to half its volume, pour in the cream. Cook this for 2 minutes until it has slightly thickened.

4 Put another saucepan of salted water on to boil. Once the water is boiling, add the chopped kale and cook for 1 minute, then drain.

5 Heat the milk in a small saucepan. When warmed through, remove from the heat and add the spring onions.

6 Mash the potatoes well in their pan and then mix in the kale. Pour over the milk and spring onions and mix again, gradually adding the cold butter.

7 Just before serving, stir the dill into the apple and mustard sauce in its saucepan.

8 Place a large spoonful of colcannon on each serving plate, put a pork chop on the side and pour over a little of the apple and mustard sauce.

HOW TO COOK PORK CHOPS WITH CRISPY EDGES

I like to cook Gloucestershire Old Spot pork chops from a delicious, happy pig. A rare breed pork chop will mean a beautiful layer of fat and fat means flavour to me. These instructions specifically refer to Pork Chop with an Apple and Grain Mustard Sauce and Colcannon (page 209).

1 Start by cutting the end off the chop (you can use this in another recipe, perhaps slow-cooked in a little soy and ginger). I want you to expose the bone.

2 Scraping the bone is called a French trim. It's really important if you don't want crispy bits of meat round the bone that will catch and stop you having a fantastic finish. Keep scraping with your knife until you go right down to the bone.

We're now going to season it. **3**

4 I want beautiful crispy pork crackling and how to achieve that is to put your pork chop in the hot pan, sit it up on the fat and leave it there, over a steady heat, until you get a golden, caramelized colour.

5 Now, seal both sides of the chop. I always put the side I'm going to serve up on the plate down in the pan first. This side will take the first colour off the pan and be more attractive.

6 Caramelization makes meat much nicer to eat. It's not just about the way it looks, the colour also helps you to enjoy the meat itself and makes it delicious.

SKILLS
- Whisking the polenta until smooth
- Making the cream cheese stuffing and pushing it under the skin of the breast
- Cooking the guinea-fowl breast
- Making a mushroom cream sauce
- Griddling the polenta
- Making a herb oil

PAN-FRIED GUINEA FOWL BREAST WITH POLENTA AND A CHANTERELLE MUSHROOM SAUCE serves 4

FOR THE POLENTA

500ml fresh chicken stock

90g quick-cook polenta

50g Parmesan cheese, grated

20g unsalted butter

salt and freshly ground black pepper

olive oil, to grease the baking tray and to oil the cooked polenta

FOR THE GUINEA FOWL

75g cream cheese

2 teaspoons chopped thyme leaves

zest of ½ unwaxed lemon

4 guinea fowl breasts on the bone, skin loosened

2 tablespoons olive oil

300ml chicken stock

FOR THE MUSHROOM SAUCE

25g unsalted butter

125g chanterelle mushrooms, halved

2 teaspoons chopped thyme leaves

100ml white wine

50ml single cream

juice of ½ lemon

FOR THE HERB OIL

4 tablespoons extra virgin olive oil

1 teaspoon Dijon mustard

1 tablespoon chopped rosemary leaves

I usually ask the butcher to cut the guinea fowl down the middle of the carcass, to keep the meat succulent, add flavour because of the bones and maintain a lovely shape. Cream cheese, thyme and lemon stuffing adds moisture and flavour to this dish. Serve with a rosemary herb oil to complement the flavours.

Preheat the oven to 180°C/fan 160°C/gas 4.

1 Place the stock in a large saucepan and bring to the boil over a medium heat. Add the polenta and whisk by hand continually for 5–8 minutes until smooth. Stir in the Parmesan cheese and butter, then season with salt and pepper.

2 Brush a baking tray with oil and pour in the polenta. Let the polenta cool, then place in the fridge until set, which will take about 20 minutes.

3 Put the cream cheese, thyme and lemon zest in a bowl and mix together. Gently spoon a quarter of the cream cheese stuffing under the skin of each guinea fowl breast, then season the breasts with salt and pepper.

4 Heat a medium-sized ovenproof frying pan over a medium to high heat and pour in the olive oil. Once the oil is hot, put the guinea fowl breasts in the frying pan skin side down and cook for 2 minutes until golden and crispy. Turn the breasts over, add the stock and place in the preheated oven for 7–10 minutes until cooked through. Then remove from the oven and let them rest.

5 To make the sauce, put the butter in another medium-sized frying pan over a medium heat and add the mushrooms and thyme. Cook for 1 minute.

6 Deglaze the pan with the white wine and cook to reduce the liquid by half. Then strain the stock and juices from the guinea fowl frying pan through a sieve into the sauce and continue to cook to reduce again. Place the sauce to one side while you prepare the polenta and herb oil.

7 Remove the polenta from the fridge and cut into 4 x 7–8cm squares or wedges. Heat a frying pan over a medium heat. Lightly brush the polenta with oil and cook on each side for 2–4 minutes, until crisp and golden.

8 To make the herb oil, put the extra virgin olive oil, mustard and rosemary in a small food processor and blend until smooth.

9 Just before serving, finish the sauce by adding the cream and lemon juice, and place the rested guinea fowl breasts in the sauce to warm through.

10 Place the griddled polenta in the centre of each plate and top with a guinea fowl breast. Pour the sauce over and dot the herb oil around the plate.

SKILLS

- Cooking the duck breasts
- Cooking the apples and
  deglazing with Calvados
- Cooking the black pudding
- Blanching the leeks
- Knife skills: cutting the leeks

PAN-ROASTED DUCK BREASTS WITH APPLES, CALVADOS AND BLACK PUDDING serves 4

4 duck breasts, skin on

salt and freshly ground black pepper

50g unsalted butter

2 Granny Smith apples, peeled, cored and cut into 8 wedges

3 tablespoons Calvados

100ml fresh chicken stock

50ml single cream

1 teaspoon olive oil

12 slices Spanish black pudding (*morcilla*)

1 leek, trimmed and cut lengthways into strips 1cm thick

extra virgin olive oil, to drizzle

Duck breasts cooked in this way can be treated like sirloin steak. The duck is garnished with cooked leek ribbons, which end up looking a little like tagliatelle. Apples and black pudding are some of the best traditional accompaniments for duck. The black pudding just needs to be heated through in the pan rather than cooked. Calvados is a wonderful drink to finish a meal with as it aids digestion; here it is the perfect spirit with which to flambé the apples.

1   Season the duck breasts with salt and pepper, then place them skin side down in a large cold frying pan over a medium to high heat. Fry for 8–10 minutes until the skin is crispy and most of the fat has rendered. Turn the duck breasts over and cook for a further 2–3 minutes, or until cooked to your liking. Remove the duck breasts from the pan and place on a plate to one side to rest. (Any rendered fat left in the pan can be strained and kept in the fridge for roasting potatoes.)

2   Heat a medium-sized frying pan and put in the butter. Once the butter is melted and hot, add the apple pieces and cook for 3 minutes over a medium to high heat until golden. Deglaze the pan with the Calvados, then set it alight to flambé the apples for a few seconds. Pour in the stock and simmer for a couple of minutes until the liquid has reduced by two thirds.

3   Finish the sauce by pouring in the cream plus any juices that have come out of the duck breasts whilst resting.

4   In a separate small frying pan, drizzle in the olive oil and fry the black pudding slices over a medium to high heat for 1 minute on each side.

5   Bring a medium-sized saucepan of salted water to the boil and put in the leek strips. Blanch for 3–4 minutes, then drain, season with salt and pepper and drizzle over some extra virgin olive oil. Toss the leek strips to coat in the oil.

6   To serve, slice each duck breast and fan out in a semi-circle to one side of the plate. On the other side make a little pile of leek strips, flambéed apple wedges and black pudding. Drizzle with the apple sauce.

SKILLS
- Poaching the veal
- Making the mayonnaise
- Knife skills: cutting the fennel, parsley and dill
- Sealing the veal
- Making the sauce

POACHED VEAL WITH FENNEL SALAD AND AN ANCHOVY AND CAPER MAYONNAISE serves 4

FOR THE POACHED VEAL
¼ celery stick
1 bay leaf
1 sprig thyme
1 sprig flat-leaf parsley
2 x 200g veal rumps, sinew and fat removed
750ml fresh chicken stock
peel from 1 unwaxed lemon
70g unsalted butter, 50g kept cold and diced

FOR THE ANCHOVY AND CAPER MAYONNAISE
2 egg yolks
1 teaspoon Dijon mustard
1 tablespoon white wine vinegar
2 anchovies
125ml rapeseed oil
125ml mild olive oil
1 tablespoon capers, finely chopped
juice of ½ lemon

FOR THE FENNEL SALAD
2 fennel bulbs, thinly sliced
1 tablespoon olive oil
salt and freshly ground black pepper
juice of ½ lemon
1 teaspoon finely chopped flat-leaf parsley
1 teaspoon finely chopped dill

This is moist, succulent and full of flavour. The veal is poached in chicken stock with a bouquet garni and lemon peel for extra flavour. A little tip to remember when cooking veal is to let the meat rest for as long as the cooking time – so if you cooked it for 10 minutes, let it rest for 10 minutes. Any juices that come out of the meat as it rests can then be whisked into the sauce for extra flavour.

1 Make the bouquet garni by tying together the celery, bay leaf, thyme and flat-leaf parsley sprigs with butcher's string.

2 Place the veal rumps, bouquet garni, stock and lemon peel in a large saucepan and bring to the boil. Simmer for 12 minutes, then remove the veal from the stock and place on a plate to one side. Remove the lemon peel and bouquet garni and discard. Continue to simmer the stock, until the liquid has reduced to one third of the original volume.

3 Meanwhile, make the mayonnaise. Put the egg yolks, mustard, vinegar and anchovies in a small food processor and pulse to blend. Gradually pour in the rapeseed oil then the mild olive oil, continuing to blend at the same time.

4 Use a spatula to scrape the mayonnaise out of the processor into a medium-sized bowl. Stir in the capers and lemon juice, then set aside.

5 Place the sliced fennel in another medium-sized bowl and dress with the olive oil. Season with salt and pepper and add the remaining lemon juice, parsley and dill. Stir well.

6 Heat a medium-sized frying pan and put in 20g of the butter. Once the butter is hot and melted, add the veal rumps and fry to seal on all sides until golden brown, then remove the rumps from the pan to a plate, cover with foil to keep warm and leave them to rest.

7 Once the stock has reduced sufficiently, whisk in the remaining 50g of diced cold butter, the resting juices from the veal and 2 heaped tablespoons of the anchovy and caper mayonnaise.

8 To serve, thinly slice the veal rumps and fan out the slices on one side of each plate. Place some dressed fennel salad alongside with a spoonful of the mayonnaise. Drizzle the warm sauce over the veal slices.

SKILLS

- Trimming and chopping the rump steak until it looks like coarse minced meat
- Shaping the burgers by hand without squashing them
- Roasting and peeling the peppers
- Blanching and skinning the tomatoes
- Making chips
- Removing bone marrow
- Using a pestle and mortar

HAND-CUT BURGERS WITH HOT PEPPER SALSA AND CHUNKY CHIPS serves 4

FOR THE CHUNKY CHIPS
4 medium baking potatoes
vegetable oil

FOR THE HOT PEPPER SALSA
2 peppers (1 red and 1 yellow), halved and deseeded
olive oil
½ red onion, peeled and thinly sliced
4 ripe medium tomatoes, skinned, deseeded and cut into wedges
2 garlic cloves, peeled and chopped
1 red chilli, deseeded and finely chopped
2 tablespoons extra virgin olive oil
1 tablespoon sherry vinegar
2 tablespoons coarsely chopped flat-leaf parsley
salt and freshly ground black pepper

FOR THE BURGERS
2 x 7½cm rounds of bone marrow
4 tablespoons vegetable oil
½ red onion, peeled and finely chopped
2 tablespoons finely chopped marjoram
400g rump steak
125g pork back fat
2 tablespoons black peppercorns, crushed in a pestle and mortar
2 tablespoons olive oil

Ready-made supermarket burgers contain all sorts of trimmings and extras, so I suggest you always make your own. This way, you know exactly what goes into them. If rump steak alone is too expensive, use half rump and half chuck. The bone marrow and pork back fat can be bought from any butcher.

Preheat the oven to 190°C/fan 170°C/gas 5.

1 Prick the potatoes and place in the preheated oven for 45 minutes. Brush the peppers with olive oil and cook under the grill for about 5 minutes, turning them over, until slightly blackened. Transfer the grilled peppers to a bowl, cover the bowl tightly with cling film and leave until cold.

2 For the burgers, remove the bone marrow from the bone, cut each piece in half and place in the fridge until you are ready to use it. Sauté the onion over a medium heat in 2 tablespoons of the vegetable oil for a few minutes until softened but not coloured. Stir in the marjoram and leave to cool off the heat.

3 Put the steak on a chopping board. Trim off and discard any excess fat and sinew, then chop the meat with a very sharp knife. Do the same with the back fat. Place the meat and fat in a food processor and pulse for a few seconds to mince even further.

4 Put the minced meat and fat in a bowl with the cooled onion and season with salt and pepper. Mix well, then shape into 4 patties, each about 2cm thick. Cover and keep in the fridge until needed.

5 For the salsa, first peel the skins off the peppers and chop the flesh. Mix the chopped peppers in a bowl with the red onion, tomatoes, garlic and chilli. Add the extra virgin olive oil, vinegar, parsley and some salt and pepper, mix well, then taste and adjust the flavourings as you like. Keep in a covered bowl in the fridge until ready to serve.

6 Prepare the chunky chips by cutting the pre-baked potatoes into wedges and shallow-fry in hot vegetable oil over a medium to high heat for 4–5 minutes, until golden brown on their cut sides.

7 Heat 2 tablespoons of vegetable oil in a heavy-based frying pan until hot. Fry the burgers over a medium heat for 3 minutes on each side if you like them medium-rare, longer if you prefer them well-cooked. Remove and set aside to rest for a couple of minutes.

8 Dust the pieces of bone marrow with the crushed peppercorns. Heat the 2 tablespoons of olive oil in the pan used to cook the burgers and fry the bone marrow for a minute on each side, until caramelized. Place a piece of marrow on top of, or next to, each burger and serve with the salsa and chips.

SKILLS

Jointing the chicken
Flouring and frying the chicken until
golden brown
Knife skills: preparing the vegetables
Making pasta and cooking pasta

CHICKEN CHASSEUR WITH FRESH TAGLIATELLE

serves 4

FOR THE FRESH TAGLIATELLE

250g '00' flour

5 eggs (2 whole eggs, 3 egg yolks)

2 tablespoons olive oil

large knob of unsalted butter

semolina flour, to dust

FOR THE CHICKEN CHASSEUR

30g plain flour

salt and freshly ground black pepper

1 chicken, cut into 8–10 pieces (see pages 222–3)

2 tablespoons olive oil

20g unsalted butter

2 shallots, peeled and cut into quarters

2 garlic cloves, peeled and finely chopped

175g chestnut mushrooms, cut into quarters

3 tablespoons thyme leaves

100ml Madeira

200ml fresh chicken stock

100ml passata

100ml double cream

4 tablespoons finely chopped tarragon

A beautiful family dish. For the pasta, you need double-zero flour. Its high gluten content makes the dough elastic, giving the pasta bite. Using free-range organic eggs is not only the right ethical choice but also gives great results. The yolks' rich colour translates into vibrant pasta. See the next page for instructions on how to joint a chicken.

1 Place the flour, eggs, egg yolks and olive oil in a medium-sized food processor and blend until the mixture forms a ball. Remove and knead until smooth. Cover with cling film and rest in the fridge for 20 minutes.

2 Place the plain flour on a plate and season with salt and pepper, then roll the chicken pieces in the flour.

3 Heat a large casserole pot and add half the olive oil and the butter. Once hot, put in the floured chicken pieces. Cook over a medium to high heat for 4–5 minutes, until golden brown. Remove the chicken and leave to rest.

4 Put the other tablespoon of olive oil in the casserole pot and add the shallots. Cook for 3 minutes until they begin to go soft. Add the garlic and cook for 2 minutes, then add the mushrooms and thyme. Cook for a further 2 minutes.

5 Pour in the Madeira to deglaze the casserole pot. Return the chicken pieces and add the chicken stock and passata. Bring to the boil, then reduce to a simmer and cook for 30 minutes.

6 Remove the pasta dough from the fridge and cut it in half. Lightly dust with some semolina flour and also dust the pasta machine. (See pages 84–5.)

7 Feed the first block of dough through the pasta machine, gradually reducing the setting each time from the thickest to the thinnest setting, until you have a thin sheet of pasta. Then attach the tagliatelle cutter attachment to the machine and feed the pasta sheet through. Carefully place the pasta ribbons on a lightly floured baking sheet and set aside. Repeat with the second block of dough, making a thin sheet and cutting it into tagliatelle ribbons.

8 Bring a large saucepan of salted water to the boil and put in the tagliatelle. Cook for 2–3 minutes, then drain.

9 Just before serving, add the cream to the chicken chasseur in the casserole pot and simmer for a further 5 minutes to reduce.

10 Melt the butter in a large frying pan and add the drained tagliatelle. Remove from the heat and toss the pasta in the pan to coat with the melted butter.

11 Place a mound of pasta on to each plate and serve 2 pieces of chicken alongside. Spoon over the delicious sauce and garnish with the tarragon.

HOW TO JOINT A CHICKEN

If you joint and bone a chicken well, even a small bird can easily feed six people, making it fantastic value. Joint into ten pieces so everyone will get some white and some brown meat. These instructions specifically refer to Chicken Chasseur with Fresh Tagliatelle (page 221).

1 Place the bird on the board with the parson's nose facing you. Pull out the wings and, using a large cook's knife, chop the wings off at the elbow joint.

2 Use your knife to search out the oyster, the soft point at the top of the chicken leg where it joins the backbone. Place your knife in the chicken at this point and cut around the oyster to allow you to pull the legs off cleanly. The oyster should stay with the leg, giving you a nice clean break.

3 Take off the end of the chicken legs by chopping through the leg just above the bottom joint.

4 Find the point in the legs that divides the drumstick and thigh and chop through to divide the legs into two.

5 Scrape back the meat with your knife to take the bone out of the thighs.

6 Cut off the parson's nose.

7 Cut round and remove the wishbone.

8 Cut a slice of breast meat from each side of the chicken. This will give you more cuts of breast meat so everyone can have a piece.

9 Trim the chicken to leave just the breast on the backbone.

10 Cut right though the backbone with your knife. Now, chop each half of the breast into pieces through the backbone, giving you the flavour from the bones too.

Lay your chicken portions out on the board, ready to cook. **11**

SAFFRON AND BALSAMIC LAMB RUMP STUDDED WITH FROZEN ANCHOVIES AND LARDONS serves 4

2 x 300g boned lamb rumps

8 fresh anchovies, frozen

50g smoked bacon lardons

2 tablespoons finely chopped rosemary sprigs

2 tablespoons thyme sprigs

salt and freshly ground black pepper

1 tablespoon mild olive oil

450ml chicken stock

¼ teaspoon saffron threads

4 tablespoons balsamic vinegar

50g unsalted butter

150g baby spinach leaves

SKILLS
- Preparing the rump of lamb
- Inserting the lardons and anchovies into the meat
- Cooking the rump so it is rare inside
- Reducing the sauce to get the right consistency
- Wilting spinach, so as not to overcook or burn

This recipe owes a lot to Anna Del Conte. Her recipe inspired me because I had never thought to add saffron to lamb, with anchovies and lardons. You might be surprised to think of lamb and anchovies together, but they are often paired up in French provincial cooking. The anchovies melt away and bring a delicious saltiness to the meat. You will need to buy 8 fresh anchovies and freeze them before starting this recipe. Lamb rump is almost like a mini leg of lamb. It is a very lean cut but it is layered with pieces of meat – you can almost see parts of the muscle. Because of this, it needs to be really well rested after you cook it.

Preheat the oven to 200°C/fan 180°C/gas 6.

1 Using a long, thin knife, make small cuts all over the lamb rumps and push in your finger to turn the cuts into small holes. Then push the frozen anchovies, followed by the bacon lardons, rosemary and thyme sprigs into the various holes you've made, and season the lamb with salt and pepper.

2 Heat the olive oil in an ovenproof frying pan over a high heat. Place the lamb rumps in the pan, skin side down, and cook for 5 minutes, turning them to make sure they brown well all over. Then place the pan in the preheated oven for 8–10 minutes. Remove the lamb rumps from the oven and let them rest for 10 minutes. This will leave them perfectly pink in the middle.

3 Meanwhile place the stock, saffron and balsamic vinegar in a medium-sized saucepan and boil until reduced by a third.

4 Pour the meat juices from the lamb rumps into the reduced sauce. Gradually stir in 30g of the butter until it melts and the sauce thickens.

5 Heat a large sauté pan, put in the rest of the butter and, once hot and melted, throw in the spinach and cook over a medium heat until just wilted. This will take 2–3 minutes.

6 To serve, place a mound of spinach in the centre of each plate. Carve the lamb rump into slices, place them on top of the spinach and pour over the sauce.

HOW TO PREPARE AND STUFF A LAMB RUMP

In my restaurant, we trim this piece of meat really, really well because although it's lean, there's quite a lot of back fat. Don't be afraid to cut off the fat to leave a nice layer and tidy it up with your knife. These instructions specifically refer to Saffron and Balsamic Lamb Rump Studded with Frozen Anchovies and Lardons (page 225).

1 Get a steel and make one, two, three, four holes right through the meat.

2 Use the tips of your fingers to open the cuts up into holes.

3 Hook the anchovies over the top of the steel and push them into the meat, threading them through like a needle.

4 Push the anchovies further with your fingers so they go right in.

5 | Push the mixture of bacon lardons and herbs into the holes. Season the meat well.

SKILLS

● Sterilizing jars
● Preparing the duck's livers
● Making soda bread without
  any proving needed

POTTED DUCK'S LIVER WITH PICKLED MUSHROOMS AND IRISH SODA BREAD serves 4

FOR THE POTTED DUCK'S LIVER

50g unsalted butter

6 shallots, peeled and finely diced

2 garlic cloves, peeled and finely chopped

1 tablespoon and ½ teaspoon picked thyme leaves

salt and freshly ground black pepper

1 tablespoon olive oil

200g duck's livers, cleaned and cored

100ml Pedro Ximénez sherry

50g melted clarified butter

FOR THE PICKLED MUSHROOMS

100ml rapeseed oil

50ml sherry vinegar

½ teaspoon fennel seeds

10 black peppercorns

2 garlic cloves, peeled and smashed

100g mixed baby mushrooms

1 tablespoon tarragon leaves

FOR THE IRISH SODA BREAD

125g wholemeal flour

125g plain flour, plus extra to dust

8g bicarbonate of soda

8g salt

250ml buttermilk

50g porridge oats

This is a pâté everyone can make. It is perfect as a Christmas starter, but it needs to be prepared at least a day in advance as the flavour improves in the fridge. It will keep up to a week in there, but you must sterilize the meat jars properly before you start cooking by washing them in boiling hot water (or in the dishwasher) or by simmering them in a pan of boiling water for 10 minutes.

1 Place a medium-sized frying pan over a low heat and put in the butter. Once the butter has melted, add the shallots and cook for 2 minutes, then add the garlic, 1 tablespoon of the thyme and some salt and pepper and cook until the shallots are soft.

2 Heat a second medium-sized frying pan and pour in the olive oil. Season the livers with salt and pepper and, once the oil is hot, add them to the pan, cooking over a medium to high heat for 1 minute on each side. As soon as the livers turn golden, add the sherry and deglaze the pan. Remove the livers from the pan to cool down.

3 Slice the livers through the middle. Place the slices in alternating layers with the shallots in 4 sterilized small glass ramekins or 4 small (200ml) kilner jars. Mix the melted clarified butter with the ½ teaspoon of thyme leaves and spoon over the top of the livers and shallots. Place the ramekins in the fridge to set. This should take an hour.

4 To make the pickled mushrooms, place the oil, vinegar, fennel seeds, peppercorns and garlic in a small saucepan and bring to the boil. Remove from the heat and pour into a bowl. Add the mushrooms and allow them to cool in the pickling liquor. When cool, add the tarragon and stir. Set aside.

Preheat the oven to 200°C/fan 180°C/gas 6.

5 Next make the Irish soda bread. In a large bowl, mix the two flours, bicarbonate of soda and salt and then stir in the buttermilk. Work the mixture into a dough and knead for a few minutes.

6 Dust a clean work surface with plain flour. Shape the dough into 8 balls and roll them in the oats. Place on a floured baking tray and put in the preheated oven for 12–15 minutes.

7 To serve, place a ramekin of potted duck's liver on each serving plate with some pickled mushrooms next to it. Put 2 soda bread rolls on the side.

PORK AND FRUIT WELLINGTON serves 4

FOR THE FRUIT DUXELLE
2 tablespoons olive oil
2 shallots, peeled and
  finely chopped
100g stoned prunes,
  finely chopped
100g dried apricots,
  finely chopped
1 Granny Smith apple,
  peeled and finely diced
juice of ½ lemon

FOR THE WELLINGTONS
flour, for dusting
800g ready-made
  puff pastry
8 slices Parma ham
4 x 120g pork tenderloins,
  trimmed
1 egg, lightly beaten

FOR THE CABBAGE
30g unsalted butter
1 onion, peeled and finely
  sliced
1 Savoy cabbage, finely
  shredded

When you think of Wellingtons you probably think of beef, but beef is so expensive, so why not use another meat? Fillet of pork is delicious, tender and very easy to cook and calls for fruit as an accompaniment here. You don't need very much; just enough for it to lift the taste of the dish. Pork is a very rich meat, so the fruit also works as an aid for digestion. Saucy accompaniment this dish doesn't need; saucy company maybe!

Preheat the oven to 200°C/fan 180°C/gas 6.

1 To make a fruit duxelle filling for the Wellingtons, place a large frying pan over a medium heat and put in the olive oil. Once the oil is hot, add the shallots and cook for 2–3 minutes until soft, then put in the prunes, apricots and apple. Cook for a few more minutes and finish off by adding the lemon juice.

2 Remove the fruit mixture from the pan and place in a food processer. Process until the mixture resembles mincemeat.

3 To make the Wellingtons, first flour the work surface and then roll out the puff pastry until it is 2mm thick. Cut out four 14cm x 18cm pastry rectangles. Lay 2 Parma ham slices on top of each pastry rectangle and spread the fruit duxelle filling over the ham. Lay each pork tenderloin on top of the fruit and then roll the pastry over the pork and press together to seal the ends. Trim any excess pastry, then brush the Wellingtons with beaten egg.

4 Place the Wellingtons on a baking tray lined with greaseproof paper and put in the preheated oven for 25 minutes. Once cooked, remove from the oven and allow to rest for 5 minutes before cutting.

5 Meanwhile, put a large frying pan over a low to medium heat and put in the butter. When the butter starts to foam, add the onion and cook gently until it begins to caramelize. Add the shredded cabbage and 50ml water, which will gently steam the cabbage, and cook for a couple of minutes.

6 To serve, neatly cut each Wellington in half. Place them with their cut-sides facing up on the serving plates, on a bed of the onion and cabbage.

SKILLS
- Sealing the pork in the pan
- Making a fruit duxelle filling for the Wellington
- Rolling out the pastry
- Covering the pork with the pastry

BALLOTINE OF GUINEA FOWL WITH CHARD AND JERUSALEM ARTICHOKES serves 4

FOR THE BALLOTINE OF GUINEA FOWL

50g breadcrumbs

200g good-quality pork sausage meat

zest of 1 unwaxed lemon

1 large guinea fowl (approx. 1kg)

2 tablespoons olive oil

100ml Madeira

100ml chicken stock

40g cold unsalted butter, cubed

FOR THE CHARD

6 large chard leaves, cut into 1cm strips

1 tablespoon extra virgin olive oil

juice of 1 small lemon

FOR THE JERUSALEM ARTICHOKES

1 tablespoon olive oil

250g Jerusalem artichokes, peeled and halved

2 garlic cloves, peeled and smashed

40g blanched almonds

1 tablespoon chopped tarragon

'Ballotine' means stuffed and rolled up. The stuffing is made from sausage meat, breadcrumbs and lemon zest; adding a little water helps to make it lighter. The most important things are to ensure you don't use the part of the guinea fowl leg or wing which has sinew, and to be very careful to remove all the shards of bone. The ballotine is poached and then fried to brown the bird beautifully.

Preheat the oven to 180°C/fan 160°C/gas 4.

1 Place the breadcrumbs, sausage meat and lemon zest in a medium-sized bowl, season and mix well.

2 To prepare the guinea fowl, first trim the tips of the legs and wings from the bird. Then cut an opening halfway along the spine and remove the breast bone and the other bones, but leave the skin intact. Lay the boned guinea fowl on cling film, skin side down, and open out like a book.

3 Season the guinea fowl and spread the sausage-meat stuffing mixture in a thick line along the length of the breast at one end. To make the ballotine, fold the breast over the stuffing and roll up tightly in the cling film, twisting the sides like a cracker. (See pages 234–5.)

4 Bring a large pan of water to the boil, place the wrapped ballotine in and simmer for 15 minutes to poach it. Remove, put aside and allow to cool slightly.

5 Blanch the chard for a minute in the same water brought back to the boil, and then toss with the extra virgin olive oil and the lemon juice to taste.

6 Meanwhile, cook the Jerusalem artichokes. Place a heavy-bottomed oven-proof casserole pot over a medium heat and put in the olive oil. When the oil is hot, add the artichoke halves and garlic. After about 5 minutes, when the artichokes have coloured, add the almonds and tarragon and cover the pot with a lid. Put in the preheated oven and cook for 10–15 minutes.

7 Unwrap the ballotine. Heat a medium-sized frying pan over a medium to high heat, add the olive oil and fry the ballotine until golden all over. This will take about 5 minutes. Then remove from the pan to a plate and rest.

8 Deglaze the frying pan with the Madeira, pour in the stock and cook to reduce the liquid by half. Take the pan off the heat and slowly whisk in the butter, until the sauce is thick and silky.

9 To serve, place some chard on each plate. Slice the ballotine and lay 3 slices next to the chard. Pile some Jerusalem artichokes on the other side and drizzle the sauce over the meat.

HOW TO MAKE A BALLOTINE OF GUINEA FOWL

1 Place half a guinea fowl skin-side up on the board and, using a large, sharp knife, remove and discard the lower half of the leg. Keeping the flesh in one hand, slowly and carefully ease the meat away from the carcass, keeping your knife as close to the bone as possible. Remove the spine. You should be left with one piece of meat, skin still attached.

2 Place a triple layer of cling film on the chopping board and rub the topmost one with a knob of butter, salt and freshly ground pepper and a few tarragon leaves.

3 Prepare the stuffing by mixing together the ingredients, plus a few tablespoons of water, to make a paste.

4 Place the guinea fowl skin-side down on the buttered cling film, and carefully spoon the stuffing along the middle. Using the cling film, gently roll up the ballotine to form a cylinder. This should be firm but not too tight, to allow the stuffing room to expand during cooking.

5 Tightly twist the ends to seal, then trim off the excess cling film.

 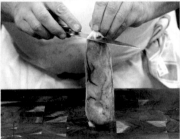 

6 Gently lower the parcel into a pan of simmering water and poach for 15 minutes.

7 Remove from the water and unwrap, discarding the cling film and tarragon leaves, but carefully reserving any cooking juices to add to the sauce.

8 Rub the outside of the meat with olive oil and fry gently in a pan, basting frequently, until the surface is crisp and browned.

Slice and serve. **9**

SKILLS

Knife skills: cutting mooli, garlic,
ginger and spring onions
Shaping the mooli
Making a parcel
Liquidizing the beetroot
Scoring the duck skin
Poaching the duck

POACHED DUCK BREAST WITH BEETROOT PURÉE AND MOOLI serves 4

1 mooli

2 tablespoons mirin

2 tablespoons rice vinegar

peel from 1 unwaxed orange

4 duck breasts, skin removed, retained and scored

4 red chillies, sliced

4 garlic cloves, peeled and sliced

100g root ginger, peeled and sliced

4 star anise

4 spring onions, trimmed and left whole

2 beetroots, boiled in their skins, then peeled and chopped

2 tablespoons orange marmalade

40ml red wine vinegar

soy sauce, to drizzle

There is a light Asian influence to this recipe, created by garlic, ginger, chillies, star anise and orange. You end up with an incredible stock that can be used again for cooking noodles or to make a wonderful broth. Duck and orange is a traditional coupling and the zesty orange theme runs throughout this dish.

Preheat the oven to 200°C/fan 180°C/gas 6.

1 Peel the mooli and cut into four 4cm x 6cm chunks. Using an apple corer, make 3 'barrel-shaped' pieces out of each chunk (these should look like the round core shape left after coring an apple).

2 Place a large square of greaseproof paper on top of a baking sheet and put the mooli pieces, mirin, rice vinegar and orange peel in the centre and mix together well. Make a parcel by bringing up the greaseproof paper sides, folding over the top and twisting the edges to seal. Place in the preheated oven for 30 minutes. Remove and set aside.

3 Meanwhile, lay the scored duck skins out flat (outer skin-side down) in a small ovenproof frying pan and place another pan on top to flatten them and weigh them down. Cook for 12–15 minutes over a medium to high heat, then place the pan, still with the other pan on top, into the preheated oven for 5 minutes. Remove from the oven and leave to one side on kitchen paper for a couple of minutes to let the skin dry.

4 Loosely tie some string around the duck breasts to hold their shape. Tie the ends around a wooden spoon, to keep the breast meat off the bottom of the pan. Place the duck breasts into a medium-sized saucepan with enough water to cover, and add the chillies, garlic, ginger and star anise. Bring the water to the boil, then take the pan off the heat and put in the spring onions. Leave the duck breasts to poach in the aromatic water for 10 minutes.

5 While the duck breasts are poaching, tip the cooked and chopped beetroots into a blender with enough water to make a purée and liquidize until smooth. Transfer the purée to a small saucepan and simmer over a medium heat to reduce. When it has thickened, stir in the marmalade and vinegar and keep warm.

6 To serve, slice the duck breasts lengthways and serve one on each plate, with a spoonful of beetroot purée on the side, the drained spring onions on top and mooli pieces on the other side. Dress by drizzling over soy sauce.

SKILLS
- Flattening the veal between cling film
- Wilting the spinach
- Grating the cheese
- Laying out, rolling up and securing the veal escalopes with a cocktail stick
- Cooking the escalopes
- Knife skills: cutting the aubergine, courgette and tomatoes
- Cooking the stir fry

STUFFED VEAL ESCALOPES WITH AUBERGINES AND COURGETTES serves 4

4 x 150g veal escalopes
50g baby spinach leaves
85g Parma ham
  (or 4 slices)
50g Pecorino cheese,
  grated
2 tablespoons olive oil
100ml Marsala wine
1 garlic clove, peeled
  and finely chopped
1 red chilli, deseeded
  and finely diced
½ medium aubergine,
  cut into 1.5cm dice
1 medium green
  courgette, cut into
  1.5cm dice
1 medium yellow
  courgette, cut into
  1.5cm dice
2 tomatoes, peeled,
  seeds removed
  and cut into 1cm dice
100ml white wine
2 tablespoons basil
  leaves, torn
salt and freshly ground
  black pepper
400g Ratte potatoes,
  boiled in their skins
2 tablespoons extra virgin
  olive oil
2 sprigs rosemary

This simple and tasty dish can be made in no time at all. Each veal escalope needs to be cut in half lengthways, opened, covered with cling film and batted out flat with a rolling pin. The flattened veal is then covered with layers of ham, spinach and cheese, and rolled into sausage shapes secured with cocktail sticks. A dash of Marsala in the cooking pan sweetens the flavours up. An extra little trick is to add a small amount of sugar to the vegetables for a touch of summer sweetness.

1 Cut each veal escalope in half, not quite cutting it through completely. Lay a sheet of cling film on a clean work surface and place the first veal escalope on top, opening it out, then lay another sheet of cling film on top of the escalope and flatten out the veal between the cling film using a rolling pin. Unpeel the top sheet of cling film and put the flattened veal escalope aside on a plate. Repeat with the other 3 escalopes.

2 Heat a small frying pan and put in the spinach and a dash of water. Cook over a medium heat for 1–2 minutes until the spinach has wilted.

3 Lay a slice of Parma ham on top of the first flattened escalope, followed by a quarter of the wilted spinach and a quarter of the grated Pecorino. Starting at the end nearest to you, roll up the escalope and filling and secure with cocktail sticks. Repeat with the other 3 escalopes and the remaining Parma ham and grated Pecorino to make 4 veal rolls.

4 Heat 1 tablespoon of the olive oil in a large frying pan and cook the veal rolls for 5–7 minutes over a medium heat, browning them on all sides. With the meat still in the pan, deglaze the pan with the Marsala and cook for another 1–2 minutes, then set aside.

5 Meanwhile, heat the other tablespoon of olive oil in a large wok or frying pan over a high heat and add the garlic and chilli. Fry for 2 minutes, then add the diced aubergine and courgettes. Fry for another 3–4 minutes, then add the diced tomato flesh and the white wine. Let the wine reduce to a couple of tablespoons of liquid. Just before serving, stir in the basil leaves and season with salt and pepper.

6 Halve the cooked Ratte potatoes lengthways and put them in a large bowl. Drizzle over the extra virgin olive oil. Remove the leaves from the rosemary sprigs and mix the leaves in with the potatoes.

7 Heat a griddle pan over a high heat, then put the dressed potatoes on the griddle and cook for 2 minutes on each side.

8 To serve, place a mound of the vegetables in the centre of each serving plate. Remove the cocktail sticks from the veal rolls, slice them thickly and place the slices next to each vegetable mound. Place the griddled potatoes on the side and drizzle over the Marsala pan juices from the veal.

GIZZI'S NOTES ON MARINADES

Marinating is a really useful technique to understand because it is a great way of getting flavour into food, especially fish, and also of tenderizing all different cuts of meat. Creating a marinade can be a chance for you to show off some personality. There are many different combinations you can create, but three core ingredient types should always be found in your marinade:

1 A fat to help the marinade cling to the meat or fish – oil is a good example. When making American fried chicken, buttermilk is used.

2 Aromatic flavour enhancers, such as chilli, garlic and herbs.

3 Some kind of acidity to tenderize the meat, like lemon or lime juice or vinegar. Buttermilk also does this, hence its heavy use in fried chicken. For a citrusy flavour in fish marinades, use the peel only otherwise the juice will begin to 'cook' the fish.

When you marinate fish or prawns you only need to leave them to soak in the marinade for a few minutes because they will absorb it very quickly.

For all meat, I would recommend leaving it to marinate for a minimum of two hours, and if possible overnight or even longer. A marinade will actually help preserve the meat so it's a great way to avoid wastage.

Grilling or barbecuing marinated food is fantastic, but you can also put marinated food in a stew or curry, which works really well.

We always go on about not having the time to cook. If on a Sunday night you were to spend a few minutes marinating some meat, you could put that in the fridge and then during the week all you've got to do is whack the meat on the grill and whizz up a vegetable side dish. Amazing.

Marinades

Jerk Marinade

2 tbl English Mustard
2 tbl Red Wine Vinegar
Zest and juice of 2 limes
4 tbl runny honey
4 habanero chillies deseeded and chopped
6 spring onions roughly chopped
A few sprigs of fresh Thyme and oregano
½ tsp Sea Salt

Butter Milk and Herb

500ml Butter milk
1 tbl dried oregano
1 tbl dried Thyme
1 tsp Cayenne pepper
2 large crushed garlic cloves
Zest of 1 Lemon
Salt and pepper

GIZZI'S NOTES ON MEAT

Here is a basic outline of different ways of cooking meat, focusing mainly on beef, and the best cuts for each method, to help you choose the right type for both your dish and your wallet. The illustration opposite shows where the beef cuts come from on the animal.

BEEF

Roasting joints

Most people tend to use **topside of beef** when it comes to roasting. It's the cut of meat that all supermarkets sell, but it's not necessarily the best. This is because it comes from a part of the animal that has done quite a bit of work so it's naturally tough, and also doesn't have any fat content or marbling to ensure a melt-in-the-mouth and full-flavoured finish. The **top rump**, which is the cut above the topside, is a great cut to roast. It's slightly fattier than topside and smaller in size, making it a fast roast. **Sirloin** makes a great roast too and is particularly easy to carve. Unfortunately, the best cut of beef for roasting, **rib of beef**, is also the most expensive, because it has a lovely large layer of fat that will melt during roasting, as well as layers of marbled flesh which hold tons of flavour. Perhaps it should be reserved for special occasions. There are some great cheaper cuts for roasting too, like **brisket**, which is best known as the cut for salt beef. When slow-roasted gently it melts in the same way pork belly does.

Steaks

For steaks, each cut has a different 'sell'. The **fillet** comes from the middle of the animal, an area that does no work, and for this reason it is very soft and tender. However, sinews and muscle give texture and for this it doesn't get better than the **rib-eye** which comes from the rib and has the same fat graduation. If you have never shared a *Côte de boeuf* (a double thick rib-eye steak on the bone) with someone, then I bid you to go out and do so. **Rump** is also fantastic. It is cheap and has flavour, but some people find it too toothsome. Another cut is **sirloin**, or **entrecote** as it's known in France.

It has bite but really good marbling, giving it tons of flavour. **Onglet steak** (also known as a thick skirt steak in the UK, or hanger steak in America) costs a fraction of the price of fillet or rib and really delivers on flavour. It is eaten a lot in France and is just so delicious. Because the muscle does more work than a fillet it is flavourful, but onglet still manages to avoid being tough at all. It will benefit from being marinaded before cooking, or simply fry it quickly – best eaten rare.

Stewing cuts

Chuck steak tends to be sold by supermarkets as the steak for stewing, and it's great because it cooks in a relatively short time. However, this does not guarantee great flavour. In fact it's the meat from the areas of the animal that do the most work that are the best cuts for stewing because they are sinewy. I tend to choose **shin of beef** for stews, which is very cheap as well as packed with taste. With slow cooking, these sinews will melt down and deliver great flavour. Yes, you put in a bit more time, but when it's in the oven, it's in the oven – right? **Beef cheek** is becoming more and more fashionable in restaurants these days. It is a very heavily worked part of the animal, (when I think of cows, I think of them chewing) and so this type of meat takes about four or five hours to cook, but it really is the most fantastic flavoursome cut. If you were to make a cottage pie out of the cheek, having previously cooked it until tender and then shredded the meat, you would end up with a truly delicious dish. Beef **short rib** and **oxtail** both make the most wonderful braises. Just think about it, stewing on the bone means a whole lot more flavour to the meat and will also give you a really super gravy!

Minced meat

Chuck steak is great for making mince for burgers and bolognese. If you can, it is a really good idea to go to your local butcher and ask him to mince some chuck steak for you. This way you know exactly what is in that mince and you can feel confident about eating your burgers cooked medium rare. If you're making burgers from supermarket-bought mince, I really wouldn't suggest eating them medium rare as the quality of meat is not good enough.

As a general note about meat, I would say that more and more cows are being fed on corn before slaughter. This is purely for the sake of fattening up the animal and getting more flavour out of the meat. In terms of cow-rearing it is totally unnatural compared to letting the animals feed on grass. If you can, always choose meat that comes from a grass-fed animal over that of a corn-fed animal.

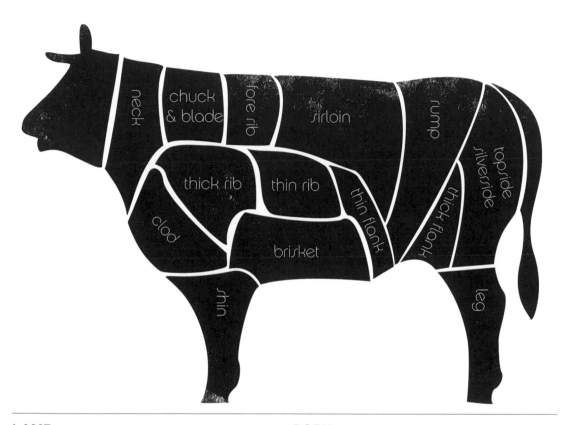

LAMB

I look at lamb in two different ways. Do you want it cooked pink or not? For a slow roast or braise, where the meat is falling off the bone, I wouldn't look further than the shoulder or shank, but for a pink juicy piece of meat I would go for leg, chops, tenderloin or rack (its posh name is 'best end of neck'). But the thing about lamb that is brilliant is that there are no rules. Most cuts can be eaten pink or slow cooked. Breast of lamb and neck fillets are wonderful braised but are also just as fantastic pink.

PORK

Pork is a whole different beast. Most people assume you should eat pork well done, but in fact I would say that depending on the cut, it is best served medium. If you want to eat your meat like this, whether panfrying or grilling, I would suggest heading towards the tenderloin, loin, eye of loin or chops. If looking for a meltingly tender cut that works brilliantly for a slow roast or stew, then pork belly, shoulder or hock is fantastic, and don't underestimate the leg for a slow cook.

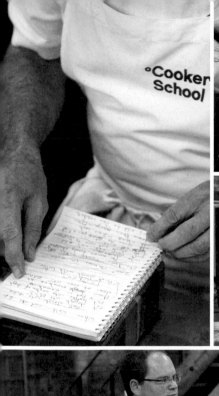

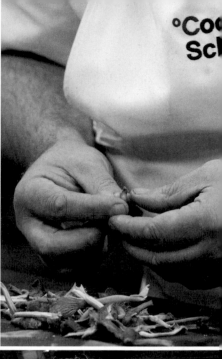

GIZZI'S NOTES ON HERBS

There are two categories of herbs: woody herbs and soft herbs. Woody herbs like rosemary are more robust and can be put in the pan for the whole duration of cooking. Soft herbs like basil are lighter and more delicate. They can be cooked along with the other ingredients but are particularly good when added at the end of cooking and when used raw in salads.

It is really important to use fresh herbs. Nothing from a jar will have as much flavour and potency as its fresh counterpart. If you buy fresh herbs and then find they start to wilt before you've used them all up, there are ways to make the most of them. You can always chop the herbs and freeze them, or whizz up a herby salsa verde with some olive oil, lemon and garlic and then freeze that. I recommend growing herbs at home because then you always have a ready supply and can pick only as much as you need. It's easy and you don't even need a garden. I live in a small flat and I still manage to fit in my herbs – by using window boxes.

Woody herbs

Rosemary is such a brilliant herb. We all know how well it works in savoury dishes – studded into a leg of lamb before roasting (see page 225), or chopped and added to a stew. I'm actually big on its use in sweet recipes – one of my signature dishes is a rosemary-infused salted caramel that I use in millionaire's shortbread or in sweet tarts. The rosemary transforms something that is usually quite sickly sweet into something elegant. Rosemary also has health benefits – it helps the body to get over colds, it aids memory and they say it sweetens your breath!

Sage is fantastic to use with pork, chicken and veal. It is also a strong medicinal herb as it has astringent and antiseptic properties. It can help with mouth ulcers and sore throats as well as being beneficial for menopausal women having hot flushes, as it reduces excess sweating.

Thyme has a great flavour that goes with virtually all meat and savoury dishes, although it can be a bit overpowering with fish. It is a herb that I think works really well on the barbeque. Medicinally, thyme is a fantastic antiseptic and antibacterial agent.

Soft herbs

Coriander is the ultimate Asian herb, but it is also used a lot in South American cooking. When you buy fresh bunched coriander, look out for long stems that taper into the root. You'll recognize the root because it looks a bit like tiny pieces of ginger. This coriander root has a much more robust and earthy flavour than the leaf or stem. In Asian cooking the tip of the root is used a lot but in Britain we usually waste it, which is a real shame. A lot of the recipes in this book call for delicate coriander cress which is baby coriander; excellent for garnishing.

Mint is not only good in desserts, but it also goes wonderfully with lamb or when added to drinks. It's not a herb that's used much in Asia, but it's fantastic in savoury Vietnamese food when used alongside lime or ginger as it really helps to bring out all the lovely flavours. Mint is fantastic for digestion – to this day, mint infusions are still drunk at the end of a meal to aid digestion and they really work!

Flat-leaf parsley is used in abundance in Mediterranean cookery. I consider it one of the most under-rated herbs here in Britain though, which is a tragedy because it is also one of the most vitamin-rich herbs available! Parsley also works really well in salads. Middle Eastern tabbouleh salad relies on parsley as a main ingredient. It's fantastic stirred into stews and sauces and really terrific in garlic butter.

Sorrel is another underrated herb, although it's one of the oldest English herbs. For me, nothing makes food more British than a taste of sorrel. Richard describes it as 'a salad leaf that has been dipped in lemon juice', which is spot on. So imagine how well that flavour works with fish and spinach or in soups. Sorrel grows in abundance in the wild but you don't tend to find it in the shops. I pick my sorrel from a schoolyard near my house where it is growing out of the tarmac! Use sorrel sparingly though, because when eaten in excess it becomes poisonous to humans. It's unlikely you will use too much of it though, as you only need a hint of the flavour.

PUDDINGS

INTERMEDIATE

- Lemon posset with butter shortbread
- Raspberry clafoutis and orange cream
- Flourless chocolate sponge with coffee cream
- Dutch apple pancakes with cinnamon and clove sugar
- Sticky toffee pudding with ginger and dates and a toffee sauce
- Chocolate mousse with praline and sauteéd strawberries
- Tiramisu
- Pear tartes tatin with star anise and vanilla

ADVANCED

- Fine apple tarts with pecan, maple and custard
- Little citrus sponges and custard
- Raspberry millefeuille
- Chocolate tart with fresh raspberries
- Saffron poached pears with spiced madeleines and lime syrup
- Crème caramel with apple compote
- Vanilla panna cotta with saffron honey-spiced figs
- Coffee and walnut cake

SKILLS
- Heating cream without splitting
- Working butter into flour (by machine or hand) to get right the consistency (i.e. not too sticky)
- Rolling out the dough

LEMON POSSET WITH BUTTER SHORTBREAD

serves 4

FOR THE LEMON POSSET
600ml double cream
140g caster sugar
grated zest and juice
   of 2 unwaxed lemons

**FOR THE BUTTER
SHORTBREAD**
255g plain flour, sifted
170g salted butter, diced
   and kept cold
125g caster sugar, plus
   extra to dust

I really rate this pudding. Who wants a crème brulée when you can have a posset? They are just so English; they always make me think of the north of England in particular. Possets date from medieval times when they were hot milk drinks curdled with ale and considered both a remedy for colds and an aid to good sleep. I love the way the punchy, refreshing smell of lemon translates on to your hands as you make this dish. When you're zesting the lemon, keep your hand on the top of the lemon because the grater is very sharp; it does enjoy meeting fingers.

Preheat the oven to 160°C/fan 140°C/gas 3.

1   Heat the cream and sugar to scalding point, not boiling, in a small saucepan. While still on the heat, whisk in the lemon zest and juice and bring to the boil for 30 seconds, whisking all the time.

2   Remove the pan from the heat and put to one side for the posset mixture to cool. When cool, pour into 4 small (150ml) glasses, then refrigerate until set. This should take around 30 minutes.

3   To make the shortbread, whizz the flour, butter and caster sugar together in a food processor, until the mixture comes together. Alternatively you can do this with your hands by rubbing the mixture together between your fingertips and then lightly pressing it together to form a ball – don't overwork the dough at this stage. Turn out on to a sheet of non-stick greaseproof paper and roll out to ½cm thick using a floured rolling pin. Using a 5cm round pastry cutter, cut out rounds of dough and carefully transfer to a baking sheet lined with more greaseproof paper. Sprinkle with some extra caster sugar and bake in the preheated oven for 10–15 minutes or until lightly golden. Once out of the oven allow the shortbread rounds to rest for 10 minutes.

4   Serve the posset chilled, accompanied by the warm shortbread.

SKILLS
- Greasing and flouring a dish, so the batter does not stick
- Whisking eggs and sugar to reach the ribbon stage
- Folding in, so as not to knock the air out of the mix so it rises well

RASPBERRY CLAFOUTIS AND ORANGE CREAM

serves 4

FOR THE RASPBERRY CLAFOUTIS

30g unsalted butter, melted

80g caster sugar

3 eggs

200g crème fraîche

35g plain flour, sifted

½ level teaspoon baking powder

200g raspberries

2 tablespoons icing sugar, sifted

FOR THE ORANGE CREAM

100ml double cream

1 teaspoon orange liqueur, such as Cointreau

2 teaspoons orange zest

seeds from 1 vanilla pod

Clafoutis is a very light batter with fruit cooked inside it – in this recipe we are using raspberries. I always line the moulds with butter and sugar as this helps to make a caramelized, crunchy, sugary coating on the outside, almost like with a soufflé. Sifting the flour helps create a lighter sweet batter, which should rise up like a sponge. Crème fraîche is a cream to which a bacterial culture has been added. It gives a great acidity and texture to any recipe where cream is required, and here I use it in the clafoutis batter. In the past, in France, turning cream into crème fraîche was a way of preserving it. Vanilla seeds, a dash of orange liqueur and the zest of an orange are the perfect flavours for the double cream to accompany this dish.

Preheat the oven to 190°C/fan 170°C/gas 5.

1   Prepare 4 shallow 200ml ovenproof dishes or gratin dishes by brushing the inside of each dish with the melted butter and then dusting with 30g of the caster sugar.

2   Next whisk together the eggs, the remaining 50g of caster sugar and the crème fraîche using a handheld whisk. Then fold in the flour and the baking powder and mix until you have a smooth batter.

3   Scatter the raspberries on the bottom of the prepared oven dishes and gently ladle the batter over. Bake in the preheated oven for 16–20 minutes, or until the mixture has browned slightly on the top and is just cooked in the middle.

4   To make the orange cream, first whip the cream to soft peaks in a large bowl. Then add the orange liqueur, orange zest and vanilla seeds and mix well.

5   To serve, sprinkle the clafoutis with icing sugar and serve straight away, while warm, with a big dollop of the orange cream.

FLOURLESS CHOCOLATE SPONGE
WITH COFFEE CREAM serves 4

4 eggs
  (4 whites and 2 yolks)
40g caster sugar
125g dark chocolate
  (70% cocoa solids),
  broken into pieces
30g unsalted butter
200ml double cream
50g icing sugar, sifted
1 shot of espresso coffee

I first cooked this recipe in the late eighties for a coeliac. It was one of those things you would think wouldn't work, but it did! Nowadays it has become more common and something that everyone can enjoy. Whisked egg yolks, sugar and usually alcoholic liqueur, whipped to a 'ribbon stage' over hot water, is called a '*sabayonne*'. *Sabayonne* works perfectly well as a dessert on its own, served with strawberries or other fruit.

Preheat the oven to 180°C/fan 160°C/gas 4.

1 Grease a 17cm x 17cm square baking tin with butter, then line it with 2 rectangular pieces of greaseproof paper. This is so you can lift the cake out of the tin when it has cooked, so overlap the pieces and leave 5cm at either side which will be your 'handles'.

2 Place the egg whites in a large clean bowl (any grease at all will stop the whites whisking properly) and add half the caster sugar. Using an electric beater, whisk until they form stiff peaks and then set aside.

3 Bring a medium-sized saucepan of water to simmering point, and place a large bowl over the pan so the base of the bowl does not touch the water below (this is a bain-marie). Put the egg yolks and the remaining 20g of caster sugar into the bowl and whisk until you reach the ribbon stage (forming thick 'ribbons' that fall off a spoon). Remove the bowl and put to one side.

4 Place a second bowl on the saucepan. Put the chocolate and butter in the bowl and let them melt, stirring occasionally.

5 Take the egg yolk mixture and stir in the melted chocolate and melted butter, then fold in the whisked egg whites.

6 Pour the cake mixture into the lined baking tin and place in the preheated oven for 12 minutes.

7 Meanwhile, using a hand whisk, whip the double cream and icing sugar together until they form soft peaks, then pour in the coffee and stir well to mix.

8 Allow the cake to rest for 10 minutes in the tin – this will allow it to set slightly. After this time, carefully lift the edges of the greaseproof paper to remove the cake from the tin. Slice it into 4 squares and serve at room temperature with a generous dollop of the coffee cream.

SKILLS
- Lining a baking dish
- Whisking egg whites
- Learning to identify the ribbon stage of egg yolks and sugar
- Folding egg whites
- Whipping cream

SKILLS
- Knife skills: cutting the apples to the correct thickness
- Making a batter for pancakes
- Cooking the pancakes for the correct time so as not to over – or under – cook

DUTCH APPLE PANCAKES WITH CINNAMON AND CLOVE SUGAR makes 2 pancakes

FOR THE APPLE PANCAKES

50g unsalted butter

1 Braeburn, Granny Smith or russet apple, peeled, cored and quartered, then each wedge cut into ½ cm slices

2 tablespoons Calvados

2 large eggs

120ml whole milk

90g plain flour, sifted

3 tablespoons caster sugar

2 tablespoons melted butter

2 heaped tablespoons crème fraîche

FOR THE CINNAMON AND CLOVE SUGAR

100g caster sugar

2 tablespoons ground cinnamon

½ level teaspoon ground cloves

English apples enrobed in a nice, thick crêpe is such a simple but satisfying pudding. Kent is known as 'the apple orchard of England' thanks to Henry VIII, who planted the orchards there that have supplied London for centuries. One apple will serve for two pancakes, but it is nice to be generous. You don't want to cook your apples through completely to a mush; they should still have some bite for a lovely contrast with the soft, creamy pancake.

1   Put the butter in a medium-sized pancake pan or large shallow frying pan (one that you can flip) and place over a medium heat. Once the butter has melted, add the apple pieces and cook for 3–4 minutes until they begin to soften. Add the Calvados to the pan and carefully set it alight to flame the apples. Let the flames go out of their own accord and then transfer half the apple mixture to a bowl and set aside.

2   Meanwhile, to make the batter, break the eggs into a large bowl. Add the milk, flour, sugar and melted butter. Whisk to combine.

3   Ladle half the batter over the apple mixture in the pancake pan and cook until the bottom of the pancake has set. Then flip the pancake over, or use two fish slices to turn it, and cook for a further minute on the other side. Slide the cooked pancake out on to a plate and keep warm.

4   Return the reserved half of the apple mixture to the pancake pan to warm through. Then pour in the remaining batter and cook the second pancake as before.

5   To make the flavoured sugar, mix the caster sugar, cinnamon and cloves in a small bowl.

6   Place each pancake on a serving plate, sprinkle with the cinnamon and clove sugar and serve with a dollop of crème fraîche and a little more sugar.

SKILLS
- Knife skills: cutting dates
- Creaming butter and sugar together
- Making pudding mixture and filling moulds
- Cooking puddings until soft to the touch in the middle
- Making a toffee sauce

STICKY TOFFEE PUDDING WITH GINGER AND DATES AND A TOFFEE SAUCE serves 6

FOR THE STICKY TOFFEE PUDDING

200g stoned dates, chopped

1 level teaspoon bicarbonate of soda

60g unsalted butter, plus extra to grease the dariole moulds if they are not non-stick

60g light muscovado sugar or light brown sugar

2 eggs

2 tablespoons golden syrup

150g self-raising flour, sifted

¼ level teaspoon ground ginger

vanilla ice cream, to serve

FOR THE TOFFEE SAUCE

75g unsalted butter

175g dark muscovado sugar or dark brown sugar

125ml double cream

This is a wonderful pudding to eat on long, cold evenings. The sticky toffee pudding itself is made with medjool dates from North Africa – a seasonal, juicy and particularly delicious type of date. In wintertime you should really look out for them in the supermarket or at your local greengrocer – they are magic! Muscovado sugar is used rather than refined sugar because it is a more natural type of sugar and the molasses are contained within the centre of the grain, which adds to the caramel taste of this dish.

Preheat the oven to 180°C/fan 160°C/gas 4.

1 Place the chopped dates in a medium-sized bowl, pour over 250ml of boiling water, stir in the bicarbonate of soda and set aside to soak for 10 minutes.

2 Meanwhile, in a large bowl cream the butter and light muscovado sugar together until pale and then gradually beat in the eggs and golden syrup. Fold in the flour and ground ginger, and then stir in the soaked date mixture.

3 Pour this sponge mixture into 6 x 180ml dariole moulds. If they are not non-stick, grease them with a little butter first.

4 Place the filled moulds on to a baking tray and put them in the preheated oven for 20–25 minutes, until the top of the puddings is just firm to the touch.

5 To make the toffee sauce, put the butter in a medium-sized frying pan over a medium heat. Once the butter has melted, add the dark muscovado sugar and stir to dissolve. Finish the sauce by pouring in the cream and cook for a further 2 minutes then remove from the heat.

6 To serve, run a knife gently around the inside of the moulds and turn each individual pudding out in the centre of a serving plate. Pour the sauce over the top and serve with a scoop of vanilla ice cream.

CHOCOLATE MOUSSE WITH PRALINE AND SAUTÉED STRAWBERRIES serves 4

250g dark chocolate (70% cocoa solids), broken into pieces

100ml single cream

1 egg yolk

4 egg whites

165g caster sugar

100g chopped roasted hazelnuts

400g strawberries, hulled and halved (if large)

40g unsalted butter

crushed pistachios, to garnish

Mousse can be a tricky thing to make. The older the eggs (within the use by period), the better they are for making mousses. I often freeze excess egg whites to use for this purpose. Another key tip is to add a pinch of salt to the egg whites as this breaks them down and makes them foam faster. Choose the smallest and nicest strawberries you can. The point of sautéing isn't to cook them, it is solely to warm them through. A homemade crunchy praline biscuit is served with this dish, which makes a wonderful contrast of texture to the smooth mousse. It's a delicate, refined chocolatey pudding and your family will bite your hand off for it!

1 Place the chocolate in a large heatproof bowl and place the bowl so it is sitting on top of a saucepan of simmering water over a low heat, without the base of the bowl touching the water. Let the chocolate melt.

2 Heat the cream gently in a small saucepan over a low heat. Take the chocolate off the heat and add the cream to it, along with the egg yolk. Stir to combine.

3 In a separate large clean bowl, whisk the egg whites with 25g of the sugar using an electric beater, until soft peaks form.

4 Add a tablespoon of egg whites to the melted chocolate mixture and fold through. Then gently fold in the rest of the egg whites, keeping the mixture airy. Cool, then place in the fridge to chill for 1–2 hours.

5 To make the praline, heat a further 100g of the sugar in a small non-stick frying pan over a high heat without stirring until it turns a golden colour. Then add the chopped hazelnuts and stir. Pour the praline out on to a silicone mat and leave to set for 1 minute. Roll out flat and cut out 4 small 4cm x 15cm rectangles (tuiles), then set aside. Keep all the offcuts of praline.

SKILLS

- Knife skills: cutting strawberries
- Melting the chocolate
- Whisking the egg whites
- Folding the chocolate into the eggs
- Making a caramel, then turning it into praline
- Cooking the strawberries

6 When the rectangles have cooled, place the remaining offcuts in a small food processor and blitz to make praline powder. Pour out on to a plate.

7 Put a medium-sized saucepan over a high heat and add the remaining 40g of caster sugar and the strawberries. Stir together to coat the strawberries, then add the butter and briefly sauté for 2 minutes.

8 To serve, shape 3 portions per person of the chilled chocolate mousse between two dessertspoons into rugby ball-shaped quenelles and very gently roll these in the praline powder. Carefully place them on the strip of rolled praline. Place some sautéed strawberries on each serving plate, next to each praline rectangle, and sprinkle with crushed pistachios.

TIRAMISU serves 4

150ml strong fresh hot espresso coffee

80g caster sugar

2 tablespoons Amaretto

1 tablespoon coffee essence

4 eggs, separated

seeds from 1 vanilla pod

100ml double cream

250g mascarpone cheese

300g sponge fingers or savoiardi ladyfinger biscuits

2–3 tablespoons cocoa powder, sifted

This creamy dessert is great for coffee lovers and comes with a touch of Amaretto to make it just a little bit naughty. When hand-whisking the mascarpone into the mixture, be careful not to beat too hard as this will knock the air out and make the dessert heavy. The egg whites are whisked together in a separate bowl and folded in gently to keep the cream mixture really light. The layers of coffee-soaked sponge fingers, cream mixture and cocoa powder look wonderful in the serving glasses and taste fantastic.

1   Pour the hot coffee into a shallow dish and stir in half the sugar. Add the Amaretto and coffee essence and stir well again. Allow the mixture to cool.

2   Meanwhile, whisk the egg whites with an electric beater in a large bowl until soft peaks form, then set aside. Clean the beaters.

3   Place the vanilla pod seeds, egg yolks and the remaining 40g of sugar in another large bowl and whisk together with the electric beater until the mixture becomes pale and light.

4   In a separate bowl, whip the double cream into soft peaks. Stir in the mascarpone and lightly whip to smooth out any lumps.

5   Fold the mascarpone mixture gently into the egg yolk mixture. Then fold in one big spoonful of the whisked egg whites until it's all incorporated, which will loosen the mixture. Continue to add the remaining whisked egg whites, folding them in gently until everything is mixed well together.

6   When the coffee mixture has cooled, start to dip the sponge biscuits into the liquid one by one, making sure they don't go too soggy, and lay half the biscuits in a layer on the bottoms of 4 wide serving glasses.

7   Pour half of the cream mixture on to the coffee-soaked biscuits in the 4 serving glasses to make the next layer. Repeat with the remaining half of the biscuits, dipping them in the coffee mixture and laying them down in the serving glasses on the cream layer. Finish by pouring the remaining half of the cream mixture on top.

8   To serve, dust the cocoa powder on top of the final layer of cream and place each glass on a serving plate.

SKILLS

- Whisking egg yolks and sugar
- Whisking cream
- Dipping the sponge fingers
- Laying the dessert

PEAR TARTES TATIN
WITH STAR ANISE AND VANILLA serves 4

2 firm Conference pears, peeled
4 star anise
1 vanilla pod, cut into four lengthways
500g ready-made puff pastry
150g caster sugar
30g unsalted butter, diced
100ml double cream
vanilla ice cream, to serve

A tarte tatin is a gooey and delicious tart made from puff pastry and sliced caramelized fruit, like apples or pears. It is baked upside-down and then flipped over before serving. The key is to layer the puff pastry thickly and wrap it tightly around the fruit. In order for the fruit to be solidly encased, the pastry really has to rest for ten minutes or so in the fridge, otherwise it will melt over the top.

Preheat the oven to 200°C/fan 180°C/gas 6.

1 Halve the peeled pears. Using a melon baller remove the core and using a sharp knife cut out the stalk. Gently push a star anise into each of the pear halves where the core has been removed, so it lodges in, and put the pieces of vanilla pod in where the stalks were.

2 Roll the puff pastry out on a floured surface until it is 3mm thick, then cut into four pieces.

3 Lay a pear half on top of one piece of pastry, cut side up, and use your hands to press and mould the pastry up around the rounded side of the pear, leaving the cut part of the pear exposed. Cut off any excess pastry. Repeat with the other 3 pear halves, and set them all aside in the fridge.

4 To make the caramel, place a large ovenproof frying pan over a high heat. When the pan gets hot, add the sugar and cook for 5 minutes, until the sugar turns a golden brown. Do not be tempted to stir the sugar, just leave it.

5 Once the sugar has turned a caramel colour, turn the heat down and slowly add the butter and stir. Do not allow the caramel to become too dark as it will continue to cook – you want it to be a lovely amber colour.

6 Carefully place the pastry-coated pears cut side down on top of the caramel in the frying pan, making sure the star anise and vanilla pod lengths don't fall out. (If they do, simply place them back in the pear but do this carefully because of the hot caramel.) Heat through, then place the frying pan in the preheated oven for 20–25 minutes, until the pastry is golden brown.

7 Remove the frying pan from the oven and, using a fish slice, carefully turn the tartes upside down on to individual serving plates, pastry-side down.

8 Holding the handle with a dry cloth, return the frying pan with the caramel to a low to medium heat. Add the double cream and stir through gently to create the sauce.

9 Drizzle the sauce over the pears and around the plates. Serve with a scoop of vanilla ice cream.

SKILLS

- Knife skills: preparing the pears
- Rolling and cutting out the pastry
- Covering the pear with the pastry
- Making a caramel
- Baking the tart for the correct time so the fruit is cooked underneath and the pastry is golden brown
- Turning out the tart

HOW TO PREPARE THE PEAR FOR THE PEAR TARTES TATIN

This beautiful presentation replaces the pear's stem and core with a stick of vanilla and a star anise in the recipe on page 265.

1 Using a vegetable peeler, peel the pears very gently as you can easily bruise them. Just take your time.

2 Halve your pear straight down the middle, leaving on the stem.

Take out the stem from the inside of the pear, cutting round it and then pulling with your fingers to leave a little channel from the exposed stem to the core.

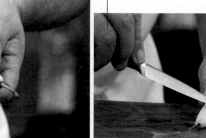

3 Using a melon baller, carefully take out the core.

4 Take a piece of star anise and place in the pear hollow.

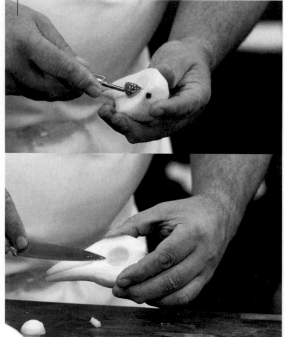

5 Add the piece of vanilla pod to replace the stem you've just removed.

HOW TO CHOP AND ARRANGE APPLES FOR THE FINE APPLE TARTS

This is a quick tart made from ready-made puff. Work speedily with your apples so they don't start to discolour before you get round to popping the tarts in the oven.

1 Cut the apples into quarters, removing the ends.

2 Peel with a sharp knife and take out the core.

3 Cut the apples into thin slices.

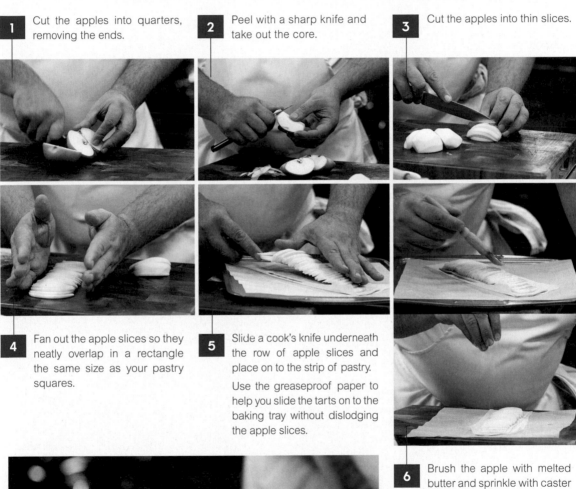

4 Fan out the apple slices so they neatly overlap in a rectangle the same size as your pastry squares.

5 Slide a cook's knife underneath the row of apple slices and place on to the strip of pastry.

Use the greaseproof paper to help you slide the tarts on to the baking tray without dislodging the apple slices.

6 Brush the apple with melted butter and sprinkle with caster sugar.

7 Cook until crispy and golden on top, adding more melted butter and sugar halfway through the cooking time to really get the caramelization going.

FINE APPLE TARTS WITH PECAN, MAPLE AND CUSTARD serves 4

FOR THE APPLE, PECAN AND MAPLE TARTS
250g ready-made puff pastry

4 Granny Smith apples

25g unsalted butter, melted

2 tablespoons caster sugar

2 tablespoons maple syrup

70g whole pecans

FOR THE CUSTARD
150ml whole milk

150ml double cream

1 vanilla pod, split down the middle

4 egg yolks

25g caster sugar

SKILLS
• Knife skills: cutting the apples
• Rolling the pastry and cutting it out correctly
• Presenting the apples on the pastry
• Baking the tart
• Warming the milk and cream
• Making the custard (see pages 272–3)

A fine tart is made with a very thin piece of puff pastry with no filling but something sliced on top – such as apples or pears – which is then cooked quickly. So simple, everyone can make one! This tart is very sugary and buttery, so by putting it on to a very hot tray, the pastry will caramelize really quickly. Because there is no filling underneath the apples, you'll end up with a really crisp pastry and delicious-tasting apples. The custard should always be made in advance because it is much nicer at room temperature.

Preheat the oven to 200°C/fan 180°C/gas 6 and heat a baking sheet in the oven whilst preparing the tart.

1 Roll the pastry out on a floured surface to 2mm thick, then cut into four 12cm strips. Place the strips on a piece of greaseproof paper and set aside.

2 Peel the apples, remove the cores with a sharp knife and cut them into thin slices. Layer the apples slices on to the pastry, neatly overlapping.

3 Brush the apple slices with half the melted butter and sprinkle over a tablespoon of the caster sugar. Take the heated baking sheet out of the oven and place the greaseproof paper with the apple-topped pastry strips on to the baking sheet, taking care not to burn yourself.

4 Place on the top shelf of the preheated oven for 20–25 minutes until the pastry has crisped up. Halfway through the cooking time, take the tarts out of the oven and brush with the remaining melted butter and sprinkle with the remaining tablespoon of sugar. This will help the apples caramelize well. Once removed from the oven, drizzle over the maple syrup.

5 Lightly toast the pecans in a dry frying pan over a medium heat for a couple of minutes. Remove from the pan and leave to cool.

6 To make the custard, pour the milk and cream into a medium-sized saucepan. Scrape the seeds from the vanilla pod and add the seeds and pods to the pan. Warm through over a low to medium heat but do not boil.

7 Place the egg yolks and sugar in a large bowl and whisk as you gradually strain in the warmed milk and cream. Remove the two vanilla pod halves from the saucepan, then pour the liquid back in. Warm over a low heat, stirring constantly, until the custard has thickened – about 5 minutes.

8 To serve, place the tarts on a serving plate. Chopped the cooled pecans roughly, mix with the maple syrup and drizzle over the tarts. Serve with the custard.

SKILLS
- Making a sponge
- Preparing moulds
- Preparing a steamer
- Making custard (see pages 272–3).

LITTLE CITRUS SPONGES AND CUSTARD serves 4

FOR THE SPONGE PUDDINGS

50g raisins

5 tablespoons sherry

2 tablespoons golden syrup

6 tablespoons lemon marmalade

2 teaspoons finely grated unwaxed lemon zest

115g unsalted butter, softened, plus extra to grease the moulds

115g light muscovado sugar

2 large eggs

115g self-raising flour, sifted, plus extra to dust the moulds

FOR THE CUSTARD

250ml double cream

150ml whole milk

1 vanilla pod, split down the middle

3 egg yolks

50g caster sugar

These fruity little sponges are easy to make and deliciously warming on a cold day. You can soak the raisins in the sherry for as long as you like beforehand. Don't be shy and think there's too much liquid when you mix them in with the batter – the sponge will soak it all up. When making the custard, make sure to keep stirring the mixture and cook it over a low heat, otherwise you will end up with scrambled eggs.

1   To make the puddings, first soak the raisins in the sherry for about 5 minutes, or until they become plump. Then butter and flour 4 x 150ml ramekins or moulds. Cut out circles of greaseproof paper big enough to line the bottom of each mould and place in the buttered moulds.

2   Mix together the golden syrup, 3 tablespoons of the lemon marmalade, lemon zest and soaked raisins. Spoon evenly into the bottom of each mould.

3   Cream the butter and sugar together in a large bowl until pale in colour with a creamy consistency. Beat in the eggs one at a time, beating well after each one is added to the mixture. Gently fold in the flour, then the remaining 3 tablespoons of lemon marmalade and the sherry from the raisins.

4   Divide the mixture evenly between the moulds so they are about two thirds full. Cover each mould with cling film or a buttered square of foil and secure with butcher's string.

5   To steam the puddings, use a saucepan big enough to hold all the moulds on a plate. Place an upturned empty ramekin or small heatproof bowl inside the saucepan, then pour in 2½cm of water. Place a heatproof plate on top of the ramekin and put the moulds on it. Cover the saucepan with its lid and steam over a low heat for 30–40 minutes. To check the puddings are cooked, insert a skewer into the middle of one of them. It should come out clean.

6   While the puddings are cooking, make the custard. Pour the cream and milk into a small saucepan. Scrape the seeds from the halved vanilla pod and add the seeds and pod to the pan. Warm through over a low to medium heat but do not boil. Remove the pan from the heat.

7   Beat the egg yolks and sugar together in a bowl. Stir in a little of the hot vanilla cream to loosen the mixture, then pour the eggs and sugar into the pan containing the rest of the cream and milk.

8   Return the saucepan to a low heat and cook, stirring all the time, until the custard thickens. Remove from the heat and pour the contents into a bowl or jug to stop it overcooking – cover with cling film to stop a skin forming.

9   Turn the puddings out of their moulds on to individual plates, and serve with the custard.

HOW TO MAKE CUSTARD

The French call custard *crème anglaise* and 'English cream' is something this country should be very proud of. What could possibly go better with all the great traditional English puddings than freshly made custard? This specifically refers to Little Citrus Sponges and Custard (page 271).

2 Whisk with a balloon whisk as the milk and cream come up to the boil. The milk is ready when it starts to sizzle at the edges and tiny bubbles appear. Take it off the heat now.

1 Pour the cream and milk into a saucepan.

3 You can't have a good custard without really good eggs. Break your egg yolks into a bowl. Add the caster sugar and beat together with a wooden spoon.

4 Meanwhile, it's time to prepare your fresh vanilla pod. Expensive vanilla is the ultimate luxury in a pudding, so carefully use a sharp knife to scrape the seeds from the pod and add both the pod and seeds to the milk.

5 We're now going to scald the eggs and sugar with the milk and cream, adding it very slowly in a thin stream, stirring all the time.

6 Pour the custard back into the saucepan and return it to a very low heat.

7 Stir the custard and start to thicken it very gently. You have to be confident with custard and take care as it thickens. If you cook it too vigorously, the egg yolks coagulate into lumps and it can turn to scrambled eggs.

8 The custard is ready when it is thick enough to coat the wooden spoon. If it looks like it's even starting to curdle slightly, put it through a sieve. Take out the vanilla pod.

9 Spoon over the puddings to serve.

RASPBERRY MILLEFEUILLE serves 4

FOR THE RASPBERRY MILLEFEUILLE

200g block of ready-made puff pastry

150g icing sugar, plus 50g for dusting

250ml double cream, whipped to firm peaks

400g raspberries, halved

FOR THE RASPBERRY COULIS

2 tablespoons caster sugar

200g raspberries

½ teaspoon cornflour

35ml framboise

This is a layered raspberry pastry with a sweetened cream and raspberry sauce. It is really easy to assemble and is one dish you can definitely prepare before your guests arrive. The skill is in handling the paper-thin puff pastry, which needs to be rolled into equally sized, long, flat, oblong strips with plenty of icing sugar. Be generous with the icing sugar as it helps the pastry strips to crisp up in the oven. Cut the corner off a freezer bag to create a homemade piping bag, so you can pipe cream in between the raspberries. This is a visually stunning and delicate dish, which will certainly impress your friends!

Preheat the oven to 180°C/fan 160°C/gas 4.

1   Using your hands, roll out the pastry into a 3cm-diameter cylinder shape. Cut it into 12 discs, about ¾cm wide.

2   Sift some of the 150g icing sugar out on to a clean work surface. Then place a pastry disc on the sugar and, pressing down, roll swiftly in one direction. Turn it over, sift over more icing sugar and roll the pastry in the opposite direction. The aim is to get these discs as thin as possible. Use strong strokes with the rolling pin to achieve this. Repeat this until you have a 1mm thin oval strip about 15cm long. Then repeat with the remaining pastry discs and icing sugar until you have 12 evenly sized sugared pastry strips.

3   Place the pastry strips on silicone mats and put in the preheated oven for around 12 minutes, or until they become golden brown. Remove from the oven and cool on a rack for 5 minutes.

4   To make the coulis, heat 2 tablespoons of water and the sugar in a small saucepan until the sugar has dissolved. Add the raspberries and cornflour and continue to cook, on a medium heat, until the raspberries break down and the mixture thickens. This should take 5–8 minutes.

5   Remove the pan from the heat and stir in the framboise, then leave to cool before blitzing the mixture in the food processor. Pass the coulis through a sieve for an even smoother finish.

SKILLS

- Rolling and cutting pastry
- Whipping cream
- Assembling the millefeuille

6   When the pastry strips have cooled, assemble the finished dish. Place one of the pastry strips on a plate and decorate it with piped whipped cream and raspberry halves. Repeat, placing a second pastry strip on top to form a second layer and decorating it as before. Top with a third pastry strip. Repeat for 3 more plates, using all 12 pastry strips. Either spoon over the cold coulis or serve it on the side.

CHOCOLATE TART WITH FRESH RASPBERRIES

serves 4

250g plain flour, sifted, plus extra to roll out

75g caster sugar

125g unsalted butter, cubed

2 egg yolks, beaten

200ml double cream

400g dark chocolate, broken into pieces

100g raspberries

100g crème fraîche

2 tablespoons icing sugar, sifted

1 tablespoon Frangelico

35g toasted hazelnuts, crushed

SKILLS

- Making sweet shortcrust pastry
- How to roll pastry out to the correct thickness
- Lining a case with the pastry; baking blind; knowing when the pastry is cooked
- Filling a pastry case
- Making a flavoured cream

This tasty dessert beautifully combines a crumbly pastry with a rich chocolate and sweet raspberry filling. The pastry is blind baked in the oven by covering the base with greaseproof paper and then adding something dry and hard over it such as rice or beans – this helps the pastry maintain its shape as it bakes. To serve, you could lightly grill the top of the tart to soften up the chocolate and sprinkle on a dusting of crushed hazelnuts. A spoonful of the sweetened and flavoured crème fraîche is an extra nutty indulgence.

Preheat the oven to 180°C/fan 160°C/gas 4.

1   To make the pastry, place the flour, sugar and butter in the food processor and pulse until it resembles breadcrumbs. Gradually add the egg yolks and process again until the pastry comes together.

2   If there's time, leave the dough to rest in the fridge for 10 minutes before rolling out. Flour a clean work surface or put a piece of greaseproof paper on your work surface (see pictures on page 278). Roll out the pastry dough using a floured rolling pin until it is about 3mm thick. Using the rolling pin to support the weight of the pastry, drape the pastry over a 22cm tart tin, pressing the pastry into the base and sides. The dough will be quite resilient, but work quickly. Cut a circle of greaseproof paper to fit the tart tin, place it inside on top of the pastry base and put some baking beans on top.

3   Blind bake the pastry base in the preheated oven for 25 minutes, then remove the baking beans and return the tart tin to the oven for a further 10 minutes. Take out of the oven and leave to cool, still in its tin.

4   Meanwhile, heat the cream in a medium-sized saucepan over a low heat. Just before it begins to boil, remove the pan from the heat and stir in the chocolate until it has all melted.

5   Once the tart case has cooled, trim any excess dough from around the edge, scatter the raspberries in the bottom and pour in the chocolate cream mixture. Leave to cool a little before chilling in the fridge for 30 minutes.

6   Place the crème fraîche in a small bowl, add the icing sugar, Frangelico and all but 1 tablespoon of the hazelnuts and stir to mix.

7   When you're ready to serve the tart, a quick blast with a blow torch over the surface brings the cocoa butter out to give a great gloss. Slice the tart into thick wedges using a sharp knife that has been warmed under running hot water. This will ensure a smooth finish. Place each slice on a serving plate, with a spoonful of the hazelnut crème fraîche and a few extra raspberries.

HOW TO MAKE AND ROLL SHORTCRUST PASTRY

The addition of egg yolks makes this a rich sweet shortcrust pastry. The 'short' in 'shortcrust' means just crumbly, so that's the texture you're after. These instructions refer to Chocolate Tart with Fresh Raspberries on page 277.

1 Place the flour and sugar in a food processor.

Add the cubed butter and pulse so you have more control. Don't work it too much. It should be like fine breadcrumbs.

2 Add an egg and pulse again. You don't want the mixture to start getting warm in the food processor because pastry needs to be cold.

3 Bring the pastry together with your floured hands. Don't work it, just pull it together into one lump. If you over-work your pastry, it will become really tough.

5 Pick up the pastry and turn it round a little to stop it sticking and get a nice shape.

Keep rolling out to the desired thickness, keeping in mind that the pastry will need to be a little thicker if your dish is large.

4 Roll out the pastry on a piece of greaseproof paper. This is a brilliant tip from professional kitchens and makes your life so much easier as it stops the pastry sticking.

HOW TO LINE A TART CASE

A pastry case is usually 'baked blind' when a moist filling is going to be added. By cooking the pastry case before you add the filling, you stop the whole tart collapsing in a soggy mess.

6 Roll your pastry off the greaseproof paper round a rolling pin and put it into the tin.

7 Push the pastry into the case nice and gently, using the soft tips of your fingers. If you do get a tiny crack in the pastry, you can squash it together.

8 Using a knife, trim the pastry roughly at the base of the tin, leaving some pastry over-hanging as it will shrink as it cooks. You can then carve the pastry off at the end to get a really nice neat line.

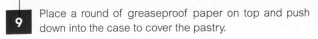

9 Place a round of greaseproof paper on top and push down into the case to cover the pastry.

10 Fill the pastry case with rice or beans. You can use anything you have left in your cupboard and they can be used time and time again. Now pop the tart in the oven to cook the pastry for 25 minutes, then return to the oven without the rice or beans for a further 10.

SKILLS
- Poaching the pears
- Making a cartouche
  (greaseproof paper lid)
- Making a sugar syrup
- Making and cooking
  madeleines

SAFFRON POACHED PEARS WITH SPICED MADELEINES AND LIME SYRUP serves 4

FOR THE PEARS AND SYRUP

300g caster sugar

peel of 1 unwaxed lime, cut in strips

4 pears, peeled and stalk left in

1 teaspoon saffron threads

zest of 1 unwaxed lime

FOR THE MADELEINES

50g unsalted butter, melted

1 large egg

50g caster sugar

50g plain flour, sifted

½ level teaspoon ground cinnamon

½ level teaspoon ground ginger

½ level teaspoon allspice

zest of ½ orange

icing sugar, for dusting

FOR SERVING

200ml double cream

2 tablespoons icing sugar, sifted

50g pistachio nuts, shelled and chopped

A simple dessert made extravagant by the addition of saffron and other spices. Be careful not to use too much saffron, though – a little adds fantastic colour but a lot will make it taste of soap! Lime zest adds a fruity kick, but take care not to include the bitter lime pith. Sweetened cream, a sprinkling of finely chopped pistachios and the madeleines on the side complete the magical combination of fruits, spice and sugar. See pages 282–3 for more instruction and step-by-step photographs.

*Preheat the oven to 190°C/fan 170°C/gas 5.

1   Place 250g of the sugar, 1½ litres of water, the lime peel, pears and saffron in a large saucepan. Make a cartouche from a piece of greaseproof paper by folding the paper in half diagonally to make a triangle, then in half again to make a smaller triangle. Keeping hold of the centre point, fold it once more to make a dart. Holding the centre point of the dart in the middle of the saucepan, measure out to the edge of the pan. This is where you need to tear the paper so that when you unfold it you have a circle roughly the size of the saucepan. Place this on top of the pears and simmer over a low heat for 10–20 minutes. The cartouche ensures a tighter fit than the lid alone.

2   Once the pears are cooked, remove them from the liquid to cool. Strain 200ml of the liquid into a small saucepan, add the remaining 50g sugar and reduce over a medium heat for 10 minutes, until the liquid becomes syrupy. Remove from the heat and stir in the lime zest, then leave to cool.

3   Brush 12 mini madeleine moulds lightly with melted butter. Break the egg into a large bowl, add the sugar and whisk until the mixture is very pale and thick.

4   Sift the flour into the egg and sugar mixture and add the cinnamon, ginger, allspice, orange zest and the rest of the melted butter, then gently fold in.

5   Fill the moulds with the madeleine batter and place in the preheated oven for 7–8 minutes. Leave to cool in their moulds.

6   Place the cream and icing sugar in a large bowl and whisk, either by hand or with an electric whisk, until it forms soft peaks.

7   To serve, warm through the syrup over a low heat. Either dip each pear into the syrup in the pan before serving, or place a poached pear on each serving plate with three mini madeleines next to it, along with a dollop of the cream. Drizzle over the reduced lime syrup and sprinkle with the chopped pistachios.

These instructions specifically refer to Saffron Poached Pears with Spiced Madeleines and Lime Syrup (page 281).

1 Using a vegetable peeler, gently peel the pears as they are very easily damaged. Leave on the stems for an attractive presentation.

2 Switch to a knife to take off the peel around the bases and tops of the pears.

3 Cut the ends off so the pears can stand to attention.

4 Carefully add the pears to the saffron-sugared water. The pears must be covered with the liquid to stop them discolouring.

5 Add a cartouche of greaseproof paper to keep the heat in and then very gently simmer with the lid on.

6 Grab a toothpick and start to check your pears after 12 minutes. Pears have very different cooking times and you don't want an overcooked pear as this will collapse. Remove from the liquid and allow to cool down.

7 Ladle the poaching liquor through a strainer into a new saucepan.

8 Add sugar for a syrup. Reduce down until thickened, then add lime zest.

9 Coat the pears in the syrup. Plate up the pears, drizzle over more syrup and serve with the little madeleines.

HOW TO MAKE MINI MADELEINES

Madeleines are miniature cakes and this is a very simple, delicious little recipe.

1 Beat the eggs and sugar in a bowl until nice and creamy. You need to beat them well as the eggs are the only raising agent in the cakes.

2 Line the mini madeleine moulds with melted butter and sprinkle over a dusting of flour. Madeleines are made from a very light batter mix and they do stick, so this will help stop them sticking.

3 Sift in the flour and add the spices.

4 Beat again with the electric beaters until you have a nice batter.

Add a little bit of butter and mix in with a palette knife, grating in the orange zest.

5 Fill the moulds up, but don't flatten them as they should have a little puff in the middle.

6 The madeleines are ready when just puffed up and golden.

The madeleines can be dusted with icing sugar before serving.

SKILLS
- Greasing and lining the moulds
- Making a caramel
- Making the custard
- Cooking the caramels

CRÈME CARAMEL WITH APPLE COMPOTE serves 4

FOR THE CRÈME CARAMEL

215g caster sugar
½ vanilla pod
650ml whole milk
5 eggs (3 whole eggs, 2 yolks)

FOR THE APPLE COMPOTE

25g caster sugar
1½ Granny Smith apples, peeled, cored and cut into 1cm dice
100g raisins, soaked in hot water
½ level teaspoon ground cinnamon
2 tablespoons rum
20g unsalted butter

This is a simple recipe but it is vital to get a few things right. Before you start making the caramel, dampen a little brush with some water and paint the inside of the pan – this will help reduce crystallization of the sugar. One absolute rule is that you should never ever stir the caramel because this encourages crystallization. When it is bubbling, you really need to ensure that the edges are kept wet or crystals will start to form.

Crème caramel is best served cold, because the whole enjoyment of eating it is to appreciate the chilled, light custard.

*Preheat the oven to 180°C/fan 160°C/gas 4.

1   To make the caramel, place 140g of the sugar and 2 tablespoons of water in a medium-sized frying pan and bring to the boil. Cook for 4–5 minutes over a high heat without stirring, swirling the pan occasionally, until the sugar has dissolved and turned a caramel colour. Be careful not to let it burn.

2   Divide the molten caramel between 4 x 150ml ramekins, carefully pouring it in and tilting the ramekins to coat the bottoms.

3   Split the vanilla pod down the centre and remove the seeds using a knife. Place the seeds and the pod in a medium-sized saucepan with the milk and warm through over a low heat – do not let the milk boil.

4   Place the whole eggs, the egg yolks and the remaining 75g of sugar in a large bowl and gently whisk until smooth – try not to let too many bubbles form in the mixture. Pour a little of the warmed milk into the bowl and whisk gently again. Then add all the milk to the bowl with the eggs – gradually, so as not to scramble the eggs – and whisk once more.

5   Strain the egg and milk mixture through a sieve, to remove the vanilla pod pieces, and pour into the 4 ramekins, on top of the caramel bases.

6   Place the ramekins in a deep roasting tin and pour boiling water into the roasting tin to two thirds of the way up the sides of the ramekins (this is a bain-marie). Put the roasting tin in the preheated oven and cook for 15–20 minutes, until the custards have just set.

7   Remove from the oven and take the ramekins out of the roasting tin. Allow them to cool and then place them in the fridge for 30–40 minutes.

8   To make the apple compote, place the sugar in a medium-sized frying pan over a medium to high heat until a light golden colour appears and then add the diced apple and the cinnamon. Cook for 2–3 minutes, or until the apple has softened, then add the rum and finish by adding the butter. Cook for a minute more and then take off the heat.

9   Using serving plates with a shallow dip to catch the caramel, turn each crème caramel upside down on to the plate so the caramel will be on the top and take off the ramekin. If you're struggling to free the caramel, gently press the top of the caramel to loosen it away from the sides of the ramekin. Place a spoonful of the compote on each plate next to the crème caramel.

HOW TO MAKE CRÈME CARAMEL

These instructions specifically refer to Crème Caramel with Apple Compote (page 285).

1 Place the sugar and water into a dry saucepan and heat very gently. Occasionally brush around the sides of the pan with a wet pastry brush to prevent sugar crystallizing around the edges. Move the melting sugar by swirling the pan in a circular motion, but do not be tempted to stir with a spoon, as this will spoil the caramel. When the sugar has melted, simmer it very carefully, watching closely until it reaches a rich dark brown, then quickly remove from the heat and carefully pour into ramekins. Leave to set.

2 Next, combine the sugar and eggs together in a bowl. They should be well mixed but not frothy.

3 Carefully split the vanilla pod, then scrape out the seeds and place them and the pod into a saucepan with the milk. Heat this gently to infuse the flavours and remove from the heat as soon as it reaches boiling point.

4 Pour the hot milk on to the sugar and egg mixture, whisking well until it thickens slightly.

5 Pass this mixture through a sieve to remove the vanilla pod and any lumps, then carefully pour over the caramel in the ramekins.

Put the ramekins in a baking tray half filled with hot water, then place in the oven and bake until just set. They should wobble slightly, like a jelly.

6

7 When cool, gently turn them out and serve.

SKILLS
- Removing the seeds from the vanilla pod
- Simmering the milk and cream
- Making the custard mix
- Using gelatine
- Toasting spices
- Making a syrup glaze

VANILLA PANNA COTTA WITH SAFFRON HONEY-SPICED FIGS serves 6

100ml whole milk
200ml double cream
4 tablespoons runny honey
seeds from 1 vanilla pod
3½ gelatine leaves
300g natural yoghurt
3 teaspoons saffron threads
1½ level teaspoons mixed spice
2 star anise
2 cinnamon sticks
2 tablespoons lime-blossom honey
9 figs, peeled and left whole

This is a simple yet indulgent pudding. Clear runny honey is added to the vanilla panna cotta. It acts as a sweetening agent with a milder sweetness and smoother texture than sugar. Leaf gelatine is used to help gently thicken the dessert, but be careful – the key to gelatine is that you must never add warm or hot water to it. Always let it dissolve in cold water, otherwise it takes on a horrible smell and the mixture will become too thick. The perfect panna cotta is one that is softly set so that you are able to slide your spoon through it. Figs should never be cooked with their skins on, so peel them with a swivel peeler. This really makes a difference to their taste.

Preheat the oven to 200°C/fan 180°C/gas 6.

1   Place the milk, cream, runny honey and vanilla seeds in a medium-sized saucepan and slowly bring to the boil, then turn down the heat and simmer for 1 minute. Take the saucepan off the heat.

2   Soak the gelatine leaves in cold water for a couple of minutes until soft, then squeeze out the excess water and whisk them into the warmed milk and cream mixture until the gelatine has dissolved.

3   Mix in the yoghurt and continue to stir until it has a smooth creamy consistency. Pour this vanilla cream mixture into 6 x 100ml non-stick moulds like mini loaf tins or mini pudding basins and leave to cool. If you have time, you can place the moulds in the fridge for 3 hours until the panna cotta has set firm but you don't have to do this.

4   Meanwhile, dissolve the saffron threads in 6 tablespoons of warm water.

5   Toast the spices in a small dry saucepan over a medium heat for a minute, then add the lime-blossom honey, soaked saffron and saffron water and stir.

6   Line a baking sheet with greaseproof paper. Dip the peeled whole figs into the warm honey glaze, remove them using a slotted spoon and place on to the lined baking sheet. Place in the preheated oven for 10 minutes.

7   Simmer the remaining glaze until it has reduced to the consistency of a syrup, then remove the pan from the heat and put to one side.

8   To serve, dip the moulds very briefly in hot water and then turn each panna cotta out upside down in the centre of a serving plate. Slice the warm baked figs in half and place 3 halves alongside each panna cotta. Drizzle the figs with the remaining glaze.

SKILLS
- Greasing and lining cake tins
- Creaming the butter and sugar and gradually adding the eggs
- Adding the flour while keeping air in the mix
- Making the praline and coating the walnuts
- Making the icing and piping rosettes

COFFEE AND WALNUT CAKE serves 8

FOR THE COFFEE CAKE

300g unsalted butter, plus extra to grease the cake tins

300g caster sugar

5 eggs

300g self-raising flour, sifted

1 level teaspoon baking powder

4 tablespoons strong black coffee, cold

a splash of whole milk, if needed

FOR THE WALNUT PRALINE

120g caster sugar

150g walnut halves

vegetable oil, to oil the baking tray

FOR THE COFFEE ICING

200g unsalted butter, softened

400g icing sugar

3–4 tablespoons strong black coffee, cold

This light and fluffy cake is a treat for coffee lovers. Use an electric beater if you can to get as much air into the cake as possible. Add the eggs one at a time to avoid the mixture curdling. Sifting the baking powder and flour adds even more air to the batter, so fold them in gently to stop that air being knocked out. If the batter becomes too tight, you can add a dash of milk as a loosener.

Preheat the oven to 180°C/fan 160°C/gas 4.

1   Grease 2 x 22cm round Victoria sandwich cake tins with butter.

2   Place the butter and sugar in a large bowl and whisk with an electric beater until the mixture becomes pale in colour. Beat in the eggs one at a time.

3   Fold in the sifted flour and baking powder. Next stir in the cooled coffee and mix well. If the mixture is too thick, add a splash of milk.

4   Divide the cake mixture between the 2 greased cake tins, pouring it in and using a spatula to level the mixture in the tins. Place the cake tins in the preheated oven for 30–40 minutes.

5   To test if the cakes are ready, stick a skewer into the centre of each one and if the skewer comes out clean, they are cooked. Take the cakes out of the oven and turn them out on to a cooling rack.

6   To make the walnut praline, place the sugar and 1 teaspoon of cold water in a small non-stick frying pan over a high heat without stirring until the sugar turns a light caramel colour. Add the walnut halves, stir well to make sure they are all coated in the caramel and pour on to an oiled baking tray or silicone mat. Using an oiled spoon, set 8 of the caramel-coated walnut halves aside on a plate.

7   Once the caramel has cooled and set – about 15 minutes – place the caramel-coated walnut from the baking tray into a small food processor and blitz to the texture of rough crumbs.

8   To make the icing, beat the butter and icing sugar together until pale and fluffy. This should take around 5 minutes. Once the mixture has reached this stage beat in the coffee.

9   Spread one third of the icing on the bottom layer of the cooled coffee cake and sprinkle generously with the praline mix. Place the second cooled cake on top. Spread the top cake layer with a thick coating of the coffee icing, using most of the remaining icing.

10 Put the final remaining icing into a piping bag with a star nozzle on and pipe 8 rosettes around the edge of the cake. Top each rosette with a reserved caramel-coated walnut half and sprinkle the middle of the cake with the remaining praline.

11 To serve, place the iced cake on a cake stand and cut into 8 pieces.

GIZZI'S NOTES ON CHEESE AND CHEESEBOARDS

A cheese course can really make a dinner party: cheeses look beautiful on the table and they are a chance for everyone to just tuck in together and enjoy themselves. However, it can be quite hard to know when to serve a cheeseboard, what cheeses to include and what to serve with them. There are no set rules, but here are some guidelines to help you create a fabulous cheeseboard with confidence.

Cheeseboards originated in France, where traditionally they are served before the pudding course. In Britain, however, they tend to be served after the puddings have been eaten. Unless you particularly want to serve your cheeseboard before, I would stick to after pudding.

Serving a form of carbohydrate – such as biscuits – with cheese complements the flavour and texture of the cheese. There is a wide range of different types of savoury biscuits and wafers to choose from. Classic water biscuits, oatcakes or charcoal biscuits go brilliantly with cheese, and even just whacking a piece of cheese on a digestive is a super way to enjoy it. You can't beat a fruit bread, like a walnut and sultana sourdough, cut really thinly. You get the carbs, the nuts and the fruit that work so well with cheese all in one hit!

Nuts have a wonderful flavour that combines well with cheese and so they make another great accompaniment. If you want to taste something a little bit different, try caramelizing some walnuts – the combination of salty and sweet just lights up your palate. Fruit and vegetables like radishes, apples and pears also provide a textural difference that works brilliantly against the creamy, crumbly texture of certain varieties like Caerphilly or Wensleydale. However, my absolute favourite way to eat cheese is with grapes – it's the ultimate pairing. Some people like to serve chutney, and there's no reason why you can't, but personally I find it a little overpowering on a cheeseboard and prefer my chutney in a sandwich.

When it comes to choosing your selection of cheeses for the cheeseboard, I would aim to include a hard cheese, a blue cheese, a goat's cheese and a soft cheese. Anything more than that is unnecessary: 'keep it simple' is my motto.

Hard cheese
A good example of a hard cheese is Cheddar. I think it's fantastic for eating during the day – it rocks in a ploughman's lunch or in a sandwich – but when it comes to cheeseboards it seems a shame to pass up on the many other beautiful hard cheeses we have in Britain, such as the delicious Warwickshire Truckle or Lincolnshire Poacher, which has a taste somewhere in between Cheddar and the Spanish Manchego cheese

Blue cheese

Stilton is a delicious blue cheese. People are often put off tasting blue cheeses by thinking of them as pungent-smelling and strongly flavoured. However, Stilton is fantastic and, compared to stronger types like Gorgonzola, it's got a lovely mild taste. I believe we make the best blue cheeses in the world in Britain and I champion Colston Basset Stilton as the king of cheeses. It originated from the village of Stilton in Cambridgeshire in the early 1700s but these days for a cheese to be called 'Stilton' it must be made by one of six dairies located in Derbyshire, Leicestershire and Nottinghamshire. The blue veins in the cheese are the result of special bacteria mixed in with the milk, which then grow a mould during the ripening process. It sounds a bit grisly, but the resulting flavour is delicious!

Goat's cheese

Goat's cheese has been made for thousands of years. France produces a huge number of different types of goat's cheese. In the UK, Ticklemore, a variety that is really trendy at the moment, is made near Totnes in Devon. It is harder than regular goat's cheese and with a firmer texture, but it's still got a lovely creaminess in the middle. Innes Bosworth Ash Log is another beautiful, flavourful goat's cheese. Made in Staffordshire, it has a black coating of ash on the outside which gives it a very smoky flavour. A lovely organic variety from the west of Ireland is St Tola.

Soft cheese

Gooey, oozy cheeses such as Brie or Camembert are called washed-rind cheeses – this means the curds are periodically bathed in hot water, which encourages the surface bacterial culture that creates the rind and keeps the inside moist. The infamous Stinking Bishop is one of my personal favourites: I could eat this until the cows come home, quite literally! It has a strong taste and is hugely creamy and quite rich.

The whole point of a cheeseboard is to have fun, taste different things and create a talking point. So don't worry too much about getting it right – just buy the most unusual and exciting cheeses you can find and you're guaranteed to inspire your guests.

1 Brie de Meaux **2** Ticklemore **3** Montgomery's Cheddar **4** Berkswell **5** Gorgonzola **6** Innes Log

STARTERS

- Salmon tartare with vichyssoise
- Mark Edwards's Scottish beef tataki with tosa-zu sauce and asparagus tempura
- Fruits de mer

MAINS

- Mark Edwards's steamed red snapper with vegetable stir-fry
- Classic roast chicken with parsnips, carrots and savoury bread pudding
- Martin Blunos's roast grouse with buttery kale and jerusalem artichoke purée
- Martin Blunos's roast partridge with mash and spinach
- Arun Kapil's poussin 'Oudhi' with pilau rice, okra and ginger kari and a spiced pomegranate and mint raita
- Arun Kapil's pot-roasted pheasant with faggots, Bombay game chips and buttered crumbs
- Roe deer venison fillet with a potato and pancetta terrine
- Roasted pork belly, pickled apple salad and celeriac and apple purée

PUDDINGS

- Tipsy trifles
- Rhubarb crumble soufflés with a rhubarb, mango and lime salad
- Eric Lanlard's Mogadores: a light chocolate mousse on a hazelnut praline feuillantine base
- Eric Lanlard's apple soufflés with a salted butter caramel sauce

SALMON TARTARE WITH VICHYSSOISE serves 4

FOR THE VICHYSSOISE

50g unsalted butter

2 leeks (white part only), finely chopped

150g Maris Piper potatoes, peeled and thinly sliced

1 bouquet garni (parsley stalks, bay leaf and thyme sprig tied together with butcher's string)

1 tablespoon crème fraîche

salt and freshly ground black pepper

FOR THE SALMON TARTARE

200g fillet of salmon, skinned, deboned and finely chopped

1 shallot, peeled and finely diced

¼ cucumber, deseeded, half peeled and all finely chopped

20ml white wine vinegar

½ teaspoon caster sugar

½ teaspoon salt

finely chopped chives, to garnish

This would be the starter for my ultimate three-course dinner, to be followed by the Roasted Pork Belly, Pickled Apple Salad and Celeriac and Apple Purée (p. 329) and Rhubarb Crumble Soufflés with a Rhubarb, Mango and Lime Salad (pp. 334–5).

1. To make the vichyssoise, heat a medium-sized saucepan and add the butter. Once the butter starts to sizzle, add the leeks and sauté over a medium heat for 5–8 minutes until soft.

2. Add the potato slices, 500ml water and the bouquet garni and bring to the boil. Simmer for 8–10 minutes, until the potatoes are tender, then take the saucepan off the heat and leave aside to cool.

3. Once cooled, place the soup in a blender and liquidize until smooth, then add the crème fraîche and mix it in. Season to taste with salt and pepper. Pass the mixture through a sieve into a jug, pressing it through using the back of a wooden spoon, and place in the fridge to chill.

4. For the salmon tartare, place the salmon and the shallot in a medium-sized bowl and season with salt and pepper. Mix together.

5. Place the chopped cucumber in a separate small bowl, add the vinegar, sugar and salt and stir.

6. To serve, place a 5cm-diameter pastry ring in the centre of the first serving bowl and place a quarter of the salmon tartare in the centre. Press down gently, then add a quarter of the cucumber mixture as the second layer and top with chopped chives. Pour soup around the ring and then carefully remove the ring. Repeat for the three other serving bowls.

MARK EDWARDS'S SCOTTISH BEEF TATAKI WITH TOSA-ZU SAUCE AND ASPARAGUS TEMPURA serves 4

FOR THE TOSA-ZU SAUCE

5 tablespoons soy sauce

8 tablespoons rice wine vinegar

4g dried bonito flakes

FOR THE BEEF TATAKI

200g beef fillet

freshly ground black pepper

vegetable, sunflower or groundnut oil, for frying

2–3 garlic cloves, peeled and finely sliced

2 tablespoons trimmed and finely sliced spring onions

FOR THE ASPARAGUS TEMPURA

vegetable, sunflower or groundnut oil, for deep-frying

200ml ice-cold water

1 small egg yolk

100g plain flour, sifted, plus extra for dusting

6 green asparagus spears, trimmed

This is a simple dish to make but it is all about technique, presentation and cleanliness. The recipe is a variation on a Japanese sashimi but in this case a Scottish fillet of beef is being used instead. 'Tataki' means to sear all the way around the outside. The dish is served with a dressing of soy sauce, rice wine vinegar and marinated bonito flakes and is then topped with fried garlic and spring onions. Bonito is a type of tuna which is cured with salt and left to dry for up to three years, using the same principle as curing ham.

Pour in the oil and preheat the deep-fat fryer to 180°C/350°F, according to the manufacturer's instructions.

1 Warm the soy sauce and rice wine vinegar (together called ponzu) slightly in a small saucepan, but do not let them boil. Add the dried bonito flakes and stir, then take the saucepan off the heat and allow the mixture to cool to room temperature. Strain out the bonito flakes.

2 Season the beef fillet with black pepper and prepare a bowl with iced water. Heat a non-stick frying pan over a high heat and put in the beef. Sear in the dry pan on each side for 5 seconds only, but make sure that the entire outside surface has been completely seared and no red meat is visible. Immediately plunge the seared beef into the iced water to stop the cooking process, then pat it dry with kitchen paper. Cover and place in the fridge to chill.

3 To cook the garlic for the tataki, pour about 2cm depth of the oil into a small saucepan and carefully heat to 150°C. Put in the garlic slices and slowly deep-fry until they turn a light golden brown colour. Then remove the garlic from the oil straight away with a slotted spoon and drain on kitchen paper.

4 Meanwhile, make the tempura batter by combining the ice-cold water and egg yolk together in a medium-sized bowl using a pair of chopsticks. Add the flour a little at a time, stirring with the chopsticks, until all the flour is combined. Using chopsticks prevents the batter becoming over-worked – you should end up with a loose batter that has some small lumps of unmixed flour, which helps to make a light, crisp batter. Always make sure the water is very cold and that you make the batter just before cooking, which will also help to make it crisp.

5 Carefully dust the asparagus spears in a little flour and shake off any excess. One spear at a time, dip them into the cold tempura batter, allowing any excess to run off, then gently place in the deep-fat fryer. Cook for 1–2 minutes until the batter is light and crisp, then remove and drain on kitchen paper.

6 Thinly slice the chilled beef into 2–3mm slices and arrange these overlapping down the middle of a flat serving dish. Top each slice with a few sliced spring onions and a slice of fried garlic, then spoon some of the tosa-zu sauce around the edges of the beef. Serve the asparagus tempura to the side.

FRUITS DE MER serves 4

**FOR THE ROCK
OYSTERS WITH
AN ASIAN DRESSING**

vegetable, sunflower or
groundnut oil, for frying

1 tablespoon sesame oil

1 small shallot, peeled
and finely chopped

2cm piece fresh ginger,
peeled and finely grated

¼ red chilli, deseeded
and finely chopped

2 tablespoons pickled
ginger, finely diced

3 teaspoons rice wine
vinegar

20ml sugar syrup

1 tablespoon light soy
sauce

1 tablespoon pickled
ginger juice

juice of 1 lime

1 teaspoon fish sauce

1 shallot, peeled and
thinly sliced in rings

4 rock oysters, cleaned
(shells retained and
cleaned)

coriander cress, to
garnish

**FOR THE SCALLOP
CEVICHE**

4 scallops, cleaned and
roe removed, shells
retained

¼ avocado, stoned,
peeled and finely diced

½ ripe medium tomato,
skinned, deseeded and
finely diced

½ red chilli, deseeded
and finely diced

¼ red onion, peeled and
finely diced

juice of 1 lime

salt and freshly ground
black pepper

This is a platter of wild shellfish and seafood from Britain, Ireland and the Atlantic – five different things for each person served on one plate. We have a wonderful large Scottish scallop served with a ceviche dressing of tomato, avocado, chilli and lime, wild native oysters served with a sour-cream *sabayonne*, Sevruga caviar and grated horseradish, a Japanese-influenced tempura, a Dublin Bay langoustine and a rock oyster with a Vietnamese dressing. An elegant and refined dish; the ingredients demand respect.

Pour in the oil and preheat the deep-fat fryer to 180°C/350°F, according to the manufacturer's instructions.

1   To make the Asian dressing for the oysters, place the sesame oil, chopped shallot, fresh ginger and red chilli in a small frying pan and cook over a medium heat for 2 minutes. Add the pickled ginger, rice wine vinegar, sugar syrup, soy sauce and pickled ginger juice and bring to the boil. Simmer for 10 minutes, then remove from the heat and add the lime juice and fish sauce. Allow to cool.

2   Place the shallot rings in the preheated deep-fat fryer for 1–2 minutes, then remove and drain on kitchen paper.

3   To make the scallop ceviche, first thinly slice the scallops into rounds and place each one back in its cleaned shell, with the slices overlapping to form a circle. Mix together the diced avocado, tomato, chilli and red onion in a small bowl and then sprinkle on top of the scallops. Squeeze over the lime juice, season with salt and pepper and set aside.

4   For the langoustines, place the potato flour and plain flour in a medium-sized bowl and mix together with a fork, whilst gradually adding the white wine and sparkling water. Do not over-mix as you want to keep small pockets of flour and air. Dip the langoustines in this tempura batter, shake them gently to remove any excess batter and then place them into the preheated deep-fat fryer. Cook for 2–3 minutes, then drain on kitchen paper and set aside.

5   To cook the prawns, heat a small frying pan over a medium heat and pour in the olive oil. Once the oil is hot, put the prawns in the pan and fry for 1–2 minutes. Turn them over halfway through cooking. Then add the garlic and butter and cook for a further 2–3 minutes. Season with salt and pepper and remove the pan from the heat. Finish the prawns by sprinkling on the chopped parsley, then set the pan aside.

FOR THE NATIVE OYSTERS WITH A SOUR CREAM FOAM AND HORSERADISH SNOW

100ml sour cream

40ml single cream

finely grated zest of ½ unwaxed lemon

2 tablespoons grated fresh horseradish

4 native oysters, cleaned (shells retained and cleaned)

1 tablespoon finely chopped chives

2 teaspoons caviar, to garnish

seaweed, blanched and cooled to serve

FOR THE LANGOUSTINE TEMPURA

50g potato flour

50g plain flour

50ml white wine

75ml sparkling water

4 langoustines, heads removed, peeled and de-veined, claws and head retained for garnishing

FOR THE PRAWNS WITH GARLIC BUTTER

2 tablespoons olive oil

8 prawns, heads removed and peeled but tail left on

2 garlic cloves, peeled and crushed

50g unsalted butter

2 tablespoons finely chopped flat-leaf parsley

6   For the native oysters, mix the sour cream, cream, lemon zest and half of the horseradish together in a small bowl. Place the mixture into an Espuma (whipped-cream gun) gun and charge with 2 bulbs of gas. Using the gun, pipe a small amount of the mixture on to each oyster sitting in its shell. Top with the remaining horseradish. Sprinkle with the chopped chives and caviar, then set aside.

7   To serve, place each rock oyster in an Asian spoon and drizzle over a little of the dressing, then garnish with the crispy shallots and coriander cress. Put a small mound of seaweed on each serving plate and sit a dressed native oyster on top of each mound. Sit a rock oyster in its spoon alongside. Place 1 langoustine, 2 prawns drizzled with butter from the pan and 1 scallop ceviche on each plate also.

MARK EDWARDS'S STEAMED RED SNAPPER WITH VEGETABLE STIR-FRY serves 2

FOR THE STEAMED RED SNAPPER

120g green beans, trimmed

1 x 500g whole red snapper, cleaned, scaled and gutted

2 garlic cloves, peeled and thinly sliced

2cm piece of fresh ginger, peeled and finely shredded

50g Hon-shimeji mushrooms

2 Erengi mushrooms, halved

180ml sake

5 tablespoons soy sauce

¼ bunch chives, finely chopped

3 tablespoons vegetable oil

1 tablespoon sesame oil

FOR THE VEGETABLE STIR-FRY

1 tablespoon sesame oil

½ red chilli, deseeded and sliced finely

1 garlic clove, peeled and finely chopped

2 spring onions, trimmed and sliced into 2.5cm slices on an angle

½ red and yellow peppers, deseeded and sliced into 2.5cm chunks

50g tenderstem broccoli, sliced into chunks

40g mange tout, trimmed

1 medium carrots, peeled and cut into rounds on an angle

3 stems of choi sum

2 tablespoons sake

1 tablespoon soy sauce

FOR THE JAPANESE RICE

150g sticky rice, rinsed and soaked

There are three elements to this dish. Firstly the saki-steamed red snapper with erengi mushrooms (otherwise known as King Oyster mushrooms), Hon-shimeji mushrooms, ginger and garlic. This is accompanied by stir-fried vegetables with chilli and saki and, finally, steamed rice. Before the fish is cleaned, make sure you have all the ingredients prepared and ready to go. Japanese cuisine is all about precision so ensure that all your vegetables are beautifully sliced and appropriately proportioned.

1 Blanch the green beans briefly in boiling water, then refresh in ice-cold water and drain.

2 Wash the red snapper inside and out with cold water, then pat dry with kitchen paper and place on to a chopping board. Make parallel diagonal cuts 2cm apart on both sides of fish, just through to the bone, which will enable the heat to penetrate and cook the fish evenly.

3 Place the fish on to a heatproof serving plate and spread the slices of garlic and ginger down the length of the tail. Arrange the Hon-shimeji and Erengi mushrooms down one side. Pour over 3 tablespoons of the sake and place the plate into a bamboo basket steamer set over a saucepan of boiling water. Steam for 12–15 minutes until cooked. Check to see if the mullet is done by cutting into the thickest part of the fish with a knife.

4 Meanwhile, cook the rice according to packet instructions.

5 To stir-fry the vegetables, place a wok over a high heat. Pour in the sesame oil and, once it is almost smoking hot, add the chilli and garlic. Stir-fry for 1 minute then put in the vegetables. Stir-fry for 2–3 minutes before adding the sake and soy sauce to finish the dish. Spoon the stir-fried vegetables into a side dish and keep warm.

6 To make a dressing for the fish, combine the soy sauce and remaining sake in a small bowl. Mix well and set aside.

7 When the fish is cooked, take the plate out of the steamer. Sprinkle the chives over the tail. Pour 3 tablespoons of the sake and soy sauce mixture over the fish, and place the blanched green beans on top. Heat the vegetable and sesame oils in a small saucepan until just smoking. Finish by pouring the hot oil over the ginger, chives and garlic slices on the tail to sear and release the flavours.

8 Serve the whole snapper with bowls of steamed rice and the vegetable stir-fry.

CLASSIC ROAST CHICKEN WITH PARSNIPS, CARROTS AND SAVOURY BREAD PUDDING serves 4

FOR THE SAVOURY BREAD PUDDING

knob unsalted butter, melted

450ml whole milk

1 bay leaf

1 thyme sprig

1 garlic clove, peeled and crushed

4 cloves

1 tablespoon olive oil

1 large onion, peeled and finely chopped

100g white bread, crusts removed, torn up

pinch freshly grated nutmeg

pinch white pepper

2 egg whites

1 egg, beaten

FOR THE ROAST CHICKEN AND GRAVY

1 unwaxed lemon, zested then cut in half

1.2kg organic, free-range chicken

salt and freshly ground black pepper

85g dried white breadcrumbs

150g unsalted butter, softened

2 tablespoons thyme leaves

2 tablespoons finely chopped flat-leaf parsley

20g unsalted butter, melted

1 tablespoon plain flour, sifted

150ml white wine

300ml dark chicken stock

This is ultimate comfort food; there is something special about sitting down to eat a beautiful roast chicken for Sunday lunch. But not just any chicken; it has to be free range, ethically produced and always organic. This roast chicken is served with perfect roast potatoes and an amazing bread pudding infused with pepper, thyme, bay leaf, garlic and cloves. The roasted root vegetables are caramelized with honey and thyme at the very end. For a family of four, this meal will cost under £15 – ultimate luxury on a budget! This is a dinner that most people attempt to do but which most struggle to get right, so have a go at this recipe.

Preheat the oven to 180°C/fan 160°C/gas 4.

1   Start by making the bread pudding. Brush the melted butter all over the insides of 4 dariole moulds and then place them in the fridge.

2   Put the milk, bay leaf, thyme, garlic and cloves in a medium-sized saucepan and bring to simmering point. Remove the saucepan from the heat and set aside for 10 minutes for the milk to infuse.

3   Heat a small frying pan and put in the olive oil. Once the oil is hot, add the onion and cook over a medium to low heat for 4–5 minutes until soft, then set aside.

4   Strain the infused milk and discard the aromatics. Place the torn up white bread in a medium-sized bowl, pour over the strained milk and add the cooked onion, the nutmeg and white pepper. Mix well, then set aside for 10 minutes.

5   Season the inside of the chicken with salt and pepper, then place the lemon halves into the cavity. Put the breadcrumbs, butter, thyme, parsley and lemon zest in a large bowl and stir together until combined. Loosen the skin on the chicken's breast and spread the butter mixture under the skin and also on the legs. Truss the bird by tying the wingtips to the knuckle joints on the legs with butcher's string and put it in a roasting tin.

6   Brush the chicken with the melted butter and season with more salt and pepper. Cover the crown of the chicken in tin foil and put the roasting tin in the preheated oven. Take the chicken out after 45 minutes, remove the foil and return it to the oven to cook for a further 25 minutes.

**FOR THE ROAST
POTATOES**

1kg Maris Piper potatoes,
  peeled and cut into
  chunks

100g goose fat

3 rosemary sprigs

**FOR THE PARSNIPS
AND CARROTS**

2 parsnips, peeled and
  cut into batons

3 carrots, peeled and cut
  into batons

knob goose fat

1 teaspoon runny honey

1 tablespoon thyme
  leaves

7   Meanwhile, finish off the bread pudding. Place the egg whites in a large bowl
    and whisk until they form soft peaks. Add the whisked egg whites and the
    beaten egg to the bread and milk mixture and stir to combine.

8   Pour the pudding mixture into the 4 chilled dariole moulds and place them in
    a deep baking tray or oven dish. Pour in boiling water to about halfway up the
    sides of the moulds and place the tray in the oven with the chicken for 1 hour.

9   Start preparing the potatoes. Parboil the potato chunks in a large saucepan
    of salted water for 10–15 minutes, then drain them and shake to roughen the
    surface of the potatoes.

10 Once the chicken and bread puddings are cooked, remove from the oven.
    Take the whole chicken out of the roasting tin, place on a plate, cover in foil
    and leave to rest while you roast the potatoes. Also cover the bread puddings
    with the foil.

11 Tip the goose fat into a baking tray. Place the tray in the preheated oven until
    the fat is hot and melted. Remove the tray from the oven and add the potato
    chunks and the rosemary, then turn the oven up to 200°C/fan 180°C/gas 6.
    Put the potatoes in the oven and cook for 30 minutes.

12 Parboil the parsnip and carrot batons in a saucepan of salted water for 2–3
    minutes. Then heat a frying pan, add the goose fat and tip in the vegetables.
    Turn the vegetables in the fat over a high heat until they are golden all over –
    about 5 minutes. Add the honey and thyme, toss well and then leave aside,
    but keep warm.

13 Pop the bread puddings back in the oven for a few minutes to reheat while
    you make the gravy. Remove any burnt bits and excess fat from the chicken
    roasting tin then put it over a medium heat. Add the flour and stir well. Pour
    in the wine to deglaze and then add the chicken stock. Bring up to a simmer
    and cook further to reduce the liquid. Finish the gravy by adding any resting
    juices from the chicken.

14 To serve, carefully turn the dariole moulds upside down to tip out the bread
    puddings. Place the chicken on a serving platter and surround with the
    honey-glazed vegetables and the potatoes. Strain the gravy into a gravy boat
    and serve with the puddings.

MARTIN BLUNOS'S ROAST GROUSE WITH BUTTERY KALE AND JERUSALEM ARTICHOKE PURÉE serves 4

FOR THE ROAST GROUSE

vegetable, sunflower or groundnut oil for frying

2 grouse

600ml whole milk, chilled

salt and freshly ground black pepper

500ml fresh game stock

100g duck livers, trimmed

50g plain flour, sifted

2 eggs, beaten

100g day-old fine breadcrumbs

100g chicken breast

½ teaspoon cayenne pepper

¼ teaspoon ground nutmeg

100ml double cream

200g caul fat, soaked in cold water

25g unsalted butter

2 tablespoons Madeira

1 tablespoon runny honey

FOR THE JERUSALEM ARTICHOKE PURÉE

500g Jerusalem artichokes, peeled and chopped, then covered in water

600ml whole milk

100g unsalted butter

FOR THE BUTTERY KALE

200g kale

20g unsalted butter

This dish has an amazing 'wow' factor. Grouse is a big bird, so only half is required here. Removing the backbone before browning the meat in an oiled pan will help it cook quicker. Once the skin has been removed from the drumstick, the whole leg is poached in stock. The glaze helps to add a bit of oomph to this dish and is made from Madeira wine, game stock, runny honey and butter. Kale really is a funky piece of veg! It has a great colour, it is seasonal and goes particularly well with roasted grouse.

Pour in the oil and preheat the deep-fat fryer to 180°C/ 350°F, according to the manufacturer's instructions. Preheat the oven to 180°C/fan 160°C/gas 4.

1   Gut the birds, reserving the livers, and remove the wishbones. Trim the livers and soak them in the milk. Cover and put in the fridge. Using a sharp knife, cut the legs from the birds and cut the drumsticks from the thighs. Remove the skin from these drumsticks and thighs, and also remove the bones from the thighs. Cut the majority of the 2 crowns from the carcasses.

2   Place the grouse crowns into a roasting tin, season with salt and pepper and put in the preheated oven to cook. Roast them for 12–15 minutes,

3   Whilst the grouse are in the oven, pour the stock into a medium-sized saucepan and bring to the boil. Add the grouse drumsticks to the stock and simmer for 10–15 minutes, then remove them from the saucepan with a slotted spoon. Set the drumsticks aside on a plate with kitchen paper to cool and dry. Retain the saucepan with the stock.

4   When the grouse crowns are cooked, take them out of the oven and carve the breast meat from the bones. Leave to rest on a plate covered in tin foil to keep warm.

5   Lay down a sheet of cling film on a chopping board, place the boneless grouse thigh meat on it and cover with a second sheet of cling film. Using a rolling pin, flatten out the meat to an even thickness, then peel back the top layer of cling film and season the meat lightly with salt and pepper.

6   Fry the duck livers very quickly in a small frying pan over a high heat, then drain and dry them on kitchen paper. Once they are cool enough to handle, wrap each fried liver in two pieces of the flattened thigh meat to form a neat ball, then wrap these balls in cling film and tie off the cling film ends. Bring the saucepan of stock back to the boil, drop in the liver-stuffed thigh balls and poach them in the simmering stock for 8 minutes.

7   Remove the cooked liver-stuffed thigh balls with a slotted spoon and set them aside on a plate to cool. Once again, retain the saucepan with the stock. Once the balls are cool enough to handle, unwrap the cling film wrappers and pat them dry on kitchen paper.

8   Lay out three shallow bowls, containing the flour, beaten eggs and breadcrumbs. Season the flour with salt and pepper. Roll the dried-off liver-stuffed thigh balls first in the seasoned flour, shaking off any excess, then in the beaten egg and finally in the breadcrumbs. Then set them aside.

9   Meanwhile, start cooking the Jerusalem artichokes. Drain the chopped pieces, then place in a medium-sized saucepan and cover with the milk. Bring the milk to the boil, reduce the heat and simmer the Jerusalem artichokes for 10–12 minutes until tender. Drain and reserve the milk.

10 Pass the Jerusalem artichokes through a ricer into a bowl. If the mixture is too stiff, add a little of the reserved cooking milk until it makes a smooth purée. Season to taste with salt and pepper and set aside.

11 Cut the meat from the grouse drumsticks and put in a food processor, along with the chicken breast meat. Season with a little salt and pepper. Add the cayenne pepper, nutmeg and cream, then blitz to make a smooth mousse.

12 Spread out a small square of the soaked caul fat on a board. Now spoon a little of the mousse mixture around the first dry cooked grouse drumstick bone, leaving the end of the bone exposed. Wrap the caul tightly around the moussed section of drumstick and trim off any excess caul. Wrap the drumstick in a layer of cling film. Repeat with the remaining mousse and drumsticks.

13 Bring the stock to the boil and then carefully lower in the drumsticks and reduce the stock to a simmer. Poach for about 5 minutes until the mousse feels firm to the touch. Allow to stand off the heat for a few minutes.

14 Remove the drumsticks from the pan. Add the butter to the stock, with the Madeira and honey. Simmer over a medium heat to reduce the liquid and produce a glaze. Unwrap the drumsticks from their cling film and place them into the glaze. Carefully roll them around over a low heat to coat with the glaze, then keep warm to one side.

15 Put 1 litre of salted water and the kale in a large saucepan and bring to the boil. Simmer until the kale turns bright green, then drain. Add the butter and toss together with the cooked kale.

16 Place the liver-stuffed thigh balls in the preheated deep-fat fryer and fry for 3–4 minutes until golden. Remove and drain well on kitchen paper, then sprinkle with a dusting of salt.

17 To make a dressing for the Jerusalem artichoke purée, place the butter in a sauté pan and heat until it begins to brown. Once you have made this beurre noisette, immediately remove the pan from the heat.

18 To serve, place some carved grouse breast meat to one side of each serving plate and drizzle on a spoonful of the Jerusalem artichoke purée criss-crossing the plate. Place a liver-stuffed thigh ball and a drumstick at the top of each plate, with a spoonful of buttery kale on the other side. Drizzle the beurre noisette sauce all around.

MARTIN BLUNOS'S ROAST PARTRIDGE WITH MASH AND SPINACH serves 4

FOR THE MASH

1kg Maris Piper potatoes, skins left on

250ml whole milk

200g unsalted butter

FOR THE ROAST PARTRIDGE

4 partridges, preferably with guts inside and feet left on

salt and freshly ground black pepper

4 garlic cloves, peeled and crushed

4 large thyme sprigs

40g clarified unsalted butter

1 teaspoon rapeseed oil

50ml brandy

50ml Madeira

500ml fresh rich game or dark chicken stock

juice of 1 lemon (if needed)

FOR THE BABY SPINACH

50g unsalted butter

200g baby spinach leaves

A simple partridge dish that is wonderfully seasonal. A Redleg partridge is used here, which is a nice-sized bird – tender and not too gamey, chewy or intense. This is the perfect dish to introduce you to eating game. It is relatively simple but there are elements of jeopardy because these birds don't have a lot of fat on them, so they are easy to overcook as it is the fat that keeps meat moist. Resting the bird is really important, to release all the juices. Partridges have been with us for centuries, since Roman times, and they are still rated very highly. Wild ones, in particular, are spectacular to eat around October/November time. You can usually pick up a partridge for about £5, so they are economical too.

*Preheat the oven to 200°C/fan 180°C/gas 6.

1   Place the potatoes in a medium-sized saucepan, cover with cold water and add a pinch of salt. Put on the lid, place the saucepan over a high heat and bring the water to the boil. Boil the potatoes until tender, then drain them and set aside to cool.

2   Prepare the partridges. Remove the guts from the birds. Pluck any rogue feathers and burn off the stubble from the skins with a gas torch or other flame. Remove the wishbones. Season the cavity of each bird with a little salt and pepper and then place a clove of garlic and a sprig of thyme inside. Truss the birds' legs with butcher's string for roasting.

3   Take an ovenproof sauté pan that is large enough to hold all the birds and place it over a medium heat. Add the clarified butter and the oil then, once the oil is hot, put in the partridges. Cook to seal the birds on all sides until they are well coloured.

4   Place the sauté pan in the preheated oven for about 12–15 minutes, to roast the partridges. Take the pan out of the oven once or twice during this time and baste the birds with the melted fat in the pan.

5   Meanwhile, remove and discard the skins from the cooked potatoes then pass them through a ricer. Heat the milk and butter together in a large saucepan until the butter has melted, then add the riced potatoes. Using a wooden spoon, beat the milk, butter and potato mixture together until fluffy. Season to taste with salt and pepper, then cover the pan to keep the mashed potatoes warm and leave aside.

6 Remove the partridges from the oven and allow them to rest for a few minutes. Then lift the birds from the sauté pan and pour off the fat. Carve the legs and breasts from the carcasses, putting the breasts on a plate and covering them with tin foil to keep warm. Place the legs into a roasting dish and put them back into the oven for about another 5 minutes to finish cooking. When they are done, remove the partridge legs from the oven and leave to rest for a few minutes.

7 Meanwhile, roughly chop the partridge carcasses and roast them in the sauté pan over a high heat with the clarified butter. Add the brandy and Madeira and set them alight to burn off the alcohol. Cook to reduce the sauce until it has a sticky consistency then pour in the stock. Bring the sauce to a rapid boil, skim off any bits that come to the surface and then reduce until the sauce has thickened again.

8 Pour the sauce through a fine sieve into a clean pan. Bring the sauce to simmering point, then adjust the seasoning, adding lemon juice to adjust the sharpness if necessary. The sauce may need skimming again at this stage. Cover to keep warm.

9 To cook the baby spinach, place the butter in another sauté pan over a low heat. Once it has melted, add the spinach and sauté until wilted. Season with salt and pepper.

10 Season the carved partridge meat with salt and pepper. Put a spoonful of mashed potato on one side of each serving plate and a spoonful of sautéed spinach on the other. Fan out the slices of breast meat over the potato along with the partridge legs. Drizzle the sauce over and around the carved partridges.

ARUN KAPIL'S POUSSIN 'OUDHI' WITH PILAU RICE, OKRA AND GINGER KARI AND A SPICED POMEGRANATE AND MINT RAITA serves 2

FOR THE POUSSIN 'OUDHI'

2 poussin
zest and juice of ½ unwaxed lemon
200ml Greek yoghurt
100g ghee
60ml single cream
75g fresh ginger, peeled and roughly chopped
4 fat garlic cloves, peeled
1 red bird's eye chilli, deseeded and roughly chopped
1 tablespoon sunflower oil
60g paneer cheese, coarsely grated
7 teaspoons Green Saffron's murgh oudhi spice blend
½ lime, to serve

FOR THE PILAU RICE

15g ghee
½ medium onion, peeled and finely diced
250g Green Saffron Aged Indian basmati rice
70g chana dahl pulses
675ml fresh vegetable stock, heated
1 teaspoon ground turmeric
2 teaspoons Green Saffron's garam masala spice blend, plus a little extra for garnish
good handful dried rose petals
good handful fresh coriander, chopped
good handful bright-green shelled pistachios, roughly chopped
1 tablespoon rose water

I'm giving a modern twist to classic buttered chicken, by revisiting the origins of the original dish and taking it in a slightly different direction. Here we are using poussin and also zeroing in on a particular region in northern India, Uttar Pradesh, and its capital city, Lucknow. When my father left home to study whilst in his twenties, he went to Lucknow. Taking ingredients and spice influences from that city, I have combined them with authentic regional dishes – also family dishes cooked by my family – to create an ultimate Indian family feast, fit for any Maharajah!

Preheat the oven to 180°C/fan 160°C/gas 4.

1   Spatchcock the poussin, then place into a sturdy, snug-fitting roasting tray. Sprinkle over the lemon zest and juice. Cover the birds with dampened greaseproof paper and set aside.

2   Meanwhile, pop the rest of the poussin ingredients into a food processor and blitz to a smooth, thick spiced paste.

3   Pour this marinade paste over the lemony poussin, scraping every last bit from the processor's bowl with a spatula. Rub the marinade into all the crevices of the bird, coating the meat well.

4   Cover the poussin with the dampened greaseproof paper again, and place in the fridge for about 10 minutes. Then pop the roasting tray, with the poussin still covered, on to the middle shelf of the preheated oven.

5   Cook for 25 minutes, then remove from the oven and take off the greaseproof paper cover. Return the uncovered bird to the oven to roast for a further 5–10 minutes, or until the meat is just cooked, but still juicy and tender.

6   Whilst the poussin is cooking, make the pilau rice. Melt the ghee in an ovenproof casserole dish over a gentle heat, then add the onion and sweat until it's good and soft.

7   Wash the rice and chana dahl pulses thoroughly and drain. Tip them into the casserole dish, then stir around for 1–2 minutes, coating all the grains with the melted ghee.

FOR THE OKRA AND GINGER KARI

2 tablespoons sunflower oil

6 okra fingers, cut on the bias into rounds

10–12 vine-ripened cherry tomatoes (large ones, halved)

20g fresh ginger, peeled and grated

Maldon sea salt, to taste

FOR THE SPICED POMEGRANATE AND MINT RAITA

200ml natural yoghurt

100ml crème fraîche

1 teaspoon Green Saffron's garam masala spice blend

seeds and juice of ½ pomegranate (no pith)

1 tablespoon chopped mint

zest of ½ unwaxed lime

8 Pour in the hot stock, sprinkle on the turmeric and garam masala, and give the pilau ingredients a quick and gentle stir. Cover the casserole dish with a tight-fitting lid and place on the middle shelf of the preheated oven.

9 After 10–15 minutes, check to see if all the liquid has been absorbed. Remove the casserole dish from the oven, take off the lid and sprinkle on the rose petals. Fluff the pilau gently with a fork, then sprinkle over the coriander, pistachios, a little extra garam masala and the rose water.

10 Whilst the pilau is in the oven, make the okra and ginger kari. In a heavy-bottomed saucepan, gently heat the oil and put in the okra slices, tomatoes and ginger. Sauté over a medium to high heat. As soon as the tomatoes begin to burst, remove from the heat.

11 Combine all the raita ingredients in a bowl, stirring gently. The pomegranate adds a glorious pink tinge to the mix.

12 Take the poussin out of the oven and allow to rest for a few minutes before serving.

13 Serve the poussin on a bed of rice with lime wedges on the side. Serve the okra and raita in separate bowls to share.

ARUN KAPIL'S POT-ROASTED PHEASANT WITH FAGGOTS, BOMBAY GAME CHIPS AND BUTTERED CRUMBS serves 4

FOR THE PHEASANT

3 clementines
1 teaspoon juniper berries
1 teaspoon ground cubeb
1 teaspoon fennel seeds
½ teaspoon green cardamom seeds
¼ teaspoon Sichuan pepper
1 star anise
1 teaspoon ground cassia
75g unsalted butter, softened
2 ready-to-cook young hen pheasants (plucked, gutted, wing bones and wishbone removed, tops of legs trimmed), offal retained
salt and freshly ground black pepper
10 rashers streaky dry-cure unsmoked bacon, 4mm thick
1 tablespoon rapeseed oil
100g pancetta, cut into lardon batons about 1cm x 2½cm
6 small shallots, peeled and trimmed, but just retaining the root
2 tablespoons Armagnac brandy
100ml dry white wine (Semillon, dry Bordeaux or dry Gascon)
75ml fresh golden chicken stock
½ teaspoon Maldon sea salt
2 tablespoons Mandarine Napoleon brandy or Grand Marnier
40g unsalted butter, cubed and kept chilled
drizzle best-quality cider vinegar or lemon juice, to taste
50g caster sugar

Whilst this recipe requires a variety of cooking skills, knife skills and presentation techniques, the real challenge is in the subtle use of spices, seasoning and how the dish is finished. For example, you could add the main spice blend to the pheasant at different stages of preparation to achieve and contrast flavour levels yet still maintain 'blend integrity'.

Preheat the oven to 180°C/fan 160°C/gas 4. Pour in the oil and preheat the deep-fat fryer to 180°C, according to the manufacturer's instructions.

1   Blanch the clementines in a saucepan of boiling water, then refresh in a bowl of iced water. Cut the peel into strips, then peel and segment the fruit.

2   Put all the spices for the pheasants in a small grinder and blitz, or grind them in a spice grinder. Mix well together. Take a quarter of the ground spices and cream into the softened butter in a small bowl.

3   Season the pheasants well inside and out with salt and pepper, then spread generously with the spiced butter. Lay the bacon rashers over the breast meat, then truss the birds with butcher's string to secure the bacon in place.

4   Take a large ovenproof casserole dish and place it over a medium heat, then pour in the oil. Brown the bacon-wrapped pheasants all over in the casserole, then remove them from the dish and set aside.

5   Pop the pancetta lardons and shallots into the casserole and cook until lightly browned. Then take the dish off the heat and place the pheasants back into the dish, sitting on their backs.

6   Pour the Armagnac into a small saucepan and warm over a medium heat. When it is hot, set the brandy alight and pour over the pheasants. When the flames have subsided, turn the birds on to their sides, so they will cook on their legs.

7   Add the wine and stock to the casserole dish, sprinkle on the remaining three quarters of the spice blend and the sea salt, pour in the clementine juice and add the strips of clementine peel. Stir all together. Cover the dish with tin foil, put the lid on and place on the middle shelf of the preheated oven for 20 minutes.

8   Whilst the pheasants are in the oven, make the cabbage-wrapped faggots. Blanch the cabbage leaves in a saucepan of boiling salted water until only just soft, then refresh in a bowl of iced water.

FOR THE FAGGOTS

4 large Savoy cabbage leaves (not the heavy, darkest green ones), destalked

retained pheasant offal – gizzard trimmings, liver and heart (washed and dried)

75g pheasant trimmings, sinews removed and coarsely chopped

100g streaky bacon, chopped

50g fatty pork belly, chopped

60g fresh white breadcrumbs

½ teaspoon Green Saffron's Quatre Epice blend

zest of 1 clementine

salt

1 tablespoon chopped flat-leaf parsley

1 egg

1 shallot, peeled and finely diced

vegetable oil, for brushing the moulds

FOR THE BOMBAY GAME CHIPS

rapeseed oil for deep-fat frying

2 large potatoes (Maris Piper or Roosters), peeled

4 teaspoons Maldon sea salt

4 teaspoons Green Saffron's bombay aloo spice blend, blitzed or ground to a fine powder

FOR THE BUTTERED CRUMBS

½ garlic clove, peeled

50g unsalted butter

150g white breadcrumbs

9   Put the various offal, meats, breadcrumbs, spices, clementine zest, salt, parsley and egg in a food processor. Pulse to a coarse texture, then use a spatula to pour out into a bowl and fold the diced shallots through the mixture.

10   Check the seasoning by frying a small teaspoon of the mixture in a little oil, and adjust if necessary.

11   Brush 4 dariole moulds about 10cm x 5cm and 3½cm deep with oil, then season with salt and pepper. Line each mould with a wilted cabbage leaf, ensuring a good amount of overlap over the sides of the mould.

12   Using a tablespoon, spoon a quarter of the faggot meat mixture into the first mould, ensuring the level comes to slightly higher than the lip of the mould. Fold the overlapping sides of the cabbage leaf over the faggot, applying a little pressure as you go, so as to seal the parcel within the mould. Cut a piece of greaseproof paper to the size of the mould to form a cartouche and place on top to cover the filling. Repeat with the other three moulds.

13   Take the casserole dish with the pheasants out of the oven (after 20 minutes), turn the birds on to their other sides, replace the foil and lid, then pop back in the oven to cook for a further 20 minutes.

14   Using a mandolin, slice the potatoes into thin rounds. Place the potato rounds into a bowl of cold water for about 20 minutes.

15   Place the faggot-filled dariole moulds into a deep baking tray, pour in boiling water to about halfway up the sides of the moulds to form a bain-marie and place in the preheated oven for 25–30 minutes. When cooked, remove from the oven and keep warm until ready to serve.

16   Meanwhile, take the casserole dish with the pheasants out of the oven (after a further 20 minutes), remove the lid and foil and turn the birds breast side up. Do not replace the foil or lid, but retain the foil. Return the uncovered dish to the oven for another 10–20 minutes.

17   For the Bombay game chips, mix the salt and spice blend together.

18   Remove the potatoes from the cold water and pat dry with kitchen paper.

19   Place the potato slices into the preheated deep-fat fryer and cook for 2–3 minutes until light brown and totally crisp – this is when the spitting stops.

20   As soon as you remove the potatoes from the hot oil, immediately season with the salt spice mix. Then set aside on kitchen paper to soak up the excess oil.

21 Check to see if the pheasants are cooked. When they're ready, the legs will move easily when gently tugged. Take the casserole dish out of the oven and remove the birds. Set aside to rest on a plate and cover with the retained foil.

22 Remove the lardons and shallots from the dish with a slotted spoon, separating out and retaining the clementine peel. Set aside and rest for a good 10 minutes, keeping the lardons and shallots warm in a bowl covered with cling film.

23 Strain the cooking juices from the dish into a jug, skim off any excess fat and reserve.

24 Deglaze the casserole dish over a high heat with the Mandarine Napoleon or Grand Marnier. Set light to the liqueur, ensuring that you burn off all the alcohol.

25 Pour the strained juices back into the casserole dish and heat up to a vigorous bubble. Add the cubed butter and vinegar, then whisk. Continue to cook over a low heat to reduce the sauce to a consistency where it clings slightly to the back of a spoon. Check the seasoning, then reserve until you are ready to serve.

26 Meanwhile, make the buttered breadcrumbs. Rub the surface of a small sauté pan with the cut garlic, then discard the garlic.

27 Place the sauté pan over a medium heat and immediately put in the butter, swirling it around to melt. Add the breadcrumbs, stirring constantly, and cook for a couple of minutes to gently colour the crumbs until crisp, golden and dry. Season with salt and pepper.

28 Turn out the golden breadcrumbs and keep warm.

29 Remove the trussing string and the bacon from the pheasants. Turn the oven up to 200°C/fan 180°C/gas 6. Place the bacon on to a baking tray and put in the oven for about 5 minutes to crisp up.

30 Carve the birds, removing and jointing the legs first, then neatly cut the breasts from the carcasses and place all the meat on a roasting tray.

31 Put the roasting tray containing the jointed birds under a hot grill for 30 seconds or so. Then trim the bird joints to neaten them up.

32 Strain the wonderful cooking juices from the roasting tray that went under the grill through a sieve into the sauce. Finish off the sauce by reheating it gently and adding the reserved clementine segments. Only just warm it through, to make sure the segments retain their integrity and freshness.

33 To serve, assemble all the components of the dish so it is visually attractive.

ROE DEER VENISON FILLET WITH A POTATO AND PANCETTA TERRINE serves 4

FOR THE VENISON AND GRAVY

4 x 150g venison saddles, taken off the bone (bones kept), trimmed and sinew removed (see photographs on pages 324–5)

pinch ground cloves

¼ teaspoon ground cumin

½ teaspoon ground coriander

zest of 1 unwaxed orange

100ml port

1 onion, peeled and finely chopped

1 carrot, peeled and chopped

100ml red wine

300ml fresh dark chicken stock

2 teaspoons thyme leaves

2 teaspoons Chartreuse

small knob unsalted butter, chilled

1 tablespoon vegetable oil

FOR THE POTATO AND PANCETTA TERRINE

50g unsalted butter

1 tablespoon olive oil

2 shallots, peeled and thinly sliced

2 teaspoons thyme leaves

salt and freshly ground black pepper

450g waxy potatoes, peeled and thinly sliced

12 slices pancetta

FOR THE BUTTERNUT SQUASH AND FENNEL

2 tablespoons olive oil

½ medium butternut squash, peeled and cut into 1½cm dice

1 fennel, cut into 1½cm dice

30g chestnuts, drained and cut into quarters

50g sprout leaves, blanched

Wild venison is absolutely delicious and one of the leanest of meats to eat. The sauce is made by chopping up the bones into small pieces and dry-roasting them with a carrot and onion until they brown. Port and red wine are used as a reduction and added to the roasted bones; and the sauce is finished off with green Chartreuse liqueur. The venison is rolled in cumin, coriander and the zest of an orange and then basted with port and orange before being sealed and roasted. A terrine lined with bacon and layered with onion confit and thinly sliced potato is served alongside, together with butternut squash and fennel. Don't forget to rest the venison before serving it. A dish of ultimate luxury!

Preheat the oven to 200°C/fan 180°C/gas 6.

1 Remove the cannon from the bone and rub the meat with the dry spices and orange zest, and brush with a little of the port.

2 Chop the bones into small pieces and place them in a roasting tin, along with the chopped onion and carrot. Put the tin in the preheated oven for 20–25 minutes.

3 Pour the remaining port and the red wine into a small saucepan and boil over a medium heat until the liquid has reduced by half.

4 Meanwhile, start preparing the potato and pancetta terrine. Heat a medium-sized frying pan and put in half the butter and the olive oil. When the butter is foaming, add the shallots and thyme. Cook for 7 minutes over a medium heat until softened but not caramelized, then season with salt and pepper and set aside to cool slightly.

5 Taking the terrine moulds (2 mini loaf tins, approx. 9 x 6 x 4cm) as a guide, trim the potato slices to the correct size to fit the mould.

6 Line each mould with 6 pancetta slices, overlapping them slightly and leaving enough hanging over the sides to be able to fold over the top and finish the terrines.

7 Put a layer of thin potato slices in the bottom of the moulds and top with some cooked shallots, then add more layers of potato slices and cooked shallots, seasoning with black pepper as you go. Finish with a final layer of potatoes and wrap the overhanging pancetta over the top.

8   Cover the tops of the moulds with tin foil and press down firmly. Place in the preheated oven for 20 minutes, then remove the foil from the moulds and return to the oven for a further 20 minutes.

9   Remove the moulds from the oven and place a weight on top of the terrines. Leave to cool, then transfer to the fridge to chill for about 45 minutes until firm.

10 When the terrines are firm, remove them from the fridge, turn out of the moulds and slice thickly. Then fry the terrine slices in the remaining butter in a small frying pan until golden on each side.

11 Next, make the venison gravy. Remove the bones from the oven and place the roasting tin over a high heat. Deglaze with the port and wine reduction, then add the chicken stock and thyme to the tin and continue simmering to reduce.

12 To cook the vegetable side dish, heat another medium-sized frying pan and put in the olive oil. Once the oil is hot, add the diced squash and allow it to colour over a medium heat for 5–10 minutes. Then add the diced fennel and cook until softened. Put in the chestnuts and sauté for another 5 minutes. Remove the pan from heat and add the blanched sprout leaves and stir to warm through.

13 Heat the oil in a medium-sized ovenproof frying pan and brown the venison fillets for 3–4 minutes on all sides over a high heat. Place the pan into the preheated oven for 5–7 minutes, then take it out and leave aside to rest for 5 minutes.

14 Stir the Chartreuse into the gravy over a low heat and whisk in the cold butter. Strain the gravy from the roasting tin into a jug,

15 To serve, slice the rested venison fillets and divide between your serving plates, overlapping the slices. Position 2 terrine slices per plate next to the venison, with a pile of the squash, fennel and chestnuts. Serve the gravy on the side or pour it over the venison and drizzle it around the plate.

HOW TO REMOVE THE CANNON FROM A SADDLE OF VENISON

This specifically refers to the Roe Deer Vension Fillet with a Potato and Pancetta Terrine on pages 321–3.

1 Remove the fat and the fillet from the bones. From the back of the bone, with the knife pointing away from you, score along the bones, leaving as little meat attached to the bone as possible.

2 Then slide a large filleting knife between the bones and the meat, taking care to separate the two and leave the meat intact.

3 Slice the fat away from the bones and fillet.

4 Using a cleaver, chop between the bones to separate them.

5 You will be left with a pile of bones and your fillet of venison.

ROASTED PORK BELLY, PICKLED APPLE SALAD AND CELERIAC AND APPLE PURÉE serves 4

FOR THE PORK BELLY

1kg pork belly, scored on the skin side, bones left on

salt and freshly ground black pepper

1 onion, peeled and quartered

4 thyme sprigs

500ml fresh chicken stock

200ml white wine

FOR THE CELERIAC AND APPLE PURÉE

50g unsalted butter

½ celeriac, peeled and diced

250ml whole milk

1 Bramley apple, peeled, cored and chopped

2 tablespoons caster sugar

3 tablespoons cider vinegar

watercress, to garnish

FOR THE PICKLED APPLE SALAD

100ml cider vinegar

100g caster sugar

2 red eating apples, peeled, cored and thinly sliced

50g watercress

Pork belly is one of those great things that years ago used to cost very little because nobody wanted to cook with it – now everyone wants it and the price has risen accordingly, but it does make an exceedingly delicious pork roast. You will need a pork belly still on the rib cage and it should be lightly salted for 24 hours (no longer or it will turn into bacon!). This draws out the moisture and firms up the texture of the flesh and makes it much more enjoyable.

1   Rub salt on the pork belly and season with pepper. Cover with cling film and leave overnight in the fridge. The next day rub off any excess salt and pat the meat dry with kitchen paper. Remove the bones from the belly and set aside.

Preheat the oven to 240°C/fan 220°C/gas 9.

2   To roast the pork, place the onion and thyme in the bottom of a large roasting tin to create a trivet, to keep the meat raised. Place the pork belly on top. Season the top with lots of salt and a little black pepper.

3   Place the roasting tin in the preheated oven for 1 hour, then add half the chicken stock to the pan. Reduce the heat to 180°C/fan 160°C/gas 4 and cook for a further 1 hour and 15 minutes. Add the remaining stock to the pan if the liquid dries out and keep an eye on the meat so it doesn't burn.

4   While the pork is roasting, make the celeriac purée. Put the butter in a large saucepan over a medium heat until it is foaming, then add the diced celeriac. Fry for 2 minutes, then add the milk and 500ml water. Bring the liquids to the boil and simmer for 30 minutes until the celeriac is soft, stirring occasionally.

5   Put the apple, sugar and vinegar into a small saucepan. Stir and cook over a medium heat until the sugar has dissolved and the apple is soft but not coloured – around 12 minutes. Tip into a blender and liquidize.

6   For the pickled apple salad, place 100ml water, the cider vinegar and sugar in another saucepan. Stir, then bring to the boil and simmer to reduce the liquid by half, so you end up with a slightly thickened syrup. When the syrup has reached this consistency, take the saucepan off the heat and put in the sliced red apples. Allow them to steep in the hot liquid to pickle for 1–2 minutes, then strain the apple slices and put in a medium-sized bowl. Once cooled, add the watercress and mix together.

7   Once the pork is cooked, remove the bones from under the belly using a sharp knife. Place the pork on a board to rest, covered with tin foil. Put the bones back into the roasting tray and deglaze with the wine over a high heat. Allow to reduce a little, then strain the juices from the roasting tin into a jug. Carve the pork into slices, placing 4 in a fan shape on each serving plate. Then spoon some celeriac and apple purée on one side and place some pickled apple salad on the other. Top the purée with a garnish of watercress and pour the strained pan juices over the meat.

TIPSY TRIFLES serves 4

FOR THE RASPBERRY JELLY

400g raspberries

60g caster sugar

2 gelatine leaves, soaked in cold water for 5 minutes

FOR THE SPONGE AND SHERRY-INFUSED SYRUP

small knob butter, to grease the cake tin

2 eggs

210g caster sugar

45g plain flour, sifted, plus extra to flour the cake tin

25g cornflour, sifted

1 level teaspoon baking powder

50ml sherry

FOR THE CUSTARD

1 vanilla pod

125ml whole milk

450ml double cream

5 egg yolks

50g caster sugar

FOR THE WHISKY CREAM AND GARNISH

150ml double cream

50ml whisky

seeds from ½ vanilla pod

25g flaked almonds, toasted, to garnish

This is a true classic and is perfect as pudding for Sunday lunch. It is a perfect example of an ultimate luxury on a budget recipe as it works out to about 75p per portion. A *sabayonne* base is used for the sponge and the key to a successful base is to keep the sponge as aerated as possible, by first sifting the flour and then folding it gently into the sponge mixture. Be careful not to knock the bubbles out of the mixture when pouring into the baking tin. Sherry is added to the stock syrup to give the trifle an alcoholic punch. Serve with whisky-infused cream and decorate with toasted almonds.

*Preheat the oven to 180°C/fan 160°C/gas 4.

1 Start by making the jelly. Place half the raspberries in a small saucepan over a medium heat with the sugar and 150ml water. Stir and cook until the sugar has dissolved and the raspberries have broken down. This will take about 3 minutes. Allow the mixture to sit for 10 minutes.

2 Push the raspberries through a fine sieve into a clean saucepan and place over a low heat. Gently squeeze the excess water from the gelatine leaves and stir into the raspberry purée until the gelatine has dissolved.

3 Pour this raspberry jelly mixture into the bottoms of 4 serving glasses and allow to cool, then chill for 30 minutes in the fridge until set.

4 While the jelly is cooling, make the sponge. Butter and flour a 20cm-diameter sandwich tin. Place the eggs and 110g of the sugar in a large bowl and whisk together with an electric beater until the mixture doubles in volume and becomes pale and thick. This will take about 5 minutes.

5 Sieve the flour, cornflour and baking powder into the egg and sugar mixture and carefully fold them in.

6 Pour the sponge batter into the sandwich tin and place in the preheated oven for 15 minutes. Remove the cake from the oven and, once cooled slightly, turn it out on to a wire cooling rack.

7   Meanwhile, make the custard. Slice the vanilla pod down its length and scrape out the seeds. Pour the milk and 250ml of the cream into a medium-sized saucepan and add the seeds and the empty vanilla pod. Warm through over a low heat.

8   Place the egg yolks and sugar in a large bowl and whisk together. Remove the vanilla pod from the saucepan, then gradually pour the vanilla-infused warmed milk and cream into the bowl, stirring as you pour.

9   Pour the custard mixture back into the saucepan and put over a low heat. Cook, stirring, until the custard has thickened, then set the saucepan aside to cool.

10 Whilst the custard is cooling, lightly whip the remaining 200ml of cream to soft peaks. Once the custard has cooled, stir in the whipped cream.

11 To make the sherry-infused sugar syrup, place the remaining 100g of sugar, 80ml of water and the sherry in a small saucepan over a low heat and stir until the sugar has dissolved and the syrup has thickened. This will take 5–7 minutes.

12 For the whisky cream, whip the cream to soft peaks, stir in the whisky and gently fold through the vanilla seeds.

13 Put the flaked almonds into a pan and dry-fry them over a medium heat until golden and toasted. Remove from the heat.

14 To assemble the trifles, take the raspberry jelly serving glasses out of the fridge. Cut the cooled sponge into 4cm cubes and dip the cubes into the sherry syrup.

15 Layer half the soaked sponge pieces on top of the jelly, followed by half the raspberries and half the custard. Repeat these layers, then return the trifles to the fridge for 10–15 minutes – this will make it easier to top with the cream.

16 Spread the whisky cream on top of the glasses and smooth over. Then garnish with the toasted almonds.

RHUBARB CRUMBLE SOUFFLÉS WITH A RHUBARB, MANGO AND LIME SALAD

serves 4

FOR THE RHUBARB CRUMBLE SOUFFLÉS

knob unsalted butter, melted

40g plain flour, sifted

30g unsalted butter, diced

15g soft brown sugar

50g roasted hazelnuts, finely chopped

500g rhubarb, trimmed and cut into 2½cm chunks

1 teaspoon grenadine

60g caster sugar

10g cornflour

100g egg whites

icing sugar, to dust

FOR THE RHUBARB, MANGO AND LIME SALAD

50g caster sugar

1 teaspoon grenadine

¼ knob stem ginger, drained then cut into julienne batons

150g rhubarb, trimmed, cut into 4cm batons and then sliced into thirds

1 Alfonso mango, peeled, stoned and flesh cut into 4cm batons, then sliced into thirds

zest and juice of ½ unwaxed lime

Soufflés can sometimes be over-sweet and lacking in texture, but the crumble on this one adds a great crunch and works really well. The base of the soufflé is made first. Butter, sugar, grenadine and a dash of water are added to the chopped rhubarb and cooked to a compote stage – until it softens. Once the crumble is made it should be placed on to greaseproof paper and toasted. Grenadine is a natural sweetener but it can also be used to enrich the colour of the rhubarb – a drop of it works wonders. Be careful though – if you use too much, things can become a little 'Disney' in terms of colour! Other fruit, like apples, or overripe pears or bananas, can be used in this recipe when rhubarb is out of season.

Preheat the oven to 180°C/fan 160°C/gas 4.

1   Brush the insides of 4 x 150ml individual soufflé moulds with the melted butter, stroking the butter upwards on the sides.

2   To make the crumble, place the flour and diced butter in a large bowl and, using your fingers, rub the butter in until the mixture resembles breadcrumbs. Stir in the brown sugar and chopped hazelnuts.

3   Tip the crumble mixture on to a baking sheet lined with greaseproof paper and spread it out evenly, breaking up any lumps. Cook the crumble in the preheated oven for 10–12 minutes until it is golden brown. Remove from the oven and allow to cool. Then pour three quarters of the toasted crumble into a small food processor and blitz into fine breadcrumbs. Chop the remaining unblitzed crumble mixture by hand and keep it to one side in a small bowl.

4   Place 2 tablespoons of the blitzed toasted crumble into each of the moulds and shake all around the mould to coat the inside. Place the prepared moulds in the fridge until needed.

5   To make the rhubarb base for the soufflé, place the rhubarb, grenadine and 10g of the caster sugar in a medium-sized saucepan, put on the lid and cook over a low heat until soft, tossing occasionally. This will take 7–8 minutes. Put the cooked rhubarb in a blender and liquidize until it forms a purée.

6   Weigh out 200g of the rhubarb purée, then pour that back into the saucepan. (Save any leftover rhubarb purée from the blender to use in another recipe.) Mix in the cornflour and cook the purée over a low heat for a few minutes more. Pass this rhubarb base mixture through a sieve into a large bowl and set aside to cool.

7   Meanwhile, make the rhubarb, mango and lime salad. Combine 50ml of water, the sugar, grenadine and ginger in a small saucepan, and stir over a low heat until the sugar has dissolved. Add the rhubarb pieces to the saucepan and stir to coat, then pour the syrup and rhubarb out on to a baking tray. Place the tray in the preheated oven and cook for 7 minutes, until the rhubarb begins to soften but retains its shape.

8   Remove the rhubarb from the oven and tip into a large bowl, reserving and chopping one piece to garnish the soufflés. Add the mango pieces to the bowl and gently toss together, then drizzle the lime juice over the mixture.

9   To make the soufflé, whisk the egg whites in another large bowl with an electric beater until they make soft peaks. Gradually add the remaining 50g of caster sugar as you continue to whisk, until the mixture forms stiff peaks, then carefully fold these whisked egg whites into the cooled rhubarb base using a spatula.

10 Spoon the soufflé mixture into the 4 prepared moulds, levelling off the tops with a palette knife. Sprinkle the reserved chopped toasted crumble and reserved chopped rhubarb on top of the 4 soufflés. Place them on an oven tray and put into the preheated oven to cook for 10 minutes.

11 To serve, place each soufflé on a serving plate, dust over some icing sugar and spoon some mango salad on the side. Top the salad with lime zest.

ERIC LANLARD'S MOGADORES: A LIGHT CHOCOLATE MOUSSE ON A HAZELNUT PRALINE FEUILLANTINE BASE serves 4

FOR THE HAZELNUT PRALINE FEUILLANTINE BASE

40g milk chocolate
40g hazelnut praline paste
100g feuillantine

FOR THE CHOCOLATE MOUSSE

125g caster sugar
75g egg yolks
125g dark chocolate
250ml double cream
250g raspberries

FOR THE COCOA BEAN GARNISH

250g caster sugar
50g glucose syrup
200g cocoa beans

FOR THE CHOCOLATE DECORATION

150g dark chocolate
4 acetate wrappers

This is one of the bestselling desserts in my pâtisserie, Cake Boy. Feuillantine is basically crushed wafers, like the fine wafers you get in ice creams. Make sure you use the very best dark chocolate you can afford for this dessert, but never use anything that is more than 70% cocoa for a chocolate mousse, as it will be too bitter. Stick to a chocolate closer to 60%.

1   Make the praline feuillantine base first. Put the milk chocolate and praline paste in a heatproof medium-sized bowl sitting over a saucepan of simmering water, so the base of the bowl does not touch the water (a bain-marie). Stir and heat gently until the chocolate and praline melt. Once the two have melted, gently fold in the feuillantine.

2   Divide the mixture between 4 small ring moulds and pat the mixture down into the moulds, to create an even base. Put the moulds in the fridge to cool.

3   For the chocolate mousse, start by making a sugar syrup. Place the sugar and 125g water in a small saucepan over a high heat and bring to the boil, stirring until the sugar has dissolved.

4   Place the egg yolks in a large bowl and start to whisk them with an electric beater at high speed. Slowly trickle in the hot syrup, whisking at the same time. Continue whisking the mixture until it is light and fluffy, then leave to cool.

5   Melt the dark chocolate in another heatproof bowl set over a saucepan of gently simmering water. Whip the double cream in a large bowl until it forms soft peaks.

6   Stir the melted chocolate into the cooled sugar and egg yolks mixture and fold in. Then gently fold in the whipped cream to the mixture as well, and again leave to cool.

7 When the mixture has cooled a little, take the 4 ring moulds out of the fridge and spoon the mixture into the moulds, levelling off the top with a palette knife. Place the filled moulds back in the fridge to set.

8 To make the cocoa bean garnish, put the sugar, 150ml water and the glucose syrup into a heavy-bottomed saucepan and cook over a medium heat until golden. Crush the cocoa beans and add them to the hot golden syrup.

9 Stir well and then pour the syrup out on to a large silicone mat. Cover with a piece of silicone paper and use a rolling pin to roll the mixture out as thinly as possible, whilst it is still hot. When you have a thin layer, peel off the piece of silicone paper and cut the solidifying syrup with a sharp knife into long strips. Immediately place the strips on to a tuile mould to give them a wave effect. Leave to cool and set completely.

10 To make the chocolate decoration, melt the dark chocolate in a bain-marie. Then, using a palette knife, spread the molten chocolate gently on to the acetate wrappers and leave to set.

11 To serve, take the ring moulds out of the fridge, place each one upside down on to a serving plate and turn out the mousses. Decorate the tops with the raspberries and the crushed cocoa bean wave garnish. Peel the acetate wrappers off the chocolate decorations and balance a decoration on top of each mogadore.

ERIC LANLARD'S APPLE SOUFFLÉS WITH A SALTED BUTTER CARAMEL SAUCE serves 4

FOR THE APPLE SOUFFLÉS

1kg Granny Smith apples, washed and dried

2 vanilla pods, split lengthways

100g dark brown sugar

2 level teaspoons ground cinnamon

6 eggs, separated

100g icing sugar, sifted

50g butter, melted

100ml Calvados

8 sponge finger biscuits

FOR THE SALTED BUTTER CARAMEL SAUCE

400ml single cream

2 vanilla pods, split lengthways and seeds removed

180g caster sugar

300g salted butter

FOR THE SPUN SUGAR GARNISH

250g caster sugar

1 sheet edible gold leaf

Granny Smith apples are best for this recipe as they are firm and tart. Keeping the peel on while they cook helps hold their shape and also adds extra flavour. In Brittany they don't use unsalted butter, and this salt–sweet idea has been around for years.

*Preheat the oven to 200°C/fan 180°C/gas 6.

1   Core and quarter the apples, then place in a large ovenproof dish. Add the split vanilla pods and sprinkle on the dark brown sugar and cinnamon. Cover with a lid and put in the preheated oven to roast for 20–25 minutes.

2   Once the apples have cooled enough to handle, remove their skins. Pass the apple flesh through a sieve into a large bowl and mix in the egg yolks.

3   Whisk the egg whites in another large bowl using an electric beater along with half of the icing sugar until they form soft peaks. Fold the egg whites into the cooled apple purée mixture very delicately using a spatula, trying to achieve the lightest possible texture.

4   Next, brush the insides of 4 individual soufflé moulds with the melted butter and sprinkle in some of the remaining icing sugar. Shake and rotate the moulds to coat all the insides with the sugar and tip out the excess.

5   Pour the Calvados into a bowl and cut the sponge biscuits in half. Dip them into the Calvados and place in the bottoms of the soufflé moulds.

6   Fill the moulds with the soufflé mixture to the top. Spread the mixture flat on top with a palette knife, then run your thumb around the edge of each soufflé mould. Put the soufflé moulds on a baking tray and put them in the preheated oven to cook for 15 minutes.

7   To make the caramel sauce, pour the cream into a large pan and add the vanilla seeds and pods. Bring to the boil, then take off the heat and leave aside to infuse for a few minutes. Remove the vanilla pods.

8   Place the sugar into a large heavy-bottomed saucepan over a medium heat. Cook without stirring to caramelize the sugar until it turns a nice deep golden colour, then remove the saucepan from the heat. Working quickly, carefully add the hot infused cream and the butter and stir well. When ready to serve, pour the caramel sauce into a jug.

9   For the spun sugar garnish, put the sugar and 70ml water in a deep saucepan and place over a medium heat without stirring until it turns to a blonde caramel. Immediately remove the saucepan from the heat and leave it to cool slightly. Next, use a fork to pull strands out from the cooling caramel and then form a ball with the strands by rolling them in your hands. Repeat to make 4 spun sugar balls. Sprinkle some gold leaf on top of the balls.

10 Remove the soufflés from the oven and dust with the remaining icing sugar. Serve with a spun sugar ball and the jug of salted caramel sauce alongside.

GLOSSARY

GENERAL SKILLS

Blanching Adding vegetables to boiling salty water for a minute or two and then refreshing with cold water to stop the cooking process and to keep the vegetables' colour.

Bouquet garni A bouquet garni is a little flavour bag of aromatic herbs, tied together in muslin with string so you can easily take it out of a soup or stew. I make my simple bouquet garni with a bay leaf, sprig of thyme, leftover celery leaves and peppercorns. Parsley stalks are also often used and sprigs of herbs can just be tied together with string. Add at the beginning of the braising time and remove just before serving.

Chilli – how to chop To chop a chilli, start by cutting it in half. The white membrane and seeds are where the chilli-heat is, so scrape out with a knife, but don't worry if some of the seeds remain (a few aren't going to make a huge difference). Chop into small pieces.

Chopping When a recipe calls for some chopping, it means to use a sharp knife to cut ingredients into small, roughly equal-sized pieces. This allows everything to cook evenly and be ready at the same time.

Clarifying butter Clarified butter is butter with the milky solids removed and it is perfect for making a hollandaise sauce where the butter actually flavours the sauce. Melt unsalted butter slowly in a small pan. As you do this, you will see the butter separate into the golden butter that we want and the milky residues that we don't. Carefully pour off the golden butter liquid to use, leaving the milky residues behind.

Crème Chantilly – whipped cream with just enough icing sugar to sweeten it – is a classic accompaniment for desserts. Whip double cream and icing sugar until fluffy soft peaks form. Watch out, though, because a lot of people over whip their cream. It should not be at all foamy and instead just hold its shape.

Eggs – how to fry an egg (see page 33 for how to poach an egg)
A perfectly fried egg is a wonderful thing, so don't keep eggs just for breakfast. Add to dishes where the melting yolk and smooth white will add texture, flavour and colour.

Pour oil into a good frying pan and heat until it begins to sizzle. Hot, but not too hot, oil will stop the egg sticking to the base of the pan.

Crack your egg into the pan, taking care not to break the yolk.

Add a little knob of butter and fry until the egg white has just set around the yolk. Don't turn the heat up too high or the base will become crispy and bubbly. Slide your egg out of the pan and on to a plate. For a restaurant-style presentation, cut out the egg using a pastry cutter. You want an attractive round shape, so trim with a knife too.

FISH
How to griddle fish (see recipe, page 139)
Season fish fillets or small whole fish and place on a very hot griddle. A griddle pan is good because it retains heat, but I never want to overcook fish so keep the heat low or even turn it off – the griddle itself is hot enough to cook the fish. Use very little oil, just a drizzle of olive, and leave the fish alone in the pan. You don't have to keep turning it because this breaks the fish up. Leave it be and let it crisp up then, at the last moment, flip it over and cook on the other side.

How to tell when fish is cooked
I like my fish just slightly undercooked. I take it almost as a compliment when fish comes back and a customer says to cook it some more because that's no problem, but if it's overdone, that's a big insult. You can tell if your fish is cooked when the flesh becomes firm and flaky, but not dry, and it just starts to change colour from translucent to opaque.

Hollandaise sauce is basically a hot mayonnaise. Egg yolks are cooked with a dash of vinegar or vinegar reduction and some melted butter to create a deliciously thick sauce. To make yours, place the egg yolks and vinegar in a glass bowl and whisk over a bain-marie, which should give a nice, gentle heat. When the egg yolks are partially cooked, whip them off the heat. Before adding the butter, check that it is warm enough to just cook the eggs, but not so hot that the yolks cook completely and the sauce splits. Gently pour the clarified butter into the egg yolks in the bowl, whisking continually until you have a smooth, thick sauce. A good tip is to pour in the butter in a really thin trickle. That trickle is important because if you add too much butter too early on, the sauce won't thicken. Sprinkle in seasoning and lemon juice to taste.

Tip Add a splash of warm water if the hollandaise gets a bit too thick.

Mirepoix is a mix of sautéed root vegetables used as the tasty base for a meaty soup or stew. Usually a mirepoix involves browning the vegetables, then placing in a pan with the meat on top for a long stretch of slow cooking. If you don't want to add any colour, leave out the carrots and cook gently, without browning, to make a white mirepoix.

Pancakes – how to make a batter (see also Crêpes on page 62)

Put your flour into a large glass bowl. Add the sugar, milk and melted butter. Stir briefly with a balloon whisk. You don't want to combine the flour and milk too quickly or the batter can be lumpy, so take it easy. Now break in the eggs. Whisk until combined and the batter is free of any lumps.

Or leave out the sugar from this basic batter, fry up some really good free-range back rashers in the pan and you can tuck into delicious bacon pancakes for breakfast.

Puréeing To purée is to liquidize, sieve or mash ingredients to get rid of lumps or smooth out the texture. You can do this by hand, with a sieve or in a blender. If using a blender, try making use of the pulse button. By pulsing a mixture, you don't liquidize it, you just mash it up for a more interesting texture.

Tip When I'm liquidizing something like a hot liquid, I'm always really nervous. What I do is to put a cloth on top of the blender to catch any hot splashes.

Reductions A reduction is all about evaporating a liquid until you get a really good, strong mixture, giving it more flavour and more colour. Pour your liquid into a small pan with any flavourings and cook that down, slowly simmering, until the liquid is about two-thirds of what you started with.

Refreshing vegetables Refreshing in iced water seals in the flavour and colour of cooked green vegetables by quickly halting the cooking process. Boil your vegetables, then briefly immerse in iced salted water (the salt gives flavour), plucking them out as soon as they get to room temperature to stop them absorbing too much water. Roll on a tea towel to get rid of any extra moisture before using.

Seasoning I cook with my heart, my eyes and my palate and I taste and season the whole time. Seasoning is not just about salt and pepper. Sugar, spices, herbs and flavourings, like lemon juice, all balance and enhance the flavours of a dish. Season carefully as you can always add more, but you can never take it back.

Tip Break sea salt through your fingers so it disperses evenly into your dish.

Tip Don't add pepper just for the sake of adding it; you don't always need another element. Pepper is for dishes with strong flavours, so I like it with meat and game, but I usually add white pepper to my soups or I leave it out altogether.

Stock (Brown fish stock for Cornish red mullet soup)

If you put fish bones and vegetables straight into water to make a stock, it would be a bit boring, but by roasting them and giving them a little bit of colour, you can even smell the difference. Rich and dark, a brown fish stock is there to add flavour to a soup or braise. Cut the cleaned fish heads and bones into large pieces and add to a heavy frying pan. You need only a tiny bit of oil as we are trying to dry roast on a low heat to colour them. Add browned, softened vegetables and your seasonings, cover with cold water and simmer for half an hour. Strain the stock before using.

The same applies to meat stocks: browning the bones first will enhance the flavour and colour.

Sweating To sweat means to slowly cook in a little bit of moisture, normally butter or oil, to soften and intensify flavours without colouring. Frying ingredients until they colour adds a caramelised, roasted flavour to a dish, so sweating is used in recipes where you don't want to change the taste of the fresh ingredients.

Tip If your pan gets too hot while sweating your vegetables, just add a little stock to get rid of the excess heat.

Toasting nuts When a recipe calls for nuts to be lightly toasted, the best way is to do this in a hot, dry frying pan for a few minutes, shaking the pan every now and then. Watch them carefully, though, as they can go from golden to burned in a matter of seconds.

Vinaigrette Nothing could be simpler. You need a little bit of white wine vinegar, not a lot, a dash of mustard (remember that mustard contains vinegar too) and a sprinkling of sugar because you don't want it too sharp. Add an oil like rapeseed and some seasoning and beat with a small whisk. I would say it's about three times oil to one times mustard, with sugar and seasoning to taste.

Tip You don't want your salad overdressed. Keep the salad nice and crispy by just tipping in a little dressing with a small spoon or dipping the leaves into the dressing at the last moment.

Zesting a lemon The zest of a lemon, or any other citrus fruit, is the part with the essential oils and most of the flavour. Zest, not the acidic juice, is what you need to add to your cooking if you want that true lemon flavour. To remove the zest, use a Microplane or citrus grater. You only want the coloured peel, so leave the bitter white pith on the fruit.

A NOTE ON INGREDIENTS

I thought it would be good to give a little reference guide to a few of the ingredients that you will come across in the Cookery School recipes. I've not included everything (as that could be a whole book in itself!) but have decided to give you my thoughts on a few things.

Balsamic vinegar If you are going to use balsamic vinegar, try to use an aged one from Modena (12 years plus). There are an awful lot of rubbish varieties out there, so choose carefully. Sherry vinegar from Spain is also delicious. Try to buy from a good delicatessen.

Bechamel This is a white sauce that is often used as a base for other sauces; it is made by whisking hot milk into a roux base of flour and butter. (See page 345).

Beef I like Hereford grass-fed beef best as it is so tasty. Animals are not supposed to eat grain as it goes against nature, so I stay away from grain-finished animals. It's ridiculous to import grain from halfway around the world to feed livestock on when our indigenous, hearty breeds do so well on pastures of green grass.

Beignet A deep-fried dumpling or doughnut made from choux pastry; there are many different sweet and savoury versions. Most associated with New Orleans, these are the state doughnuts of Louisiana.

Black pudding Traditionally the best black puddings are made from pig's blood, but today many are made from dried chicken's, cow's or lamb's blood.

Bonito A type of tuna that is cured with salt and left to dry for up to three years. It is one of the basic building blocks of Japanese cuisine and used to make stocks and miso soup or sprinkled on to dishes to give a smoky flavour.

Bouquet garni A bundle of herbs used to flavour stocks and stews, it is removed from the dish before serving.

Beurre noisette Otherwise known as brown butter; a butter which hasn't been clarified.

Butcher's string This is not an ingredient, but something that crops up in a few recipes. Also called 'butcher's twine' this is string that is made especially for cooking, so don't use any old string that you might have lying around in the shed!

Caul fat Traditionally used to wrap faggots, caul fat is the lining of a pig's stomach. It's a membrane, which is a soft fat that disintegrates with cooking. Be careful not to use too much.

Celeriac A variety of celery that is grown just for its root. It tastes and smells like celery. It should be washed and scrubbed really well.

Ceviche A South American dish, and the national dish of Peru, whereby seafood or thin slices of fish are 'cooked' in citrus juice.

Chartreuse A green liqueur made with wild mountain herbs; it is named after the monastery on the border of France and Belgium in which it is produced.

Chicken The minimum standard for the chicken that we eat should be free-range. Even better is free-range and organic. Anything below that is not good enough in terms of animal welfare. I've visited lots of chicken factories and I'd rather be a vegetarian than eat a chicken from those places. When I was growing up on a farm, chicken was always treated as a royal lunch – let's try and treat it like that again.

Choux pastry Used for éclairs, buns, profiteroles and beignets. Heating this pastry helps to stabilize the mixture and works the gluten into the flour so it becomes more durable.

Colcannon A traditional Irish dish of mashed potatoes mixed with cabbage or kale.

Consommée A clear stock soup usually made out of meat bones.

Dahl A thick, spiced Indian stew made from pulses or lentils.

Duxelles A term for finely chopped mushrooms that have been fried off, which is generally used as a stuffing. Usually found in a Beef Wellington or the base of a mushroom paté. It's a versatile method, which with different flavourings can be added to a variety of dishes.

Erengi mushrooms Otherwise known as King Oyster mushrooms. They are thick, meaty and great grilled or added to steamed dishes. It is all about texture with these mushrooms. The great thing is that many mushrooms are grown here now in the UK so they don't have to be imported.

Frangelico A hazelnut liqueur.

Game There are two types of game: furred (rabbits, venison) and feathered (pheasant, guinea fowl, partridge, to name a few). The feathered game season runs from August to January so get hold of some and try out the great game recipes in this book. The wonderful thing is that it is readily available, in season. There is nothing so pure as feathered game.

Goat's curd This is a light cream cheese and works really well as an alternative for dips and stuffings.

Grenadine A red syrup made from pomegranates.

Grouse This is a much more expensive bird compared to partridge. It is a thoroughly wild bird which eats young heather shoots. The grouse moorlands must be very well managed to encourage the breeding and survival of grouse. The twelfth of August is the start of the shooting season for grouse.

Guinea fowl Otherwise known as the African hen, a guinea fowl is like an African pheasant because it is a wild bird. It has been domesticated in Britain and cross bred. There isn't a lot of meat on guinea fowl because they are very slim like pheasant with long slender breasts. Sometimes with guinea fowl you need to fold them up and moisten them with butter before you roast them because they can be very dry.

Hash A coarse, chunky mixture of meat (usually beef or corned beef) with cooked potatoes, onions and other flavourings, usually mixed together and fried off to finish.

Lamb Why would anyone want to eat lamb from anywhere but the British Isles where it is incredibly well produced? The perfect time to eat lamb in the UK is from March to midsummer. It's great used in hotpots, stews and when roasted or grilled and is astonishingly good value for money.

Langoustines Otherwise known as Dublin Bay prawns. This is not to do with the bay itself but rather with the Atlantic around the coasts of Ireland and Scotland. They are absolutely delicious and can be madly expensive, but they have to be tried now and then.

Lardo The delicious fat from Parma ham; great when wrapped around firm white fish, like monkfish, and roasted.

Lemons Should be given a good wash and a rub. Only use organic and unwaxed lemons otherwise you will get a mouthful of wax and pesticide residues. (A waxed lemon is an older lemon and so there will be less juice.)

Madeira This is a fortified wine from the island of Madeira.

Mirin Saki which has been turned into a cooking wine.

Mooli or daikon Asian white radishes, with the peppery taste of a radish.

Oils There are many different types and they all have their different uses. The key is to buy them in small quantities because they are perishable goods so it's better to use a small bottle quickly and replace it with fresh. Olive oil, for instance, doesn't belong in a clear bottle sitting above your cooker. Good olive oils and extra virgin olive oils should be kept in secure dark bottles away from oxygen and light.

Sunflower oil and groundnut oil are good for light frying. Rapeseed oil is a naturally pressed oil – it's a bit of an eyesore when you see it growing in the countryside but it's found its place as a natural cooking oil with some healthy benefits, as it has a high content of vitamin E. I like to use it because it's a light oil suitable for cooking and for dressing salads. Cobb nut oil, from Kent, is also starting to show its face in some places and can be used as a groundnut oil.

Orzo Pasta made in the same shape as wheat or rice. It is big in Turkey and Greece and is known as Italian wheat but made from pasta.

Oysters Rock oysters are delicious. They were imported into British and Irish waters in the 1960s when our own Portuguese variety was wiped out. Historically, they have never bred themselves but now this is happening. The varieties are numbered 1, 2 or 3 and this denotes their size. From the start of September they are readily available in great oyster bars around Britain and Ireland – go and enjoy some. My favourite way is to serve them *au naturel* or with a little squeeze of lemon juice and a grinding of black pepper leave off the Tabasco as they are just too delicate.

Polenta This is made from ground cornmeal and can be cooked into a loose consistency, like porridge, or a hard compacted cake which can then be sliced up; used in a lot of Italian cookery.

Pork The minimum standard for pork, as laid down by the Soil Association, is that it should be free-range, and the perfect time for pigs to go to slaughter is at 6 to 7½ months old after that they start to put on lots of extra fat. I want to buy meat from people I know, so go and talk to your local butcher and ask him questions about where the meat has come from. Try to find a butcher with direct links to farms. When it comes to pork, ask the butcher about the different breeds then try a few – as with anything, it's all about experimenting and finding out what taste you like best.

Puff pastry Made with layers of butter, flour and water. The pastry puffs up when the butter melts through these layers.

Quails' eggs Delicious little eggs that can be quite fiddly to peel once they are boiled, but they are worth the effort.

Remoulade A French condiment similar to tartare sauce but often more yellow in colour. In its most basic form it is mayonnaise mixed with herbs, capers and cornichons, but it can be taken in many different ways with the addition of other ingredients.

Rhubarb There are two different seasons for rhubarb and it comes in two guises natural rhubarb and forced rhubarb. Forced rhubarb is grown in the dark, before the season for natural rhubarb, so no light gets to it. The stems tend to be very slim and you will never have anything else out of season that tastes so beautiful as forced rhubarb. It is okay to use this out of season!

Rice There are so many different types of rice pilaff, long grain, short grain, Basmati, and different types of risotto rice. Always use the type of rice advised in a recipe as there is always a reason behind its use. A risotto won't work with anything other than risotto rice, for instance.

Rouille A French sauce made from olive oil, garlic, saffron, breadcrumbs and chilli; usually served alongside seafood.

Roux The base of a white sauce, a roux is equal measures of butter and flour stirred over heat. After sieving and adding in milk a little at a time, a silky roux is made by beating the milk in using the back of a wooden spoon to get rid of the lumps. This makes the gluten get to work and become really elastic. This sauce is the base of so many dishes. Definitely one to have in your little black book of essentials.

Saffron This expensive spice of crushed crocus stamens can simply be sprinkled into a liquid dish like a soup, but for something like a saffron mayo you must soak it in water first or you'll end up with lots of saffron but no flavour.

Salmon I only ever like to use organic salmon, not farmed, and would encourage you to do the same.

Salt I use salt to bring out the flavour, to make the food taste better. I don't want to poison anyone, so when I talk about seasoning in the kitchen, I only ever use natural rock or sea salt (non-iodized). Stay away from chemically enhanced salts. To flavour soup, I grind the salt flakes really quickly in my fingers but for something like a salad I will leave them whole.

Scampi In the UK and Ireland this term refers to a way of battering or breadcrumbing and deep-frying pieces of lobster or monkfish tail; it can also refer to different varieties of prawn.

Schnitzel A traditional Austrian dish of breadcrumbed escalope of veal or pork, which is then fried until golden and crisp.

Sourdough A delicious artisan bread that is risen naturally using wild yeast.

Steak tartare A dish of finely chopped or minced raw beef which should only be made using fresh meat of the highest quality.

Tempura A light Japanese batter made with two flours I usually mix plain flour and potato flour. White wine and fizzy water help to puff the batter up.

Tomatoes An incredibly nutritious fruit with a very low calorific content. It is one of the only fruits or vegetables that actually improves its nutritional value with cooking. In this country we grow a huge range of heritage tomatoes in natural soil that taste delicious. Do try and get hold of some or, even better, grow some of your own: they will always taste better than any tomato that you'll ever buy.

Tomato purée If you're adding tomato purée to a dish, it's always good to let it sit in the dry pan for a few minutes. Tomato purée can be just a little bit sharp, but by toasting it you cook that out, making it taste so much better.

Veal When you're buying meat, a high standard of animal welfare is so important and you will also find that it always produces the best-quality meat. You must buy veal that meets Assured British Meat (ABM) standards to ensure that the calves have been fed and looked after well and have had plenty of space to run about in. Rather than being a white–beige colour (from being raised in restricted conditions on a milk-based diet), the meat will be a pale pink.

INDEX

*Page references for photographs are in **bold***

celeriac

  à la minute vegetable soup
    with bacon dumplings **18**, 19

  celeriac and apple purée
    328, 329

  cream of celeriac soup
    with chicken and girolles **42**, 43

  crispy confit duck leg with
    celeriac remoulade **186**, 187

chanterelle mushroom sauce
  212, 213

chard **232**, 233

cheese 292–3

  cheese and ham toastie **54**, 55

chervil: tarragon and chervil sauce
  194, 195

chestnuts: pepper-crusted tuna
  with carpaccio of mushrooms
  and chestnut beignets **158**, 159

chicken

  how to joint 222–3

  baby chicken with puy lentil dahl
    198, 199

  chicken chasseur **220**, 221

  chicken Kiev **64**, 65, 66–7

  chicken schnitzel with crispy
    capers and a fried egg
    174, 175

  classic roast chicken **306**, 307–8

  cream of celeriac soup with
    chicken and girolles **42**, 43

  crispy chicken liver rolls
    204, 205, 206–7

  mushroom tortellini with chicken
    consommé **90**, 91

  poussin 'oudhi' 314–15, **316–17**

chickpeas: sautéed prawns with
  chickpea mayonnaise **46**, 47

chillies: squid-ink gnocchi with
  Brussels sprouts and chilli
  152, 153

chips

  Bombay game chips 318–20

  chunky chips **218**, 219

chives: poached haddock with
  salsify fricassee and a salmon
  egg and chive sauce **142**, 143

chocolate

  chocolate mousse 336–7

  chocolate mousse with praline
    and sautéed strawberries
    260, 261

  chocolate tart with fresh
    raspberries **276**, 277, 278–9

  flourless chocolate sponge
    with coffee cream **254**, 255

chorizo: baby squid stuffed with
  chorizo and feta **134**, 135

chowder: clam chowder
  160, 161–2

cinnamon and clove sugar
  256, 257

clafoutis: raspberry clafoutis
  252, 253

clams

  how to cook 162

  clam chowder **160**, 161–2

  razor clams with a tomato sauce
    140, 141

cloves: cinnamon and clove sugar
  256, 257

coffee

  coffee and walnut cake **290**, 291

  flourless chocolate sponge
    with coffee cream **254**, 255

  tiramisu **262**, 263

colcannon **208**, 209

compote: apple compote **284**, 285

consommé: mushroom tortellini
  with chicken consommé **90**, 91

coriander 246

courgettes

  clear tomato soup with an
    aubergine, courgette and
    tomato ratatouille **88**, 89

  stuffed veal escalopes with
    aubergines and courgettes
    238, 239

couscous: citrus and herb roasted
  vegetable couscous **44**, 45

crab

  how to prepare 112–13

  crab bisque with sesame crab
    toasts **156**, 157

  crab and orange salad **110**, 111

  dressed crab with seasonal
    vegetables **136**, 137

crème caramel

  how to make 286–7

  crème caramel with apple
    compote **284**, 285

crêpes

  how to make 62

  mushroom crêpe gratin **58**, 59–60

crisps: smoked garlic aioli with root
  vegetable crisps **38**, 39

croutons

  how to make 72

  Cornish red mullet soup with
    crispy croutons and rouille
    68, 69

curd: tea-smoked mackerel with
  beetroot stew and fresh curd
  148, 149

custard

  how to make custard 272–3

  how to make a savoury custard
    53

  blue cheese and bacon tarts
    50, 51

  fine apple tarts with pecan,
    maple and custard **268**, 269

  garlic custard with snails **92**, 93

  little citrus sponges and custard
    270, 271

D

dates: sticky toffee pudding with
  ginger and dates **258**, 259

dressings

  how to make 22–3

  griddled leeks with a honey and
    mustard dressing **20**, 21

  lime and ginger dressing **76**, 77

duck

  crispy confit duck leg with
    celeriac remoulade **186**, 187

  crispy duck, bok choi and black
    beans with a lime and ginger
    dressing **76**, 77

  pan-roasted duck breasts with
    apples, Calvados and black
    pudding **214**, 215

  poached duck breast with
    beetroot purée and mooli
    236, 237

  potted duck's liver **228**, 229

duck's eggs

  griddled leeks with a honey
    and mustard dressing **20**, 21

  smoked salmon with duck egg
    omelette **104**, 105

E

Edwards, Mark 301, 305

eggs

  how to poach 33

  chicken schnitzel with crispy
    capers and a fried egg **174**, 175

  griddled leeks with a honey
    and mustard dressing **20**, 21

  guinea fowl hash with fried quail's
    egg **188**, 189

  poached haddock with salsify
    fricassee and a salmon, egg
    and chive sauce **142**, 143

  smoked salmon with duck egg
    omelette **104**, 105